D0915916

Japan's Foreign Policy in an Era of Global Change

Japan's Foreign Policy in an Era of Global Change

Takashi Inoguchi

St. Martin's Press
New York

© Takashi Inoguchi, 1993

First published in the United States of America in 1993

Printed in Great Britain

ISBN 0-312-09951-7

Library of Congress Cataloging-in-Publication Data

Inoguchi, Takashi.
    Japan's foreign policy in an era of global change / Takashi
Inoguchi.
        p.   cm.
    Includes bibliographical references and index.
    ISBN 0-312-09951-7
    1. Japan—Foreign relations—1945–   I. Title.
DS889.I376   1993
327.52—dc20   93-7278
                                                                            CIP

Typeset by BookEns Ltd, Baldock, Herts.
Printed and bound in Great Britain by Biddles Ltd of Guildford and King's Lynn

Contents

Acknowledgements   vii

Introduction   ix

Part I: Constituting Japan's foreign policy   1

1. The ideas and structures of foreign policy: looking ahead with   3
    caution

2. Japan's uncertainty and unease with itself: international structure   57
    and international role

Part II: Redirecting Japan's foreign policy   69

3. Japanese responses to Europe 1992: implications for the United   71
    States

4. Change and response in Japan's international politics and strategy   91

5. Japan's response to the Gulf crisis: an analytic overview   98

Part III: Envisioning Japan's foreign policy   115

6. Japan's foreign policy in a time of global uncertainty   117

7. Japan's role in international affairs   139

Part IV: Two historical appreciations   157

8. Asia and the Pacific since 1945: a Japanese perspective   159

9. Awed, inspired and disillusioned: Japanese scholarship on American   179
    politics

Select bibliography   201

Index   205

Acknowledgements

I acknowledge with gratitude the advice and assistance that I have received during the course of completing this book. Since the chapters of this book were originally written amidst the greatest transformation since World War II, it would have been very easy to lose sight of the basic nature and direction of that great transformation and of the impact on Japan's foreign policy without such sound advice and indispensable assistance.

Chapter 1, 'The ideas and structures of foreign policy: looking ahead with caution', was written for the Japan Political Economy Research Conference project and published originally in Takashi Inoguchi and Daniel Okimoto (eds)., *The Political Economy of Japan, Vol. 2: The Changing International Context* (Stanford: Stanford University Press, 1988). Although some of the information in this chapter, such as the position of Nakasone; the relations between the USSR and Japan and the GATT talks is somewhat outdated, it deserves close reading to understand how Japan perceived international changes and its later repositioning. I am grateful to Yasusuke Murakami and Hugh Patrick for their intellectual leadership and Daniel Okimoto and all others in the project for their enthusiasm about deciphering the Japanese phenomenon. Chapter 2, 'Japan's uncertainty and unease with itself: international structure and international role', was written for presentation at the Round Table of the International Political Science Association, Seoul, May 1990. I am thankful to Sungjoo Han for enabling me to think further on the subject. Chapter 3, 'Japanese responses to Europe 1992: implications for the United States', was originally written for presentation at the East-West Forum Workshop, Washington, DC, October 1989. I am grateful to Sewelyn Bialer and William Griffith for inviting me to work on new terrain. Chapter 4, 'Change and response in Japan's international politics and strategy', was written for the workshop organized by the Northeast Asia Program of Australian National University in early 1990 and published originally in Stuart Harris and James Cotton (eds.), *The End of the Cold War in Northeast Asia* (South Melbourne: Longman Cheshire, 1991). I thank Stuart Harris and James Cotton and all other Asianists at Australian National University for their ever-deepening interest in Pacific Asia. Chapter 5, 'Japan's response to the Gulf crisis', was originally published in the *Journal of Japanese Studies* (Vol. 17, No. 2, Summer 1991). I thank Susan Hanley, its editor, for inviting me to write the article on a fascinating topic. Chapter 6, 'Japan's foreign policy in a time of global uncertainty', was originally published in the *International Journal* (Vol. XVI, No. 1, Winter 1991-92). I am grateful to Robert O. Matthews and Charles Pentland, its co-editors, for inviting me to write the lead article for the main theme of 'Japan's cultural role'. Chapter 7, 'Japan's role in international affairs', was originally published in Robert H. Taylor (ed.), *Asia and the Pacific: Handbooks to the Modern World* (Facts on File, 1990). I thank Robert H. Taylor for inviting me to write a historical article. Chapter 9, 'Awed, inspired and disillusioned: Japanese scholarship on American politics', was originally published in Richard Samuels and Myron Weiner (eds.), *The Political Culture of Foreign Area and International Research: Essays in Honor of Lucian W. Pye* (Brassey's, 1992, McLean, Virginia). I am grateful to Richard Samuels and Myron Weiner, the volume's co-editors, for inviting me to think afresh about the subject.

I am grateful to the following publishers for permission to reproduce the above materials: Stanford University Press for Chapter 1; Longman Cheshire for Chapter 4; the Society for Japanese Studies for Chapter 5; *International Journal* for Chapter 6; International Institute for Strategic Studies for Chapter 7; Facts On File for Chapter 8; and Brassey's for Chapter 9.

For the thorough task of scrutinizing my non-native English sentences appearing in those chapters that have not been published before, I am, as always, immensely thankful to Martha Lane Walsh, a friend and an editorial colleague as the managing editor of the *Journal of Japanese Studies*.

Frances Pinter has been an angel to me in encouraging me to publish books in English and accepting my proposal to do so. I am immensely fortunate that my proposal has passed her high standards.

Last but not least, Kuniko Inoguchi, my wife and colleague, has been most helpful in terms of boosting my morale during the entire period of publishing this book when she has had to spend most of her time with our new twin daughters. It is not an exaggeration to say that she is also the spiritual mother of my twin books from Pinter Publishers.

Takashi Inoguchi
Tokyo

Introduction

Two competing images of Japan's diplomacy at this time of great transformation-cum-transition after World War II can be identified. One is the image of Japan adrift, with an *ad hoc*, opportunistic, and short-term pragmatism. The other is the image of Japan being determinedly and tenaciously steadfast to its national interests. Ironically, both images can cite the same examples as evidence to advance their arguments. For instance, Japan's fairly strong resistance to liberalization of the rice market can be used to support the argument that Japan is drifting without being able to maintain a more enlightened position of facilitating the formation of a global free-trade regime in the framework of the Uruguay Round of GATT. Yet from the other angle such resistance can be interpreted as the tenacious pursuit of Japan's national interest in producing at least one kind of principal grain, rice, when its food consumption is overwhelmingly dependent on imports from abroad, and especially when there is little likelihood of an accord in the negotiations on agricultural subsidies between the two major giants, the United States and the European Community. Another example is the territorial issue between Japan and Russia. The former argument holds that, despite the demise of the Cold War and despite the urgent need to extend aid to Russia for its fledgling democracy and to rescue its free-market system, Japan has been narrow-minded and opportunistic in its attempt to settle the territorial issue first before further rapprochement is made and large-scale financial assistance offered. Japan is considered adrift for its short-sighted attempt made without seeing through sea changes in its diplomatic environment. The latter argument goes that Japan is steadfast in its attempt to do first things first, namely, conclude a Treaty of Peace with Russia, including a territorial settlement, since Japan and Russia have achieved diplomatic normalization in 1956 and nothing beyond that since then. Japan is to be lauded for exercising political leadership in adopting this course despite the calls made by Europeans and Americans for Japan to do something, although they themselves have made no further large-scale commitments to financing aid.

Perhaps both images coexist, first because Japan has been unable to convey clearly how it conceives its own interests, and second because Japan has been unable to demonstrate a 'world vision' which it is supposedly beginning to realize. First, Japan's conception of its own interests is perhaps less articulated in terms of goals and means and defined more in terms of pragmatic rules of thought and behavior such as 'seek consensus before acting', 'do not swim against the great tide of market forces', and 'respect coexistent harmony more than competitive discord'. The salience of pragmatic rules in guiding Japan's diplomacy is fathomable if one understands how Japan perceives its standing in the global community since 1945: Japan has been a semi-sovereign state with its right to resort to war denounced even for the settlement of international disputes, according to the still-dominant view in Japan. Therefore, Japan has opted for a course largely confined to the economic sphere. In the market-place, pragmatic rules are clear. Such dicta as 'build economic infrastructure', 'consolidate manufacturing capabilities throughout sectors', 'put the market in command', and 'pool money in such a way that it can be lent to critically important sectors' have been shared by many Japanese leaders. These could be regarded as a set of instructions to a market actor, but never as guidance to diplomats representing the state. But it would not seem far-fetched if I were to say that post-1945 Japanese diplomacy has been grounded on these dicta.

On top of this reliance on strategic pragmatics, the general uncertainty prevailing in the post-Cold-War world has been counseling virtually every actor to be cautious. Punishment of Saddam Hussein in Iraq has been far less effective than was assumed at the triumphant end in spring 1991 of the breathtaking US-led Gulf War, and the euphoria of a European Monetary Union dissolved suddenly in mid-1992 with the breakdown of the European Exchange Rate Mechanism after national referenda in Denmark and France gave strong warnings against a smooth transition to the union. Japan has every reason to be more skeptical of grandiose designs, whether for destruction or construction.

Second, the fact that Japan does not possess much of a 'world vision' may be normal for a non-hegemonic power. Georg Hegel correctly noted that Minerva flies out only at dusk. In other words, ideological theorization becomes perfect only at the beginning of hegemonic decline. Given the fact that Japan is not a hegemonic power nor is it declining, expecting Japan to have a world vision may be slightly excessive. If an American were to say that Woodrow Wilson's 14 points were something of a world vision expressed at the dawn of the American century and that a non-hegemonic power can manifest its world vision, one could argue easily that that was because of American exceptionalism and that Japan is a non-exceptional state. As a matter of fact, one would have a hard time finding powers acting, more or less successfully, on the basis of their world visions. Not many would agree that the the United States has been acting on a world vision. Rather, it has been acting without knowing clearly the direction in which it is heading. Nor would many argue the same with regard to, say, France trying to contain Germany within a single Europe, often with the effect of failing to achieve its dream of deeper integration. It is acting on the basis of its unachievable vision and thus harming its own political and economic life.

From the totally opposite angle, one can argue that Japan possesses a world vision in fledgling form and that the only pity is that Japan's world vision is not universally applicable. Former Prime Minister Noburu Takeshita's pet words, 'when you do something, sweat by yourself and give credit to others', may be the epitome of humility, generosity, and altruism. But, it is argued, it cannot be a kind of world vision like freedom and democracy. Nor are those guidelines of strategic pragmatism such as 'don't swim against market forces', 'strategic fuzziness may be better than misplaced precision', and 'go multilateral rather than bilateral, or unilateral'. Yet one can argue that such pragmatism can be restructured as the guiding principles of the post-Cold-War era into the twenty-first century. They represent the spirit of conciliation, consultation, and cooperation along with deep acknowledgment of the global economic, technological, and environmental forces shaping our political and military life. Rather than asserting great-power sovereignty reminiscent of the nineteenth-century European powers, Japan is aspiring to adapt presciently to the normalcy of the twenty-first century—that of sharing responsibility and shaping the future. Naturally one can argue that such pragmatism is merely behavior models or at best principles guiding action but not values nurtured and shared among nations. To this one can counterargue that in tandem with the globalization of human life—technological, economic, and political—those values many aspire to achieve are increasingly common, especially since the end of the Cold War which coincided with the breakdown of European communism. Freedom, democracy, equality, human rights, and environmental preservation, for instance, are values widely shared and aspired to by many people including the Japanese. Not many questions need to be posed with respect to the type of values in any world vision, one can argue.

I do not intend to give full justification to the two arguments and two counterarguments regarding Japan's allegedly myopic conception of its own interests and alleged lack of any world vision on the basis of which Japan could assume global leadership and share many values with others. My only intention here is to demonstrate that both arguments and counterarguments can be cogently made and to introduce readers to the main text of the book concerning Japan's foreign policy under global transformation.

Part I
Constituting Japan's foreign policy

1

The ideas and structures of foreign policy: looking ahead with caution

On August 2, 1985, a leading economic daily, *Nihon keizai shimbun*, carried articles on the following topics.

1. The US Congress discusses anti-Japanese trade legislation in response to Japan's Action Program for trade access.
2. US government guidelines for the new round of GATT focus on market access for investment in high-tech areas.
3. A Bank of Japan study suggests a stronger yen to solve the current-account deficit problem.
4. The Resource and Energy Agency of the Ministry of International Trade and Industry (MITI) publishes a report on cooperative utilization of coal in the Pacific area.
5. US biotechnological advances may undercut Japanese rice production.
6. The Soviet vice-minister of foreign trade proposes joint Soviet-Japanese production of machinery and technological cooperation in high-tech areas.
7. CANON decides to produce 100 per cent of its photocopying machines in the EEC to avoid trade frictions.
8. Fujitsu establishes Fujitsu Canada, Inc., to expand computer sales in Canada.
9. 'Japan bashing' heats up in Washington, DC; relations with US states remain relatively cordial.
10. Prime Minister Nakasone comments in a television interview on the US use of atomic bombs in Hiroshima and Nagasaki and pleads for more understanding of the Action Program that the Japanese government will implement in the following three years.

With Japan's economic growth, the almost daily newspaper coverage of topics such as these have contributed to the complexity of views of Japan as a phenomenon. Several contending images of Japan have dominated recent debates throughout the world. Perhaps at no time in history have images of Japan been so complex.[1] At one extreme, some critics of Japan tenaciously perceive it as a free-rider. This perception seems vindicated if one looks at Japan's small defense spending compared with that of the United States. These critics note that even compared with the military outlays of the United States' Atlantic allies, Japan's defense budget has been exceedingly small.[2]

The argument seems convincing given, for example, the lack of a direct Japanese contribution to the defense of the Persian Gulf, whose security assures 65 per cent of Japanese oil consumption but merely 3 per cent of US oil consumption.[3] Why should the United States spend so much money to defend remote areas where its Japanese and West European allies have much more at stake? Why can't Japan send aircraft carriers to the Indian Ocean and the Persion Gulf to secure its oil?

More generally, it is argued that US responsibilities for defending Japan should be steadily lessened to allow Japan to shoulder a larger load. Burden sharing commensurate with Japan's economic capability is the basic formula implicit in this argument.[4] To restore and reshape a sounder US hegemony, it is vital that the United States 'discipline' its allies to follow US policy lines by playing up the Soviet threat to the nonsocialist world as a whole.[5] Since Japan has long benefited from US security assurances and economic benevolence, it is high time, the argument goes, that a rich Japan do more for the rest of the world community.

A similar perception persists in the area of foreign aid. Although the absolute amount of Japan's official development assistance (ODA) amounted to half that of the United States in 1984, as a percentage of GNP or of total grants, it was not very high.[6] The argument is thus that Japan is stingy and irresponsible and does not understand the responsibilities of noblesse oblige. Furthermore, citing the Japanese emphasis on industrial infrastructure building, critics argue that Japan donates aid only to serve its own politico-economic interests, especially its own manufacturing and financial interests, which are allowed to grab the bulk of the business associated with Japanese foreign aid.[7] It is further argued that Japan's aid should extend to areas not immediately adjacent to Japan. As a global economic power, Japan should shoulder more responsibilities in regions beyond East and Southeast Asia—the Middle East and North Africa, sub-Saharan Africa, the Caribbean, and Central and South America.[8] The underlying assumption is that Japan has benefited enormously without shouldering many international responsibilities. In short, Japan is the world's ultimate egoist.[9]

At the other extreme, Japan's potential as a challenger is mentioned with increasing frequency and intensity.[10] (This image is often compatible with the free-rider image.) The first sign is found in manufacturing and trade.

The Japanese advances in exports of televisions, automobiles, steel, video tape recorders, and electronic goods tend to foster this image. Skillful translation of technological breakthroughs into commodity production and world-wide marketing is seen as a Japanese characteristic. Japanese mass production allows for both variety and quality, and market targeting enables Japan to capture large portions of the market quickly. Japan's export-led economic recovery after the first oil crisis further reinforced the challenger impression.

Japanese advances in robotics, enabling production of manufactured goods with efficiency and precision, has also strengthened its image as a challenger. This makes some uneasy about the future prospects for their own economies, where unemployment rates are already high. With the largest percentage of robot-aided manufacturing facilities in the world, is Japan producing commodities more efficiently and causing unemployment abroad and thereby weakening the economic abilities of importing countries? The image that friends are in fact foes has been gaining a secure position in some quarters.[11] The nightmare is that the increasing Japanese share of the world automobile and electronics markets might extend to other areas as well. What if Japan achieves a superior competitive position vis-à-vis the United States in all manufacturing sectors, as Chalmers Johnson sees for the year 2000, between the two extremes of 'hamburgers and ICBMs'?[12]

If the US Defense Department's procurement of Japanese electronics components for high-precision weapons goes beyond a certain threshold, will Japan not acquire enormous leverage over the United States? Indeed, former CIA Director William J. Casey denounced Japan's large holdings in US computer companies as 'Trojan horses'.[13] With the steady increase in direct Japanese investment (from $32 billion in 1980 to an estimated $150 billion in 1990), the national security argument is gaining strength.[14]

Japan is also portrayed as a challenger in international finance. One finance economist has calculated that Japan will seize a commanding share of the global financial market by 1990. Japan's overseas lending, which amounted to $42.6 billion in 1982, is likely to grow to $211 billion in 1990, with

Japanese trade surpluses and influx of foreign portfolio investment abroad providing the Japanese banks with plenty of new dollar deposits, which can then be onlent through the Euromarket. . . The Yen dominated-bond market will exceed the Eurobond market in new issues. . . Oil will be priced in yen, speeding the development of the yen currency bloc in the Far East. . . Interest rate movements in Japan will be completely liberalized. . . A relentless series of mergers through the 1980s will make the world's five largest banks all Japanese. . . In 1990 one yen will equal one cent, the Japanese GNP will be the largest in the world.[15]

This image is further reinforced by the recent Japanese military buildup and the average 7.1 per cent annual budgetary increase between 1980 and 1985.[16] Japan could become a formidable military power in two or three decades if it so chooses, given its advanced technological level and vast economic and demographic size. According to this image, the gradual Japanese economic advance is nothing but a step toward overall Japanese supremacy. If Japan assumes a military burden commensurate with its economic capability, as opposed to the current $10 billion or 1 per cent of GNP,[17] this will strengthen the notion of Japan as a challenger. The uneasy asymmetry between Japan's economic and military power will be broken sooner or later, the argument goes, since historically no major economic power has remained such without transforming itself into a major military power.[18]

A third image portrays Japan as a supporter of international economic and political arrangements. Recently, however, the other two images have tended to overshadow the supporter image. According to this argument, Japan's increasingly positive role in military burden sharing, political cooperation, foreign aid, debt rescheduling, and foreign direct investment are best characterized as those of a supporter.

Japan is now the second largest aid donor next to the United States and the largest aid donor in many countries east of Pakistan. It is argued that Japan's emphasis on foreign aid to build industrial infrastructure compensates for the two major US priorities: basic needs and weapons. In terms of geographical coverage, Japan has significantly expanded its aid donations from East and Southeast Asia to other parts of the world. The major recipients of Japanese foreign aid are not only the resource-rich countries on which Japan is fundamentally dependent but also the countries whose security is a major concern for the United States and therefore, at least indirectly, for Japan as well. Not only such neighboring countries as South Korea, China, and Indonesia but also countries like Pakistan, Turkey, Egypt, Saudi Arabia, and pro-US Central American countries are now major recipients of Japanese foreign aid.[19] Furthermore, Japanese foreign aid increasingly emphasizes humanitarian aid and basic needs as it comes to focus on sub-Saharan Africa and South Asia.[20]

Japan has recently become the second largest contributor to the World Bank after the United States. Japan's contribution to the Asian Development Bank has been the largest since the bank began. Despite its large contributions to such organizations, Japan is said to maintain a low profile and to be interested more in the economic health and growth of recipient countries than with outright promotion of narrowly conceived Japanese national interests.[21]

Moreover, by 1983 Japan had become the second largest country after the United States in terms of outstanding net external assets. In proportion to the increase in these assets, Japan's syndicated loans and foreign direct investment have grown by leaps and bounds in the 1980s. Japan's syndicated loans, which amounted to $32.1 billion in 1982, have three major characteristics that, when combined, corroborate Japan's supporter role very well. The first is lower spreads and higher maturity on average than OPEC or most of US lending. The second is that Japanese agents have been taking risks as leading managers or co-managers of consortiums, often in cooperation with US banks. In 1983, the Bank of Tokyo was the number-two leading manager next to the Bank of America. In 1986 Nomura Securities was the number-two leading manager of Eurobonds, after Crédit Suisse First Boston, and in fixed-rate Eurobonds it was the leading manager. The third is that Japanese banks have shown themselves adept in conducting debt rescheduling to some developing countries, again in cooperation with US banks.[22]

Japan's foreign direct investment has grown radically in the 1980s. In 1983 it registered $32.2 billion, fourth in the world.[23] In 1986, it rose to $105.9 billion. Japan's foreign direct investment in the United States increased fivefold between 1977 and 1982. Japan's overall willingness to accept minority ownership also befits its supporter role.[24]

In terms of security, the increasing burden sharing with the United States is prominent, ranging from budget sharing for US bases in Japan to the Japan-US division of labor in naval intelligence and blockade activities in joint military exercises in the Western Pacific.[25] It is argued that the Japanese government's strong support for the deployment of Cruise and Pershing II missiles in Western Europe in 1983 is an indication that Japan quite cautiously plays a supporter's role.[26] Similar instances of political cooperation often cited are (1) resolving the loan issues with South Korea before Prime Minister Yasuhiro Nakasone's visit to the United States in 1981; (2) keeping diplomatic channels open with Iran and Iraq and trying to mediate between them since shortly after the Gulf war started in 1978; (3) supporting the United States in calling for a new round of GATT negotiations sometime after 1986 and prodding other countries to join it in the economic summit of May 1985; and (4) helping the United States in September 1985 by jointly persuading initially reluctant West Germany, France, and Great Britain to make concerted interventions in the market to lower the value of the dollar.

These three contending images of Japan—free-rider, supporter, and challenger—coexist with amazing ease if only because Japan is an enigma to the rest of the world. The confusing coexistence of the three images in the minds of many reflects the complex position Japan occupies in various areas of the international system, Japan's wide-ranging options vis-à-vis the international system, and the various ways Japan's policy mix determines its role in the international system.

In the following, I first summarize three characteristics of the third quarter of this century with longer-term implications for Japan. Then in greater detail, I focus on the post-1973 world, delineating major environmental changes and corresponding modifications in Japanese assumptions about economic and security policies. Third, I describe the domestic context that allowed Japan's ascension as a world power and that determines and con- strains the way it adapts to international changes and modifies its role, focusing on domestic preferences and policy priorities. Fourth, I speculate on the prospects for Japan and the rest of the world, discussing Japan's aspira- tions and capabilities and the sustainability and stability of alternate systemic possibilities.

Japan, 1950–2000

Japan's basic preoccupations before the early 1970s concentrated on internal economics and politics. Following the difficult immediate postwar years, its economy, effectively insulated from external disturbances, performed well for most of the 1960s. The real economic growth rate averaged about 10 per cent until the first oil crisis in 1973, and political stability, with a major emphasis on economic growth, reigned. From July 1960 until July 1972, there was only one change of prime minister.

Despite occasional disturbances both inside and outside Japan, most years of the third quarter of the century provided a favorable international environment, compared with the first decade of the fourth quarter, 1975–85. Aside from the immediate postwar years, Japan had a 'sort of vacation' from most of the painful international and political complications that it experienced between the mid-nineteenth century and the mid-twentieth century.[27] During those one hundred years, Japan was plagued and shaped largely by national insecurity.[28] The third quarter of the century was an exceptional period compared with the more tumultuous fourth quarter.

Many favorable conditions enabled Japan to achieve high economic growth and continuous political stability. Among them, the most important are (1) the upward trend of the world economy in the third quarter of the century; (2) latecomer effects in industrialization; and (3) the resilient US hegemonic umbrella in both the military and the economic areas.

Even the most cursory comparison of the 1950s and 1960s with the 1930s and 1940s or with the 1970s and 1980s makes the overall differences between them clear. The four criteria Kondratieff utilized to identify long-term conjunctional change—wars, technological innovation, gold production (or, in more contemporary terms, money supply), and agricultural production (resource constraints)—are useful measures in this regard.[29]

The third quarter of the century was an era of global economic upturn by most criteria. World War II, the Cold War, the Korean war, and the Vietnam war played important roles in initiating or accelerating an upward trend or in effect precipitating the end of such an upturn. The waves of technological innovations and their rapid diffusion over the globe, in fields from steel to automobiles to petrochemicals to nuclear energy, were largely unprecedented in terms of their variety and enormous impact on production. The money supply expanded greatly in many countries, accommodating flourishing business activities and accelerating inflation. Resource constraints were hardly felt during most of the period. For the most part, commodity prices remained low during the 1950s and 1960s.

It was quite fortunate for Japan that it underwent its recovery and expanded growth during a period of world economic prosperity. Without this coincidence, Japan's economic growth would have taken a much longer and more hazardous path. Japan's previous spurt in industrialization took place in the increasingly unfriendly environment of the 1930s and 1940s.[30] Difficulties on a worldwide scale in trade and monetary transactions, in technology transfers, and in resource utilization and the eventual involvement in hostilities on all fronts forced Japan to mobilize economic resources for war. At least temporarily, this prematurely terminated Japan's industrial growth. Furthermore, national insecurity heavily influenced the forms of economic and political institutions throughout the period. The strong duality in industrial structure (with more secure, larger industries, on the one hand, and less secure, smaller industries, often the former's subcontractors, on the other hand) and political authoritarianism were two examples.[31] In the 1950s and 1960s, such unfavorable conditions did not exist.

Latecomer effects give a certain advantage to being industrially backward.[32] A latecomer can achieve more rapid economic growth because of lower costs and technological improvements by learning from the forerunners. Most crucially, a latecomer can dispense with a large amount of R&D because the pioneers have already explored the technological frontiers and the subsequent technological diffusion usually enables cheaper acquisition of new technologies.[33] Japan's contributions to technological innovation were concentrated more in manufacturing than in scientific discovery. With the markets for certain products already created by the early starters, those Japanese products with quality, cost, and other comparative advantages slowly and steadily penetrated the market. It is sometimes difficult to recall that Japan was the lonely forerunner of the newly industrializing countries outside Western Europe and North America in the 1950s and early 1960s and that Japan was a recipient of IMF loans until the mid-1960s. The latecomer effect accounts for much of the Japanese economic expansion.

The US hegemonic umbrella ensured Japan access to the world market and allowed Japan to dispense more or less with military expenditures. The US hegemonic position in the international system came about during World War II. First, the United States was the most effective contributor to the military and economic weakening of Germany and Japan.[34] Second, the United States steadily rooted out British colonial positions around the world in the process of working out the postwar international economic, political, and military framework of the US-dominated neo-liberal imperium.[35] Although the Soviet Union also emerged as a victor, the contrast between the two countries was stark: the United States lost 290,000 men in the war whereas the USSR lost about 20 million; the United States had an enormous supply arsenal, the USSR found it difficult to acquire production facilities and fuel; the United States produced more than 60 per cent of the world's manufactured products, the USSR a much smaller amount. In short, the US preponderance in the economic and military fields far outweighed the rest of the world.[36] Owing to these dominant economic, military, and even cultural positions, the United States shaped and remolded the postwar international system. The IMF and World Bank as economic institutions, NATO and other alliances as military institutions, and the United Nations and other organizations as political institutions were imprinted with US hegemony in loosely institutionalized forms.[37]

For Japan, the US hegemonic umbrella meant primarily three things.[38] With Japan's security tied to US global strategies and US military bases in Japan, Japan could dispense with most military expenditures. The ratio of military expenditures to overall government spending has been about 5 per cent and its ratio to GNP has been less than 1 per cent for the past two decades. This is a minuscule amount compared with that spent by the other major OECD powers (approximately 10–30 per cent of total government spending).

Economically, Japan enjoyed liberal access to the world market, both for exports of manufactured goods and imports of natural resources. Without this unprecedented liberal economic order, Japan would have found it difficult to develop its present-day trading pattern with the rest of the world. The yen-dollar exchange rate was favorable to Japanese exports, and Japan benefited much from this for most of the third quarter of this century. The fixed exchange-rate system provided much needed stability and predictability for Japanese manufacturers and traders.

Politically, US support of the conservatives during the Occupation allowed them to recuperate from the disgrace of defeat and the damages of the early Occupational reforms. Without active US support, it would have been more difficult for the Japanese conservatives to occupy what is called in political theory the Downsian center of the electoral spectrum, as they gradually did during the early 1950s after labor unions were fully legitimized, tenants liberated, business conglomerates disbanded, and many political and economic leaders purged from office by the early Occupation reforms. If the predominant party system was, as is often said, a major source of political stability and economic success in the 1950s and 1960s, then some credit goes to the United States, at least from the Japanese conservatives' point of view.

A major turnabout became increasingly clear in the 1970s and 1980s, when the three major conditions supporting Japan's political economy in the third quarter of the century eroded to a considerable extent. First, the world economy is experiencing a reversal in the fourth quarter of the century. The average growth rate in real income in the OECD countries registered an unmistakable decline in the beginning of the fourth quarter.[39] The Vietnam war, a major conflict in terms of its consequences on the belligerent countries and the world as a whole, ended with an unequivocal outcome in 1975. With the beginning of détente in the early 1970s, military activities slackened, at least in the United States. Although technological innovation continued to be as vigorous as before, its ability to stimulate economic activities became less powerful, despite its variety. The expansion of the money supply, however, did not increase as rapidly as the economic growth rate because of prolonged stagnation; resource constraints were felt less strongly because some resources, like oil, had already reached their upper limits shortly before. In the early 1980s, the worldwide supply of oil and the US supply of wheat and corn, for example, were plentiful; manufactured products were also in oversupply, but demand was sluggish and unemployment soared.

Second, much of the latecomer effect became less pronounced because of Japan's admirable success. Such phenomena as the high population growth rate, the high percentage of the population working, the high investment in production equipment and socioeconomic infrastructure, the high growth rate of real gross fixed-capital formation, and the preponderance of the manufacturing sector in the economy either ceased to exist or weakened substantially. During the past decade, some of the latecomer attributes characterizing the Japanese model disappeared, although they continue to be much commented on both inside and outside Japan.[40]

Yet Japan's economic performance is still one of the best in the world, causing nightmares for both North America and Western Europe. Many articles published in the United States portray Japan as engaging in an economic Pearl Harbor.[41] As one of the few beneficiaries of the Reagan boom of the mid-1980s, Japan has caused envy and enmity throughout the world, including in the United States itself. But Japan is facing an unenviable situation in which the weakening of its latecomer attributes and its increasing international burden sharing will steadily slow its growth potential. Economic liberalization and higher integration with the US economy increase Japan's vulnerabilities to a US recession, as well as to US whims.[42] In Europe, many Japanese visitors have been told that European life would be much easier without a militarily threatening USSR and an economically formidable Japan.[43]

Third, US hegemony has been eroding slowly. The abandonment of the gold standard in 1971 was taken as a painful US announcement of its abjuration of its position as the preponderant and sole responsible molder of the international monetary system. The US withdrawal from Vietnam in 1973 was viewed as a grudging US admission of its inability to assume the role of the sole arbiter of international conflict. Militarily, the USSR has been catching up steadily with the US, especially during the 1970s, when the United States slowed or stopped much of its military expansion efforts. Neither the United States nor the USSR, however, seems clearly superior to the other. A series of large-scale US and Soviet military and naval maneuvers at various key spots in the past decade seems to document both their difficult-to-hide insecurity and their drive for power.

The Reaganite response to the US decline was manifested first in the form of a prosperity based on a large-scale tax cut and second in the form of ever-increasing defense spending financed by unprecedented government deficits.[44] Although US military hegemony and monetary sovereignty have not changed fundamentally, during the first decade of the fourth quarter of the century, they have become major disturbing, disquieting, and disorganizing forces in the international system.

Altered environments and modified assumptions

Global economic metamorphoses

The two basic changes in the international economic environment since 1973 are the floating exchange-rate system and creeping protectionism combined with trade liberalization. The United States, which created and sustained after World War II what Ronald McKinnon calls the world dollar standard system, abandoned it abruptly in 1971 because it could no longer maintain it.[45] Keeping the US dollar as virtually the sole international currency created three difficulties.[46] First, the overvalued dollar according to the fixed exchange-rate system with dollar-gold convertibility is considered to have contributed to the enormous US trade deficits. Second, the large amount of dollars flowing easily in and out of the United States is thought to have lessened the effectiveness of domestic economic management. Third, the enormous capital outflows following multinational companies abroad are believed to have caused a gradual shortage of capital investment for domestic industries, resulting in a steady loss of competitiveness.

Since 1973, a more efficient floating exchange-rate system than that of 1971 has been installed. Its most important feature is credit expansion. Throughout the post-oil crisis period, the major factors contributing to credit expansion have been the separation of the dollar and gold, the institutional innovation of credit lending through consortia, the financial liberalization spearheaded by the United States, and the great fluctuations in the US money supply expansion rate. Other than credit expansion, this capital regime was not a perfect solution. Two important problems are that exchange rates have been subject to somewhat wild vibrations and domestic macroeconomic management is no more effective than before.

Instability and disorder in the international system in the 1970s and 1980s have further accelerated speculative flows of capital. The long business slump since 1974 has led many banks and firms throughout the world, especially in surplus countries (first the OPEC countries and then Japan) and US-based banks and and multinational companies, to earn profits by investing in stocks and bonds. The decade-long global economic slowdown has meant surplus capacity for business firms, which have become large conglomerations of banks, security houses, mutual security societies, general trading companies, and think tanks, in addition to their primary function as manufacturing factories. Many big business firms are now speculators. Money moves across borders on the order of $150–200 billion a day.

Most troublesome for the first half of the 1980s was the overvalued dollar, caused primarily since the late 1970s by high US interest rates. The dollar's high value has contributed to the US trade deficits. It encouraged the alarming amount of capital inflows into the United States that made it a world debtor country by the end of 1984, seventy years after its status changed from debtor to creditor. The possibility of vast amounts of foreign capital leaving the United States, thus causing a sudden large-scale depreciation of the dollar once interest rates are lowered drastically to encourage the economy, has been a real possibility, especially for the past few years.[47]

Furthermore, the United States has asked and pressured Japan to liberalize its domestic financial institutions toward fully accommodating foreign financial institutions' activities in Japan and to internationalize its domestic financial markets to enable Japanese financial firms to conduct business abroad freely.[48] The floating exchange-rate system has so encouraged short-run capital flows that Japan cannot remain an exception in international finance. Second, the saturation and suppression of domestic demand in Japan and the large amount of surplus funds have forced Japanese firms, banks, and security houses to pursue more opportunities abroad in terms of syndicated loans, Eurobond underwriting, and foreign direct investment.

The transition to the floating exchange-rate system was thus the first important change in the international economic environment that effected an economic metamorphosis in Japan. Since the shift to the floating exchange-rate system was beyond the control of the Japanese authorities, we can call it environmental. The sheer size, the extraordinary resource dependence, and the ever-growing economic interdependence that characterize the Japanese economy fostered a strong sense of vulnerability throughout the 1970s and into the 1980s.[49]

The second environmental change is creeping protectionism combined with trade liberalization.[50] The onset of the global recession in 1973 accelerated the significant advances of economies that had not been major forces in world production and trade.[51] There are, along with Japan, a dozen or so newly industrializing countries (NICs). Taking advantage of the relative decline in competitiveness in certain manufacturing sectors of the major industrialized countries in Western Europe and North America, they have captured increasingly large export-market shares in the industrialized countries in, among other sectors, textiles, shipbuilding, steel, automobiles, electric appliances, and electronic components and equipment. Industrial adjustment in such industries has been slow and faced dogged resistance, revealing their inability to phase out, in large part because of self-complacency and sociopolitical rigidities.[52]

The result has been creeping protectionism in Western Europe and North America. Often, overt nontariff barriers are used. Manufacturing sectors benefiting from overt nontariff barriers in the 1970s and early 1980s accounted for 34 per cent of the market for US manufacturing, 10 per cent for Canada, 20 per cent for Germany, 32 per cent for France, 34 per cent for Italy, 22 per cent for Great Britain, and 7 per cent for Japan.[53] An economist has estimated, however, the overall loss to Japanese exports incurred because of the toughest measures threatened by protectionist hard-liners at 10 per cent.[54] Sometimes outright restrictions are imposed, as in France with Japanese videotape recorders. Sometimes bilateral agreements curtail the expansion of imports, as with NIC textiles and Japanese automobiles. New entrants have posed a serious problem to old GATT members, who are accustomed to dealing with problems emanating from economies 'similarly structured'. They use protectionist threats to induce the up-and-coming countries to 'behave well', that is, according to their norms and rules.[55]

The Tokyo Round Free Trade Agreement, concluded in 1979 and to be implemented by 1987, will lower tariff barriers to an unprecedented degree. Since 1979, there has been a combination of free trade rhetoric on the one hand and a delayed implementation of the agreement and creeping protectionism using nontariff barriers on the other hand. The high export dependence and the lack of 'similarly structured' economies in Asia have made Japan all the more concerned about the creeping tide of protectionism.

Yet a larger trend is the increasing volume of trade across and against national barriers. For the dozen years since the global recession began in 1973, only once—in 1982—did world trade register an absolute decline. Creeping trade protectionism seems, therefore, a politico-economic manifestation of the relative maladjustment of a sector or an industry in the face of increasingly strong global forces penetrating national economies.

Two Japanese assumptions altered

Along with these two fundamental changes in the international economic environment have come two fundamental changes in Japanese assumptions on economic management in the 1980s. The first assumption is that a small economy does not influence other economies, whereas a large economy does. The second is that an economy can be isolated and regulate external forces at its borders.

The small economy assumption was discarded with the rapid expansion of the Japanese economy, an economy that has come to affect the world economy significantly. Starting with geographically adjacent economies, a number of countries bordering the Western Pacific are strongly affected by Japan. Business conditions in the latter often crucially affect economic directions in the former. Most noteworthy are the Far Eastern NICs, whose manufacturing and trade crucially depend on the imports of capital goods from Japan and enormous borrowing of Japanese capital.[56] Japan is the number-one trade partner and/or the number-one aid donor for more than half the countries in the Western Pacific.[57] Many of them have trade deficits with Japan.

More important from a global point of view is the increasing trade interdependence of the United States. The ratio of exports to GNP in the United States almost doubled during the 1970s. The United States could no longer realistically aspire to become an independent Fortress America, as was the case with the Energy Independence project of the early 1970s. A large part of US trade is its Pacific trade, which by 1977 had surpassed its Atlantic trade.

Not only in trade but also in finance, Japan has ceased to be a small country.[58] Japan's foreign direct investment tripled between 1981 and 1983. Japan's direct investment in the United States accounted for 87 of the 325 cases of foreign direct investment in the United States in 1984.[59] Capital inflows into the United States from Japan as well as from elsewhere have become so immense that the United States could not risk alienating foreign capital by suddenly lowering interest rates, which could result only in a sharp decline in the dollar's value. Japan's financial ties with the rest of the world have become very tight and dense over the past few years.

The closed economy assumption has also become unsustainable. Before 1973, the Japanese economy was characterized by a constellation of localized competitive systems.[60] Since business firms desperately needed financial resources for high-level investment in a high-growth economy and since the Japanese economy was basically closed, financial authorities were effectively able to regulate financial flows to firms, sector by sector, through commercial banks with official guidance and financial intermediation. The large amounts of savings captured by quasi-governmental financial institutions like the Postal Savings system enabled the financial authorities to adopt this system of regulation. The consequences were that the financial market was highly regulated whereas the product market was not and that intrasectoral competition was fierce (localized competition) whereas the national market as a whole was compartmentalized. Thus, the somewhat enigmatic picture emerged of strict state regulation in finance coexisting with fierce market competition in manufacturing.

After the first oil crisis, however, the direction of financial flows was reversed.[61] Instead of money flowing from the public sector to the private sector in large amounts, as was the case before 1973, money has come to flow more from the private sector to the public sector, primarily in the form of government bond purchases. Overloaded by swollen expenditures created especially by the large-scale introduction of social security programs at the end of the high growth period, the government was forced to issue an enormous amount of government bonds and requested that the private sector 'digest' them.[62]

One of the structural components that enabled the government to regulate the private sector has been eroded by the change in the tide of monetary flows. Since the net savings rate remained as high as before, government bonds were digested without causing inflation in Japan, unlike the case in the United States.[63] The consequence was, however, to strengthen the influence of private financial institutions vis-à-vis the government.[64] This trend was furthered by the strong global tide of financial liberalization and internationalization ushered in by the transition from the world dollar-standard system to the floating exchange-rate system.[65] Under the floating exchange-rate system, short-term capital movements have become a major feature of international transactions. Hand in hand with this trend, the overall demand for financial liberalization and internationalization has been intensified, starting with the United States and then proliferating steadily among other OECD countries and the NICs.

This tide partly resulted from the expansion and performance of the Japanese economy. First, the rapid expansion of the Japanese economy in terms of GNP, gross fixed-capital formation, exports and imports, and foreign reserves has made it difficult for the Japanese economy to remain isolated from foreign economic influence. The enormous success of the Japanese economic expansion has made Japan more visible and more susceptible to criticism that it does not guarantee reciprocity in the openness of markets, both product and financial. Japan's soaring trade balances and growing foreign market shares for certain products have made it difficult to argue against this contention. Second, the good performance of the Japanese economy has been evidenced twice since the first oil crisis in the overall appreciation of the yen. Over the long term, demand for the yen as an international currency will increase. As of 1983, yen-dominated foreign reserves account for a mere 3.9 per cent of total world reserves.[66]

For these reasons, the days of the neatly insulated and effectively managed economy are gone, and the economy has become far more susceptible to international market forces. As domestic demand for manufactured goods is saturated, foreign direct investment increases. As allegations that Japanese exports generate unemployment in importing countries grow harsh, foreign direct investment again increases. As accusations of Japanese resource exploitation increase, foreign direct investment and official development assistance rise. As domestic bond markets become saturated, business firms increasingly draft foreign bonds or Eurobonds abroad, denominated either in dollars or in yen. Conversely, foreign business firms will increasingly draft yen-denominated bonds in Japan. As Japan's surplus capital increases, given its high saving rate, the volume of syndicated Eurocurrency credits increases. The consequences of these changes for international manufacturing and financial patterns are not yet clear. But there is one positive consequence that can be surmised but not yet empirically proved.

The horizon of activities in financing and marketing has been broadened and globalized. Financing and sales abroad are now much easier, and business firms are likely to depend far more strongly on foreign markets. Unless a thorough domestic financial liberalization is achieved simultaneously and unless Japan moves upward in technological and industrial innovation by not comforting itself with manufacturing abroad and foreign sales in markets it now dominates, the possibility exists that the international competitiveness of Japanese products will decline.

The US experience in the 1950s, 1960s, and 1970s is instructive in this regard. Production abroad by US multinational firms mushroomed when opportunities abounded under US hegemony.[67] By the mid-1960s, however, capital outflows from US banks financing these multinationals became unbearable because of balance-of-payments problems. Moreover, the Euromoney market developed beyond US regulation, and capital outflows continued in the form of offshore markets. The fixed exchange-rate system with dollar-gold convertibility was finally abandoned by 1971. Since then, enormous amounts of capital have flowed out of the United States. These capital outflows seemed to have contributed considerably to the 'deindustrialization' of the US economy.[68]

As a result, domestic manufacturing sectors have not received sufficient investment. When the economy finally started to recover, enormous capital inflows from abroad attracted by high interest rates helped make the United States a debtor country.[69]

To sum up, Japan has ceased to be a small and closed economy in the past decade. It made the transition to the floating exchange-rate system in 1973, agreed to trade liberalization at the Tokyo Round of GATT in 1979, signed the Japan-US agreement on Japanese financial liberalization and internationalization in 1984, and announced the three-year Action Program of economic liberalization and market access in 1985. In other words, Japan is now a large and rapidly liberalizing economy.

Global security metamorphoses

Japan's security environment has not changed as dramatically as its economic environment; continuity has been stronger than discontinuity in this area. Nevertheless, two significant changes in the security environment have occurred: renewed competition between the United States and the USSR, and US hegemonic pressure on its allies.

The first change, from détente to renewed hostility between the United States and the USSR,[70] is the most important change in the Japanese security environment since the heyday of détente in the early and mid-1970s. Since Japan has been under the US security umbrella, any alteration in basic US foreign policy needs careful attention from Japan.

During the 1970s, the Americans and the Soviets interpreted détente very differently. The United States viewed détente as mutual restraint in excessive military buildup. (Recall Harold Brown's testimony: 'When we build, they build; when we cut, they build.'[71]) The USSR took détente as US restraint in furthering US nuclear superiority vis-à-vis the USSR, given the US difficulties in Vietnam and the post-oil crisis recession. The United States thought of détente as moderation of Soviet expansionary efforts; the USSR took détente as US restraint in blocking the forces of liberation and revolution in the Third World, especially since the Soviets perceived the 'correlation of forces' as favoring the progressive forces of the world.

Besides these interpretive differences, the domestic contexts of the two countries, especially the conservative resurgence in the United States and secondarily the post-revolutionary stagnant conservatism in the last Brezhnev and post-Brezhnev eras, have been conducive to renewed animosity.[72] The resumption of a large-scale nuclear arms race in the late 1970s coincided with increasing strains and conflicts within each of the two blocs loosely headed by the two countries. Some Soviet clients and ex-clients were openly defiant (the turmoil in Poland, the anti-government war in Afghanistan, and China's invasion of Vietnam).[73] In the view of the US government, some of its Western allies were moving toward 'finlandization', and Japan was becoming an economic menace and hindering the US restoration and reindustrialization program.[74]

The second change, the US attempt to align its allies under its schemes far more strongly than before, is related to the first change. With a somewhat exaggerated perception of the Soviet military threat, the United States has been attempting to make its allies more cohesive and more supportive of its scheme to restore a reinvigorated hegemony. Efforts to reassert US hegemony have focused on three areas of US superiority: sophisticated weapons, high-tech communications, and international finance. In particular, the reinforced US nuclear superiority over its allies has no parallel since 1945.[75] The principal US concerns have been not to let the Europeans be lured into finlandization or Euroneutralism and not to allow either the Europeans or the Japanese to conduct business as usual with the Soviet bloc.

Two Japanese assumptions shaken

With these environmental changes as systematic constraints, Japan's security policy has undergone a metamorphosis. Like the small-country assumption in the economic area, the Japan-as-a-free-rider assumption rested on its small size and light weight. The sheer economic size of Japan, however, had rendered the first assumption ridiculous to many observers by the late 1970s. Similarly, the fast advances of Japanese high technology—in communications equipment, new materials, robotics, and electronic components—had made Japan very visible and rendered the free-rider assumption obsolete by the late 1970s.[76]

Nonetheless, the Japanese economy has not expanded to such a degree as to enable Japan to pursue a 'go it alone' posture. The policy line of Mao's China in 1957 (both economic and nuclear) has not been a viable option for China, let alone for Japan. De Gaulle's 1964 decision to depart NATO has not been considered an attractive option either. Most thoughtful Japanese apparently think that working with the United States as a second-rate power—or a junior partner—is the prudent choice for Japan in the foreseeable future.[77] Japan's course is thus to contribute as much as possible to US policy out of its abundant economic resources since few in Japan have fundamentally questioned the US-Japan security alliance.

One way that Japan plays this positive supportive role is to emphasize the multidimensional nature of national security, using the notion of 'comprehensive security' proposed by a study group established during Prime Minister Ohira's tenure (1978–80).[78] The hope hidden in this notion is that Japan's contributions to global economic welfare (foreign aid, debt rescheduling, and contributions to international organizations) will be conceived as security-related, supportive contributions. The notion of comprehensive security succeeded an emphasis on economic security in the mid 1970s.[79] The first oil crisis brought home to the Japanese that Japan's survival depended virtually on every corner of the world and forced Japan to plan for emergencies with such economic security programs as energy and resource diversification, energy conservation, and self-sufficiency in food. When the notion of economic security was discussed after the first oil crisis, many people still assumed that Japan could avoid involvement in conflicts in other parts of the world. What Japan has to do is to secure energy, food, other natural resources, and, of course, product markets, all despite wars. With the advent of the second cold war, this assumption has also been rejected.[80]

The other aspect of the Japanese security metamorphosis is the gradual erosion of the island of peace assumption, the mindset of most Japanese that grew out of the lesson they drew from the events of the 1930s and 1940s.[81] Most Japanese assume that as long as Japan is not armed and does not harbor any intent of military aggrandizement, foreign countries will respect Japanese sovereignty. Therefore, Japan ought to refrain from any activities that might involve Japan in an armed conflict. The postwar appeal of pacifism to most Japanese has not yet subsided.

The Ohira government considered policy alignment with the United States vital, and it came to describe Japan as 'a member of the Western alliance'.[82] The drastic change in tone of the 1979 White Paper on Defense reflects the government's fine-tuning in line with the change in US policy during the late Carter administration. The Suzuki government (1980–82) took 'two steps forward, one step backward' on the question of policy alignment, using the word 'alliance' in the Japan-US joint communiqué of 1981, but later giving the word an interpretation tailored to the domestic audience. The Nakasone government (1982–1987) has unequivocally supported the Reagan administration against the USSR. Its vehement opposition to the

Soviet introduction of intermediate-range nuclear forces targeted at Western Europe and its explicit linkage of Japanese security with European and thus global security were a clear departure from past policy. On the whole, however, the Nakasone government's policy toward Japan's military buildup, security-related technological cooperation, and joint naval and military exercises is largely a continuation of the Ohira and Suzuki governments' policies.

Countering this trend of policy alignment with the United States is pacifism, which has undertones of isolationism, unilateralism, and free-ridership. Isolationism is manifested in the belief that if Japan avoids weapons and conflicts, peace is bound to prevail. The unilateral pledge to the cause of peace in Article 9 of the Japanese constitution is thought to have had good effects for Japan. The importance of free-ridership is clear. The island of peace has been kept intact under the US security umbrella and sphere of influence since 1945. The Japanese have been ambivalent about acknowledging the US umbrella since they fear that the US forces in Japan (with or without nuclear weapons) might induce or invite an attack by a third party against Japan.

The reinvigorated military and naval forces of the Soviet Union over and adjacent to Japanese territories and general Soviet provocations since the mid-1970s have, however, aroused dissonant feelings within the Japanese government. This has been especially true since the Soviet provocations followed the adoption in 1976 of the Self-Defense Policy program based on the assumptions of the détente period of the early and mid-1970s.

On top of this, US pressure for burden sharing led the Japanese government to be more conscious of the security ties with the United States. The overriding motive of the Japanese government in accommodating the US government's requests and pressures in this respect and others is a strong sense of Japan's vulnerabilities and the incalculable cost associated with security independence.[83] Japanese compliance over the past few years with US demands in such areas as defense cooperation, trade liberalization, and liberalization of finance and capital markets cannot be explained without fathoming Japan's deep sense of vulnerability.

The government has moved cautiously toward accommodation while being attentive not to arouse public pacifism. The basic cost-benefit calculation of the Japanese government seems to be that the economic costs of accommodation are basically manageable and that the psychological costs have to be lowered by 'educating' the Japanese public.[84] Gradual intensification of the key words used to characterize the security ties with the United States are part of this process: 'a member of the Western bloc' (Ohira), a US ally (Suzuki), and 'an unsinkable fortress' (Nakasone). The inevitable retreats associated with the revelation of these characterizations are designed to appease the intensely pacifist domestic audience and evidence some of the difficulties that lie ahead for the government. Although the Japanese government has been scared by the seriousness with which the US government has been thinking about the possibilities of Japanese fighting together with Americans, it has so far cooperated.

How far the Japanese government can go is a moot question, however. The Japanese military capability is still extremely limited, especially in light of the contingencies that the US government expects the Japanese Self-Defense Forces to meet. Since the Japanese government does not believe that the Soviet intermediate-range nuclear forces are primarily and massively targeted at Japan, it can avoid the hard decision over which defense posture Japan should develop in relation to the Japan-US alliance.[85]

In sum, Japan has cautiously been modifying the two assumptions that governed its security policy until recently—the free-rider assumption and the island of peace assumption—and has started to assume more of a supporter's role in direct response to changes in the security environment as well as in US policy.

Internal logic

If changes in the global, economic, and security environments include systemic requirements that demand Japanese adaptation, then domestic values and structures work as a basis and a filter for adaptation and thus render change more compatible with internal logic and more amenable to it.[86] Internal logic is robust and resilient to change when values and structures have been shaped and restructured incrementally over forty years of successes in achieving the two basic priorities of maintaining peace and achieving prosperity.

A resilient pattern of priorities

Most revealing of the Japanese preference pattern is the record, shared by few countries, of having waged no wars since World War II.[87] This contrasts with the fifty years preceding 1945, when Japan was one of the most intensely war-waging nations in the world.[88] The postwar Japanese commitment to self-restraint in this respect cannot be overexaggerated.

Having been barred from heavily rearming itself because of its defeat in World War II and the subsequent US occupation, Japan's policy with respect to economic well-being and military spending has been weighted overwhelmingly in favor of the former. Japan relegates most of its critical military roles to the US forces inside and outside Japan. It was President Truman who overruled Prime Minister Churchill's advice to allow Japan to retain a small army after the war and provided the Japanese with a constitution in which Japan relinquished any military role.[89] In other words, the United States imposed security free-ridership on Japan.

During the Occupation, the United States maintained its policy on Japanese national security, but did drastically alter its policy in order to transform Japan into an industrially strong ally from which US forces could operate effectively to contain communist forces nearby, whether they were Soviet, Chinese, or North Korean. This response emerged from the intensified cold war in the late 1940s, particularly after the outbreak in 1950 of the Korean war, but US policy on Japanese national security as such was consistent.[90]

The US and the Japanese governments' positions on Japan's national security formula roughly converged. The Japan-US Mutual Security Treaty signed and ratified in 1951 and put into effect in 1952 in tandem with Japan's regaining its independence makes it crystal clear that the US forces bear most of the responsibility for assuring Japan's national security.[91] The Japanese government and most Japanese wanted the Self-Defense Forces to play a minor role. The primary and secondary roles of the Self-Defense Forces in the early years were to help maintain law and order at a time of political and economic turmoil and Left-Right confrontation and to serve as a disaster-relief force. Only gradually has their role in national defense come to be perceived as primary.[92]

The primary concern of the Japanese government during the first two postwar decades was economic recovery and reconstruction. Few would have welcomed a defense burden during this period. As GNP expanded in the 1960s and 1970s, defense expenditure declined in proportion to the total budget. When the growth rate of government revenues far exceeded the estimated growth rate of the economy in the early 1970s, the Tanaka government (1972–74) decided to expand social welfare to an overwhelming proportion.[93] Cries for improvements in social welfare and the environment in reaction to some of the negative social consequences of growth-first economic management, together with criticisms from abroad, encouraged the government to do so.[94] Shortly after the government reaffirmed its butter-first policy in the 1970s, the Miki government (1974–76)), leaning to the left within the Liberal Democratic Party (LDP), put a cap on the expansion of the defense budget in relation to GNP.[95] Aided by the sheer growth of GNP, this semibinding threshold was maintained for the succeeding ten years, even when both superpowers began the second cold war in the late 1970s. All this amply illustrates the stability and robustness of the Japanese government's guns-and-butter policy mix.

Table 1.1 Major categories of Japanese expenditure, General Account Budget, 1955–87 (¥100 million)

Expenditure	| Fiscal year							
	1955	1965	1975	1980	1984	1985	1986	1987
National debt	434 (4.4)	220 (0.6)	10,394 (4.9)	53,104 (12.5)	91,551 (18.1)	102,241 (19.5)	113,195 (10.7)	113,335 (0.1)
Local government	1,374 (13.9)	7,162 (19.6)	44,086 (20.7)	65,452 (15.4)	88,864 (17.5)	96,601 (18.5)	101,850 (5.1)	101,841 (−0.0)
General account Social security	1,043 (10.5)	5,183 (14.2)	39,282 (18.5)	82,124 (19.3)	93,211 (18.4)	95,737 (18.2)	98,346 (2.7)	100,896 (2.6)
Veterans pensions	895 (9.0)	1,693 (4.6)	7,558 (3.5)	16,399 (3.9)	18,859 (3.7)	18,637 (3.6)	18,501 (−0.7)	18,956 (2.5)
Education/science	1,308 (13.2)	4,751 (13.0)	25,921 (12.2)	45,191 (10.6)	48,323 (9.5)	48,409 (9.2)	48,409 (0.1)	48,497 (0.1)
Local finance	—	—	215 (0.1)	8,425 (2.0)	1,829 (0.4)	—	—	—
Defense	1,349 (13.6)	3,014 (8.2)	13,273 (6.2)	22,302 (5.2)	29,346 (5.7)	31,371 (6.0)	33,435 (6.6)	35,174 (5.2)
Public works	1,635 (16.5)	7,333 (20.0)	29,120 (13.7)	66,554 (15.6)	65,200 (12.9)	63,689 12.1	62,233 (−2.3)	60,824 (−2.3)

Economic assistance	101 (1.0)	271 (0.7)	1,926 (0.9)	3,826 (0.9)	5,439 (1.1)	5,863 (1.1)	6,232 (0.3)	6,492 (4.2)
Small business	26 (0.3)	217 (0.6)	1,273 (0.6)	2,439 (0.6)	2,292 (0.5)	2,162 (0.4)	2,052 (−5.1)	1,973 (−21.4)
Energy	— —	— —	884 (0.4)	4,241 (1.0)	6,032 (1.2)	6,288 (1.2)	6,297 (0.1)	4,952 (−21.4)
Food management	— —	1,055 (2.9)	9.086 (4.3)	9,556 (2.2)	8,132 (1.6)	6,954 (1.3)	5,962 (−14.3)	5,406 (−9.3)
Others	1,670 (16.8)	5,182 (14.2)	26,870 (12.6)	42,775 (10.0)	43,694 (8.6)	43,244 (8.2)	40,837 (−5.6)	39,163 (−4.1)
Emergency items	80 (0.8)	500 (1.4)	3,000 (1.4)	3,500 (0.8)	3,500 (0.7)	3,500 (0.7)	3,500 (0.0)	3,500 (0.0)
Gen'l acc't subtotal	8,107 (81.7)	29,199 (79.8)	158,408 (74.4)	307,332 (72.1)	325,857 (64.4)	325,854 (62.1)	325,842 (−0.0)	325,834 (−0.0)
TOTAL	9,915 (100.0)	36,581 (100.0)	212,888 (100.0)	425,888 (100.0)	506,272 (100.0)	524,696 (100.0)	540,886 (100.0)	541,101 (100.0)

Source: Zaisei Seisaku Kenyukai, ed., *Korekara no zaisei to kokusai hakko* (Finance and bond issues in the future) (Okura zaimu kyokai), 1985, p. 60; 1987, p. 30.

Note: Figures in parentheses are percentages of total.

The data in Table 1.1 further support this evaluation. It is clear that the expansion rate of defense expenditures was held lower than other categories of expenditures such as social security, public works, and education until the onset of the second cold war and the subsequent change in the international economic and security environments. The small size of Japan's defense expenditures in comparison with those of other major countries is shown in Table 1.2.

Table 1.2   *Defense expenditure patterns of selected OECD countries, 1978–86 (percentages)*

Year	Japan	US	UK	FRG	France
1978	5.5	23.5	14.4	19.4	17.5
1979	5.4	23.5	14.8	19.0	17.3
1980	5.2	23.6	14.7	19.0	17.4
1981	5.3	24.2	14.6	19.0	17.5
1982	5.5	26.2	15.8	18.8	18.3
1983	5.5	26.6	13.1	19.6	17.1
1984	5.8	26.8	13.5	19.7	18.2
1985	6.0	27.2	11.6	19.8	18.2
1986	6.2	27.6	—	19.9	—

Source: Nihon ginko chosa tokei kyoku, *Nihon keizai o chushin tosuru Kokusai hikaku tokei* (Comparative Economic and Financial Statistics, Japan and Other Major Countries) (Tokyo: Nihon ginko), 1986, p. 88; 1987, p. 88.

Table 1.3   *Japanese expenditure patterns before and after the first oil crisis, 1973 and 1985* (¥ billion)

	1973	1985	Growth rate %
Tax revenue	13.370	38,500	2.9
Size of General Account Budget	14,780	52,500	3.6
Social security	2,220	9,570	4.3
Education and science	1,640	4,840	2.9
Public works	2,560	6,370	2.5
Defense	950	3,140	3.3
CPI (1980 = 100)	55.4	112.1[a]	2.02
Annual GNP	116,600	314,600	2.7

Source: Same as Table 1.1; p. 61.

[a] 1984

It is immediately clear from Table 1.1 that Japanese 'butter' is produced mostly on a small scale. The level of Japanese wealth is not reflected in a proportionate level of investment in nonindustrial socioeconomic infrastructure. Most salient in this regard are houses, roads, sewers, and parks.[96] One could argue that the financial and administrative austerity policy of the past few years has led the government to rely more on the private sector than before, even in the area of infrastructure consolidation, and that the austerity policy accords well with the public's mild distrust of government spending habits. Even if this argument is accepted, one cannot deny that government expenditures on public works have been the primary target of the austerity policy. In fact, among government expenditures on social security, education, public works, and defense, public works recorded the lowest expansion rate between 1973 and 1985 (see Table 1.3).

Judging from the far from admirable achievements in this area, it seems that the Japanese miracle was a Pyrrhic victory based largely on the ephemeral advantage of economic backwardness and the adroitness in adaptation the Japanese were forced to acquire by perceived structural weaknesses, such as relative geographical isolation and the relative lack of natural and financial resources and of military might. One could even argue that both the wise allocation of resources to industrial manufacturing and infrastructure in the 1950s and 1960s and the respectable management of the economy in the 1970s and 1980s were made possible, however reluctantly, by sacrifices in the area of nonindustrial infrastructure.[97] The primacy of economic growth over social well-being in the former period and the primacy of anti-inflation policies over public spending in the latter period aptly sum up the priorities of the Japanese government and people. Since this policy priority pattern seems so robust, we need to look more closely at the most recent decade when policy priorities have shifted incrementally but without fundamentally altering the basic pattern of expenditures.

Self-restructuring under recession

The most salient feature of domestic management from 1973 to 1985 was the preoccupation with internal equilibrium. Domestic management of the economy and polity continued to absorb much of the government's energy and effort throughout the 1970s. This strong internal orientation contributed to the diffusion of externalities to the rest of the world, to the exacerbation of external issues, and thus to the difficulty of restructuring Japanese foreign policy in the 1980s.

In economic management, the first oil crisis was the watershed of Japanese economic development. It looked then as if the two mechanisms of Japanese economic growth for the preceding 20 years had foundered. The cheap and abundant supply of energy and other resources from abroad for refueling Japanese manufacturing halted abruptly. The subsequent economic recession replaced favorable conditions of easy access to basically expanding markets of the industrialized and industrializing worlds for Japanese exports of manufactured goods with increasingly stiff competition and creeping protectionism. These changes led some to conclude that the Japanese miracle had come to naught and that the Japanese future would be bleak at best. Contrary to this somewhat prematurely pessimistic view, however, the Japanese economy from the first oil crisis through the second oil crisis demonstrated that it was still robust and resilient, though not without problems and some important changes in its structure.[98] Various indicators of economic performance for the major industrialized countries clearly show that Japan's performance was among the best; inflation was effectively curtailed; real economic growth rate, though half of what it had been, still ran at a respectable 3–5 per cent on average; the unemployment rate doubled, but remained the lowest in the OECD (see Table 1.4)[99]

In monetary policy, the foremost policy emphasis after the first oil crisis was overcoming inflation.[100] The already overheated economy of the early 1970s was conducive to further inflation created by the first oil crisis. In 1974, Japan's inflation rate was the highest of the major industrialized countries. The hyperinflation of 1974 was, however, effectively tamed by 1976 through the fairly tight money supply policy pursued by monetary authorities. Since 1974, money expansion in terms of M2 and CD has averaged about 11 per cent.[101] The major considerations that led the monetary authorities to adopt this policy line were (1) the disappearance of the built-in economic discipline of the balance-of-payments ceilings since abandonment of the fixed dollar-yen exchange rate in 1973 and (2) the relative ineffectiveness of interest rate manipulation and public works spending in the stagflated economy.

On the whole, this 'price stability first', or deflationary, policy set the tone of economic management for the decade after 1974. For the most part, however, business activities still remained sluggish. The economic upturns of 1977 and 1978 were not full-fledged. The second oil crisis triggered another recession, although consumer price stability was on the whole maintained. The policy thrust has undoubtedly been to preserve internal equilibrium even at the cost of leaving intact much of the external equilibrium, thus arousing further international complications. Such disturbances as trade surpluses and wild exchange-rate movements were considered to be of secondary importance and were handled more or less on an ad hoc basis.

In fiscal policy, on the one hand, there has been a steady accumulation of government debts because of the sudden large-scale decrease in tax revenue (especially corporate tax revenue), a steady increase in social welfare spending since the enactment of the social security reforms of 1973, and the consequent large-scale government bond issues, especially since 1975. On the other hand, Keynesian economic management has been perceived as ineffective.[102]

The continuing expansion of government expenditures during the high growth period (1952–73) did not pose much of a problem to the government because GNP expanded more rapidly than government expenditure. The sudden advent of an economic recession in 1974, however, meant that government revenue was far below government expenditure, which was already structurally committed and thus difficult to alter. Most serious was the steady increase in social welfare expenditures, which was the direct result of the 1973 social welfare laws and the aging of the population. The most dramatic revelation of this imbalance appeared in 1975 with the issuance of the so-called deficit bonds. Although this was not a new practice, the enormity and severity of the revenue-expenditure gap in 1975 were unparalleled and encouraged the fiscal authorities to go ahead with the scheme. By 1985, the cumulative total of government bonds reached more than 42.3 per cent of GNP.[103]

Since government bond issues themselves do not cause inflation, this pattern of fiscal management was most convenient and most comfortable to the government, at least in the short run. Efforts to cut expenditures started only in the 1980s. Prime Minister Zenko Suzuki commissioned the Provisional Council on Administrative and Financial Reform, instituted into law in 1981. It presented its proposal to the cabinet in March 1983 after intensive study and discussion. The reform efforts represent a cumulative policy package and aim to change expenditure patterns and underlying policy priorities.

The economic authorities thought that Keynesian demand management would be ineffective in their attempts to stipulate demand in the stagflated economy and would only aggravate both inflation and unemployment. Rather, as summarized above, a tight money supply policy became the key policy instrument. Even when internal and external criticisms against the tight economic policy were raised in 1976–78, Keynesian management was not wholeheartedly adopted. The major thrust of fiscal policy is directed not at Keynesian macroeconomic management but at resource allocation and income redistribution. Again, this represents the primary preoccupation with internal equilibrium. Price stability and provision of largely divisible public goods are two of the major concerns of the Ministry of Finance.[104]

Two changes in the Japanese economy take on special significance because they are directly related to, if not necessarily caused by, the two macroeconomic policy thrusts outlined above. The ratio of government outlays to GNP increased from 12.7 per cent in 1973 to 17.7 per cent in

Table 1.4 *Major economic indicators for selected OECD countries, 1976–87*

Indicator	1976	1977	1978	1979	1980	1981	1982	1983	1984	1985	1986	1987
JAPAN												
Nominal GNP	12.4	11.0	9.9	8.0	8.7	5.9	4.9	4.3	6.7	5.9	4.4	4.6 est.
Real GNP	4.6	5.3	5.2	5.3	4.0	3.3	3.2	3.7	5.1	4.3	3.0	3.5 est.
CPI	9.5	6.9	3.8	4.8	7.6	4.0	2.6	1.9	2.2	1.9	0.5	1.6 est.
Unemployment	2.0	2.1	2.2	2.0	2.1	2.2	2.5	2.7	2.7	2.6	2.8	—
Current account ($100 million)	47	140	119	−139	−70	59	91	242	370	550	880	770 est.
Official interest rate	6.50	4.25	3.50	6.25	7.25	5.50	5.50	5.00	5.00	5.00	2.50	—
UNITED STATES												
Nominal GNP	11.5	11.7	13.0	11.5	8.9	11.7	3.7	7.6	10.5	6.2	5.2	6.5 est.
Real GNP	4.9	4.7	5.3	2.5	−0.2	1.9	−2.5	3.6	6.4	2.7	2.5	3.1 est.
CPI	5.8	6.5	7.7	11.3	13.5	10.4	6.1	3.2	4.3	3.6	1.9	3.0 est.
Unemployment	7.7	7.1	6.1	5.8	7.1	7.6	9.7	9.6	7.5	7.2	7.0	6.7 est.
Current account ($100 million)	4.2	−145	−154	−10	19	63	−91	−466	−1,065	−1,177	−1,406	—
Official interest rate	5.25	6.00	9.50	12.00	13.00	12.00	8.50	8.50	8.00	7.50	5.50	5.50 est.
UNITED KINGDOM												
Nominal GNP	17.3	15.2	15.4	15.8	16.0	8.9	8.7	9.3	7.6	9.6	5.4	—
Real GNP	2.6	2.6	2.8	2.7	−2.2	−1.2	1.5	3.4	2.8	3.4	2.6	3.0 est.
CPI	16.5	15.8	8.3	13.4	18.0	11.9	8.6	4.6	5.0	6.1	3.4	3.75 est.
Unemployment	4.5	4.8	4.7	4.3	5.4	8.5	9.8	10.7	11.1	11.3	11.5	—
Current account ($100 million)	−17	−2	19	−15	68	125	69	47	16	45	−5	—
Official interest rate	14.25	7.00	12.50	17.00	14.00	14.375	10.00	9.00	—	11.3125	10.8125	18.875 est.

FRG

Nominal GNP	9.4	6.5	7.7	8.1	6.3	4.0	3.4	5.1	5.0	4.8	5.5	4.0–4.5 est.
Real GNP	5.6	2.7	3.3	4.0	1.5	-0.0	-1.0	1.8	3.0	2.5	2.4	2.5 est.
CPI	4.4	3.6	2.7	4.2	5.4	6.3	5.3	3.3	2.4	2.2	-0.2	1.0 est.
Unemployment	4.6	4.5	4.3	3.8	3.8	5.5	7.5	9.1	9.1	9.3	9.0	8.5 est.
Current account ($100 million)	39	41	92	-60	-157	-52	41	41	70	132	3.58	—
Official interest rate	3.50	3.00	3.00	6.00	7.50	7.50	5.00	4.00	4.50	4.00	3.50	3.00 est.

FRANCE

Nominal GNP	15.5	12.3	13.6	14.1	13.4	12.3	14.7	10.5	8.9	7.5	6.9	5.7 est.
Real GNP	4.9	3.1	3.3	3.2	1.4	0.6	2.0	0.8	1.6	1.6	1.9	2.0 est.
CPI	9.6	9.4	9.1	10.8	13.6	13.4	11.8	9.6	7.4	5.8	2.7	2.5 est.
Unemployment	4.3	4.8	5.2	6.0	6.4	7.8	8.7	8.8	10.0	10.2	10.5	—
Current account ($100 million)	-34	-4	71	51	-42	-47	-121	-47	-8	-2	37	—
Official interest rate	10.50	8.875	6.375	12.125	10.75	15.125	12.75	12.00	9.50	8.75	7.25	7.75 est.

Source: Same as Table 1.1, 1987 ed., pp. 150–1.

1980.[105] In 1985 it reached 16.8 per cent. Though still low compared with comparable figures for most West European countries, the Japanese figures document the rapid expansion of the government's role in the economy over the past decade as an inevitable consequence of the government's accommodation of various public demands during the high growth period. The most important factor was a disturbingly steady increase in the amount of social security-related expenses. The welfare reforms enacted early in 1973 before the first oil crisis guarantee an automatic expansion in social welfare as long as the weight of the nonworking elderly population among the total population increases, which is indeed the case in the post-high growth period.[106] Moreover, although in 1969 the Diet passed a law prescribing a ceiling on the number of central government personnel, this did not limit the expansion of local government personnel, which increased in the 1970s with the expansion of educational and social welfare expenditures at the local level.

The second change is the increasing importance of foreign demand vis-à-vis domestic demand. Until the early 1970s, two features kept foreign trade from accounting for a large percentage of Japan's GNP: a large population with a high income level and Japan's effective isolation as a latecomer industrializing country. These two features caused a limited integration of the Japanese economy into the world economy in terms of the ratio of foreign trade to GNP, which belies the conventional image of Japan's reliance on exports. The figure was 22.2 per cent in 1970 and 26.1 per cent in 1980.[107]

However, the Japanese economy has become increasingly exposed to the world economy. The primary factor in this has been the saturated domestic demand since 1974. Deflationary economic policy, de facto tax increases, and semi-forced savings have all contributed to economic conservatism and made domestic demand sluggish. One extreme example of this is automobile sales. In January 1984, the domestic market accounted for 28.9 per cent of Japanese automobiles sold and the foreign market for 71.1 per cent.[108] A secondary factor is the liberalization of the Japanese economy. Macroeconomic management primarily oriented at maintaining internal equilibrium led manufacturers to rely increasingly on exports, but consumers were not much lured by less appealing, foreign-manufactured goods. Hence, growing external disturbances, such as criticisms of export drives as exporting unemployment and of high trade surpluses as originating from nontariff barriers against foreign products, have been almost inevitable.[109] In the mid-1980s, the aggravation of external economic frictions virtually forced the government to tackle such issues as the trade surplus and economic liberalization.

The politics of restructuring

Political management is the second facet of internal equilibrium. The predominantly internal preoccupation of the Japanese government throughout the 1970s was perhaps inevitable not only because of the economic recession but also because of the concurrent political problem of a possible loss of power to the opposition. The conservatives focused on restoring the internal equilibrium in their favor.[110]

Perhaps reflecting the complexity of problems facing incumbents, changes in government were far more frequent after 1972 than before throughout the democratic world. Japan was not an exception. Six prime ministers have ruled since 1972, whereas the decade before 1972 saw only two. The overall lower figures of public support for the LDP reflected the enormity of these problems. It looked during most of the 1970s as if the government might change hands at any moment. Nothing of that sort happened. Instead, support for the LDP started to increase in the late 1970s. Since Nakasone's ascension to power in 1982, the LDP has enjoyed extremely high opinion poll support. The most recent evidence of this high level of support was the landslide victory of the LDP in the elections for both Houses on July 6, 1986.[111]

Public support for the LDP reached a nadir in the 1970s. A series of external disturbances in the first half of the 1970s shocked, bewildered, or at least reinforced the feeling of uncertainty about the government. In addition, domestic upheavals were also pronounced. Accelerated inflation in the early 1970s was a major political issue for both Prime Ministers Sato and Tanaka. Environmental deterioration in the early 1970s enabled the opposition to gain control of many local governments. The Lockheed scandal and related malaise of the LDP delayed most major policy initiatives that needed to be tackled immediately. Intraparty conflicts within the LDP were aggravated by the handling of the issue of political ethics. The economic recession after the first oil crisis was prolonged until 1977. These unpleasant issues and concerns, along with the management of various external constraints and disturbances, dominated political developments in the first half of the 1970s. It is not surprising that public attitudes toward the incumbent party were not favorable.

Although external events occasionally gave cause for disquiet and uncertainty and the internecine struggle within the LDP was reinforced rather than resolved, political developments in the latter half of the 1970s and into the 1980s were more stablizing and reassuring from the viewpoint of the incumbent party. As business conditions picked up slowly in 1976–77, the incumbent party steadily regained public support. Although the second oil crisis delayed a fuller business recovery, the public's attitude toward the economy changed unmistakably during 1977–78 to quasi satisfaction verging on resignation with the status quo. With per capita income reasonably high, inflation effectively tamed, and annual real economic growth registering a respectable rate, the public increasingly exhibited economic conservatism.[112]

The perception of economic improvement in the recent past and the expectation of economic improvement in the near future tended to converge year by year. Economic conservatism seemed easily channeled into political conservatism. Public support for the LDP reached a high level in the early 1980s. The strong internal equilibrium evident in the political developments of the 1970s and the early 1980s, assisted very much by economic resilience, seemed to restore the composure of the incumbent party. Nonetheless, to a remarkable degree the conservatives seemed to achieve this not so much by longer-term design as by short-term muddling through.[113]

The primacy of restoring the internal equilibrium in the conservatives' favor can be seen in public as well.[114] Farmers and small-business owners represent the two most loyal and trustworthy constituencies of the LDP. Their support, however, declined considerably and reached a nadir between 1973 and 1976. Regaining the strong support of traditional conservatives was of utmost importance to the LDP. The instinctive LDP response was to favor these groups by passing laws that channeled the benefits of public policy to them or to protect them from internal and external structural forces by not changing laws in a more market-conforming direction.

The LDP's selective and differential wooing of different social groups was particularly pronounced in the decade after the first oil crisis. At this time, the agricultural population was declining rapidly, and food (except rice) was increasingly imported from abroad. By 1982, Japan exceeded the Soviet Union in the total amount of food imports. Small businesses found it increasingly difficult to resist competition and penetration by supermarket chains, department stores, and other kinds of stores run by big business. Small family-owned factories have been subject to competitive pressures from big business, especially when economic conditions were not favorable. Although small-business owners have not dwindled in number as rapidly as farmers, their number is more or less stable.

Specific target policies seem to have helped the LDP regain the support of the majority of farmers and small-business owners. For 1976–79, the average rate of increase in the Ministry of Agriculture's budget was 11.1 per cent. For small-business budget items, the average increase for 1974–79 was 19.8 per cent. These groups' support for the LDP increased by 8 per cent and 4.3 per cent, respectively, between 1976 and 1980.[115]

The LDP's adaptation in the new policy areas of social welfare and the environment was remarkable. Contrary to its previous policy priorities, in the 1970s the LDP geared its policy emphasis to these new areas. In 1971 the Environment Agency was established, and since 1972 social welfare expenditures have received a strong emphasis. Overall, social welfare expenditures annually registered a 24.5 per cent increase (1973–79), and environmental expenditures (facilities and equipment for an amenable living environment) a 25.6 per cent increase (1973–79).[116] By 1980, Japanese social welfare standards had reached a level roughly on a par with those of the major OECD countries, and Japanese environmental regulation was among the strictest in the world.[117] Many factors favored the LDP's pursuit of these policies, including a still respctable economic growth rate and a favorable demographic age profile.

A major consequence of this policy for the LDP was to dissipate criticisms from the opposition parties, who had gained control of many local governments by pointing to the central government's neglect of social welfare and the environment. The result of this unabashed policy adaptation was unequivocal. Among the social groups that showed the strongest interest in these two issues, LDP support increased significantly.[118] In support of the government's emphasis on social welfare were the jobless, the elderly, and managers and professionals; supporting its policies on environmental issues were white-collar workers, urban residents, and youth.

The reincorporation of traditional clients into the LDP camp and the winning over of those social groups agitated by the opposition characterized government-public relations in the 1970s. Consequently, the restoration and restructuring of internal equilibrium dominated political developments during this decade. Overall economic resilience helped the government, although the government's macroeconomic policy may be given equal credit. Internal equilibrium between the government and the public was restored, and although political concerns were focused primarily on domestic issues, exogenous disturbances helped the government in a small way to retain public support since the people tend to rally around the government during a time of foreign pressure and national crisis.

Meeting external requirements

That the basic orientation of government is toward internal equilibrium is not uncommon. By and large, the primary concerns and daily preoccupations of most central governments are about internal economic and political affairs. Japan is, however, an extreme example in its orientation toward internal affairs.

During the period of crisis absorption and management in 1973–78, the government was primarily concerned with assuring a stable supply of energy and nonenergy resources and with securing and expanding export markets around the world. During this period, the government favored the notion of 'economic security';[119] that is, security involved protecting and consolidating economic efficiency in light of the unstable international business environment. This notion fitted nicely with the then-prevailing mood in Japan that (1) national security is economic in nature and (2) national security is ensured by paying costs that do not derive from economic considerations alone. The government's efforts were largely confined to consolidating the Self-Defense Forces slowly but steadily within bureaucratic and political constraints, without directly articulating its strategy.

In the period of initial recuperation and restructuring in 1979–83, the government focused on the intricate matrices of economic, political and military aspects of the global transformation. The notion of 'comprehensive national security' became a favorite during this period.[120] The emphasis was national security, relying on all conceivable resources, albeit with an undeniable emphasis on economic power. Although the government increasingly recognized the need to tackle national security issues squarely, it was painfully aware of Japan's shortcomings in military power and, at the same time, of the foolishness of publicizing this fact. Clearly influencing the thinking of the government were the Vietnamese invasion and occupation of Kampuchea, the Chinese invasion of Vietnam, the Soviet invasion and occupation of Afghanistan, the Iran-Iraq war, the Israeli and Syrian occupation of Lebanon, the US military involvement in Nicaragua and other Central American republics, and the Soviet downing of a Korean Airline aircraft.[121] In addition, the increasingly stern economic and business environment clearly disturbed government and business leaders. Particularly worrisome were the rash of protectionist bills introduced in the US Congress, growing agitation in the EC against Japanese imports, the arresting of several Japanese nationals on charges of technological spying, and unfriendly takeovers of Japanese subsidiaries in the United States.

The path from economic security to comprehensive security was not linear. Rather, it involved a zigzag course reflecting the solid pacifist-isolationist sentiments of the public.[122] Furthermore, because of its strong internal preoccupation, even during this period it was necessary for the government to overhaul its whole range of public policies in order to redirect its foreign policy. Two actions are noteworthy.

The first was Prime Minister Ohira's creation of nine policy study groups on the future of Japanese culture, urban living, family life, lifestyle, science and technology, macroeconomic management, economic foreign policy, Pan-Pacific solidarity, and comprehensive national security.[123] Many of these groups attempted to grasp the nature of global and national transformations to help develop ways of restructuring national policies. Three of them directly addressed the question of Japan's foreign policy. In addition, there was a subtle stress on Japaneseness in the proposal: reevaluation of Japanese culture, Japanese family life, postindustrial society in Japan, Japanese urban life, and Japanese macroeconomic management.

The second action by the government, the administrative and financial reform, was initiated by Prime Minister Suzuki and continued under Prime Minister Nakasone.[124] The major goals of this reform package were the restructuring of administrative and financial patterns to fine-tune them to changing policy priorities and the retention of the grand conservative coalition of 1955 by not causing excessive strains on the public during implementation of transformed policy priorities.[125]

Administrative reform and the redressing of financial difficulties had several thrusts. First, they were intended to slash the excesses of previous expenditure patterns, especially in social welfare, education, public works, and personnel salaries, in favor of such items as defense, foreign aid, and science and technology. These high policy priorities were very significant in conjunction with the ceiling imposed on budget requests. The increases in defense and foreign aid spending are outstanding. Although these cuts are not enough to decrease the accumulated government deficit drastically, at least the direction of policy emphasis seems to have been set unequivocally.

Second, the reforms were aimed at reorganizing the state bureaucracy to facilitate high-level policy management to handle crises and emergencies of a higher order than was customarily envisaged earlier. Although the initial attempt at creating a comprehensive management agency directly under the prime minister did not materialize in the final proposal, bureaucratic functions of coordination and management and of policy analysis and planning were stressed.

Third, the reform emphasized the nonintroduction of a large-scale tax increase, which the government wishes to avoid for electoral reasons. Prime Minister Ohira's careless allusion during the 1979 election campaign to the possibility of a tax increase and the subsequent loss of votes seem to be behind this decision. With the LDP's landslide victory of 1986, tax increases are likely to become slightly more manageable. Even without a large-scale tax increase, the income tax has been increasing because of bracket creep. Even with these substantial de facto tax increases, however, the government debt cannot be reduced much for the rest of the 1980s.[126]

The period since 1984 has been characterized by the government response to intensified US pressure for economic liberalization and international burden sharing. Two programs constitute the core of meeting and adapting to pressure from outside. One is a series of economic liberalization measures symbolized by the Action Program, announced in July 1985 for implementation by 1987. The other is the Self-Defense Forces' New Defense Capability Consolidation Plan for 1986–90. Both aim at overcoming the previously strong image of Japan as an economic spoiler and military free-rider and at creating an image of Japan as an economic and military supporter. The Action Program is expected to end much of Japan's activities as a high-tariff mercantilist state, and the new defense plan is expected to place Japan in the category of a nonnegligible military power supporting the United States in the Pacific region.[127]

During this most recent period, the administrative and financial reform packages have still been on the government's agenda. This has meant continuing budget austerity, with only foreign aid, defense, and science and technology targeted for more expansion and with socioeconomic, non-industrial infrastructure set aside as a secondary policy priority—a continuation of the pattern since the 1950s.[128]

Conspicuous in these government attempts to reorient Japan's course are mobilization of the public by utilizing a wide spectrum of leaders for the articulation and deliberation of policy and the translation of many policy-related ideas into legislation and budget items. In this, bureaucrats have played an important role. These two features and the steady progress in implementation are a demonstration of the government's strength. Although not all of the proposals were implemented, the whole self-searching process seems to have set the basic tone of Japan's internal and external management.

However, because the exacerbation of major issues such as government debt, trade, and defense issues was partly the result of the government's previous semi-exclusive preoccupation with restoring internal equilibrium, primarily at the sacrifice of external issues, any policy reorientation must start by overhauling a whole range of public policies, which makes the task more difficult. Yet the government's promise not to increase taxes, together with the basic anti-inflationary preferences of the majority of the governmental actors and people, has effectively nullified a more fundamental budgetary restructuring than that necessary to accommodate all the internal and external problems.

Thus, the government's efforts to cast a Japanese image of an economic and military supporter have not been wholly successful in large part because domestic factors have inhibited or postponed otherwise timely and effective actions. When the United States, Japan's major ally, faces the tasks of enhancing its economic competitiveness and military buildup while plagued by trade and budget deficits of extraordinary proportions, it is inevitable that the United States is no less strongly pulled by concerns for its internal equilibrium. When the two largest economies put their externalities on the other's shoulders, it exacerbates their overall relationship. As one newspaper put it, 'It is as if both actors push their garbage into the other's garden in order to clean up their own garden.'[129]

Looking ahead with caution

Japan's rapid transition over the past decade in terms of macroindicators has provided Japan with complex and often conflicting images. The strength of the economy, the adaptability of industry, and the swiftness of technological innovation are sometimes contrasted with political-military passivity. Yet the same images of economic strength and efficiency are sometimes combined with a potential for political-military assertiveness. In between lies the ironically uneasy image of the increasing contribution of healthy economic growth and political resilience to general global welfare. Underlying these conflicting images are the increasingly wide policy options that Japan and the rest of the world have come to envisage and entertain for the future, even if only vaguely. These policy options have not been articulated often in the recent past.

Policy options in the economic sphere are basically divided into trilateralism and regionalism. This policy choice hinges on the degree of protectionism that develops in Western Europe and North America and the speed of economic development in the Western Pacific region.[130] If the protectionism that has developed in the EC over the past decade continues, it will leave de facto the multilateral free-trading system of GATT, and Japan will be forced to find other markets far more vigorously.[131] If in addition US protectionism further develops in the same direction and if the United States substantiates its free-trade bilateralism with countries such as Canada and Israel, then Japan's policy choice will slide further toward regionalism.[132]

Yet the protectionism that has developed in Western Europe is not of a kind that would lead immediately to vicious political and economic conflicts reminiscent of those of the 1930s. Rather, it represents a combination of benign mercantilism and regionalism.[133] It is not likely that Western Europe will degenerate into a malign political and economic bloc reluctant to have economic transactions with others, even if it further develops its current version of protectionism. It is, after all, the largest economic bloc in the world and is sufficiently open in terms of trade relations, technological cooperation, and capital transactions. It would benefit the United States and Japan to do more for Western Europe in terms of technological cooperation and overseas direct investment in exchange for continuing West European membership in the GATT system.

Although protectionism has been gaining strength in the United States, especially in Congress, the US government is determined to maintain the multilateral free-trade system and has been working hard to extend GATT coverage to the service, agricultural, and high-tech areas.[134] Although the United States has been generating its own version of sectoral protectionism, it is not likely that it will succumb to overall protectionism in principle. Sectoral protectionism is a rather temporary, limited device to appease maladjusted sectors affected by the rapid inroads of Japanese products and to facilitate the recovery and readjustment of the US economy in the 1980s. For the largest economy and the greatest technological power in the world to pursue protectionism as it becomes increasingly interdependent with the rest of the world would be suicidal. Bilateral deals in trade, finance, technology, and weapons represent new tactics to enhance US bargaining power with other kinds of influence over its negotiating partners.[135]

The economic size of the Western Pacific region is far from sufficient to compensate Japan for the loss of North American and West European markets.[136] Even if their economic growth rates were high, the Pacific countries are in a different development stage from Japan, let alone from America and Europe. Even if their income levels were to become roughly comparable to Japan's, the lack of a geoeconomic core in the basin may prevent Japan from developing a policy line for the area in isolation from other lines. Yet the Pacific Basin idea has been kept alive as insurance. Furthermore, the Western Pacific region as a whole is fairly evenly interdependent with the United States, Japan, and the EC. Japan is not economically predominant in the region. For example, Japan and the United States compete almost evenly as the largest trade partners. More important, the EC is a close third in international trade, and foreign direct investment in the region (excluding Japan for the moment) has been on the rise since some of the region's economies reached the status of the NICs or an even higher stage.

Whereas the Western Pacific line gravitates toward Southeast Asia, Northeast Asian regionalism will encompass Japan, the two Koreas, China, the USSR, and Outer Mongolia. The two dynamic forces, Japan and South Korea, might develop the kind of economic relations with their socialist neighbors that West Germany has developed with Eastern Europe.[137] If recent trends continue, Northeast Asian economic relations will become substantial in the future.[138] In addition to the already strong linkages with each other, Japan, the United States, and Hongkong have been enhancing their economic ties with China quite significantly, and Taiwan and South Korea have been strengthening their subterranean links with China.[139] However, the conceivable difficulties associated with strengthening trade and resource dependence on socialist countries might discourage Japan from pursuing this line very far.

In this regard, the USSR poses a far graver problem to Japan than China does. It is unlikely that Japan will be lured into the embrace of the USSR for such reasons as resources or anti-American nationalism. Most of the natural resources in the Soviet Far East and Siberia are available in other parts of the world. The question about China is whether the policy line of economic modernization and relative openness will continue. Although the Japanese government is basically optimistic about the steadfastness and stability of the current Chinese policy line, it is not quite certain about it.

Thus, for the foreseeable future, it seems that nothing fundamental will change. Basic trilateralism will continue as the core of Japanese economic interactions with the rest of the world; the regional components, both Southeast and Northeast Asian, will acquire more weight, but most likely will not surpass that of the trilateral components in the 1980s.[140]

There are basically two policy choices in the security sphere: a continuing link with the United States or the ending of this link. Crucial to Japan's policy choice are the cost-benefit calculations associated with the Japan-US security ties and the geopolitical conditions constraining Japan's choice. It is not necessary here to recount the reasons why the current mode of Japan-US security ties seem likely to last for the foreseeable future. However, if the inclusion of Japan in a US-led joint action against the USSR threatens to make Japan a target of Soviet nuclear and nonnuclear attacks without involving US forces throughout the rest of the world, Japan will think more than twice about the desirability of continuing Japan-US security ties. Intermittently intense economic pressure from the United States based on its security hegemony would also encourage Japan to reconsider.

However, departing from the Japan-US security relationship is easier said than done. The joint deterrence formula can be questioned in light of West European experiences with US introduction of theater nuclear weapons, which enable the United States to decouple itself from Western Europe in case of a Soviet attack.[141] Thus, Japanese nuclear armament combined with the Japan-US security relationship is a possibility.[142] But this formula has increasingly high costs of overcoming various easily aroused forces both at home and abroad. Most serious is the US reaction to a nuclear Japan. Would the United States allow Japan to take policy steps that might lead to Japan's becoming more than a second-rate power?

The departure from the Japan-US security relationship could take various forms. It might follow the French pattern of an independent military command with a close economic and security relationship with the United States. It could follow the Indian pattern of nonalignment and the resulting high prestige despite its weaker economic bases. It could also take a nonnuclear pattern. A Japan without nuclear weapons yet protected by extremely powerful antinuclear forces that render nuclear weapons antiquated is theoretically possible. Such a possibility still awaits a major technological breakthrough. Should Japan dissociate itself from the security relationship with the United States, Japan may well be lured into membership in a group 99, namely, a group of countries not strictly under the umbrella of either of the two superpowers.[143]

This is not the place to discuss all these and other policy options in detail. The task would require a book-length treatment. For the foreseeable future, however, Japan's security policy seems to rest on security ties with the United States. Despite all the discussions about the hegemonic decline of the United States, US hegemony, if in a somewhat reduced form, will continue to be sufficiently robust for the foreseeable future. As Edward Gibbon wryly noted of the decline of the Roman Empire. 'This intolerable situation lasted for about three hundred years'.[144]

The main point here, however, is to show that Japan and the rest of the world have come to envisage Japan's options more widely than before. This is precisely because of Japan's growth and the altered configuration of power in the international system of which Japan is a part. This suggests that Japan's policy choice could affect the world far more strongly than was possible before.

It is widely believed that social systems, whether groups, firms, states, or empires, always face major difficulties because past successes encourage them to adhere tenaciously to the methods that brought about those successes. Japan today is a case in point. The once-astute policy mix of a low profile in high politics (security and money) and a high profile in low politics (production and trade) has now become more difficult to sustain because of its previous admirable success. By flying low in the community of nations, Japan has achieved peace for the past forty years. By single-mindedly pursuing economic growth and prosperity, it has achieved worldwide status as a first-rank economic power. These are admirable achievements for a country that had no choice but to surrender unconditionally to the Allies. Yet success does not breed success forever. Japan's successful adaptation to the turmoils of the 1970s and 1980s has made obvious both the positive and the negative aspects of Japan's policy mix.

On the positive side, Japan has performed respectably in the area of economic growth, inflation, employment, social welfare, and environmental control.[145] It has contributed to the growth of global welfare by sustaining stable economic growth, making developmental loans, and thus helping to prevent many from following the vicious cycle of a zero-sum game.[146] Moreover, Japan has increased its share of international responsibilities in such areas as defense, aid, and contributions to international organizations, in a remarkably resolute and steadfast manner.

On the negative side, the maldevelopment of the socioeconomic infra-structure, seen most prominently in housing, roads, and sewers, is high-lighted by the accumulation of savings, which creates nothing other than interest income for savers and financial institutions purchasing foreign bonds and stocks. The economic surplus in trade that Japan has recorded intermittently has been seen as constraining industrial adjustment and macroeconomic management in the deficit countries.[147] And Japan's economic success has encouraged less adaptive countries to criticize Japan for its lighter burdens in the management of the international politico-economic system.[148]

These three externalities of the Japanese miracle are not in the forefront of the Japanese consciousness. In the short term, Japan will probably adhere to the policy line it has followed since 1945. But it would not take much reading in Japanese history to realize that the opposite of 'plus ça change, plus c'est la même chose' better fits the Japanese reality, namely, 'change and metamorphosis come about under the disguise of continuity and constancy'.

What we have seen since the first oil crisis is the stable process of change, internally patching this or that without losing sight of the overall balance among the various social sectors and externally adjusting to disturbances with a clear sense of national purpose and international environmental direction. Looking at a deeper level of public policy for the past decade enables one to fathom more clearly the extent of Japanese adaptation in an age of transition. Rather than meticulously setting details for a long-term strategy, which is difficult in a time of transition, Japan seems to set its course by selectively following the overall US policy line in the security and economic spheres and yet leaving its options open as much as possible. In the security area, US prodding for a Japanese defense buildup and technological cooper-ation helps Japan strengthen itself. In the economic area, US pressure for economic liberalization helps Japan become more competitive.

Yet on matters deemed essential or crucial to the Japanese future, Japan is consistently tough and resistant. Communications equipment, fighter bombers, and space shuttles immediately come to mind, to name but a few of the high-tech products that Japan tenaciously refuses to buy abroad. Since the first oil crisis, Japan has diversified its sources of natural resource supplies such as oil and iron ore. Japan's increasing imports from China of such grains as corn and beans are designed to mitigate excessive dependence on the United States for food supplies as well as to reduce China's bilateral trade deficit with Japan.[149] Cooperative business arrangements with tech-nology and capital exports as key elements have been a Japanese answer to the rising protectionism and nationalism of the past few years.

All these represent adaptation, Japanese style, to an age of transition from an assured US hegemony to a disorganized and disquieted US hegemony. This has not been easy since the world now looks at Japan with jealousy and enmity; because the United States, by reasserting its hegemony, is causing major disturbances for its friends and foes; and, no less important, because the robustness of Japan's internal logic—both ideas and structures—makes drastic restructuring efforts look more tardy and more superficial than many wish to see, at least in the shorter term. Japan's efforts to be accepted fully as an economic and military supporter have been significantly hindered by domestic factors. But any policy restructuring not supported by internal logic is bound to be ineffective. Japan's policy restructuring may be slower but steadier and longer lasting than many are inclined to think. The title of a newspaper article aptly catches Japan's mood, 'Japan: Uneasy on World Stage'.[150] Japan is cautiously, and with such ad hoc improvisation, searching for its proper role in the world, knowing its capabilities and constraints and living with its aspirations and apprehensions. Assessment of the virtues and vices of the Japanese restructuring over a longer term remain a task for the future.

Notes

Some of the material in this chapter originally appeared in Takashi Inoguchi, 'Japan's Images and Options: Not a Challenger, but a Supporter,' *Journal of Japanese Studies*, Vol. 12, No. 1 (Winter 1986), and in Takashi Inoguchi, 'Foreign Policy Background', in Herbert J. Ellison, ed., *Japan and the Pacific Quadrille* (Boulder, Col.: Westview Press, 1987). The author is grateful to the *Journal of Japanese Studies* and to Westview Press for permission to reproduce that material here.

1. For a discussion of the contending images of Japan and their relation to its place and status in the world, see Johan Galtung, 'Japan and Future World Politics', *Journal of Peace Research*, Vol. 10, No. 4 (1973), pp. 355-85; and Takashi Inoguchi, 'Japan's Images and Options: Not a Challenger, but a Supporter', *Journal of Japanese Studies*, Vol. 12, No. 1 (Winter 1986), pp. 95-119.

2. For a recent example of this argument, see Zbigniew Brzezinski, 'Japan Must Take Steps to End Free Ride on Defense', *International Herald Tribune*, Aug. 23, 1985. Japan spends around $10 billion on defense versus $300 billion for the United States. Cumulative expenditures for 1961-80 are $1,820 for the United States, $239 billion for West Germany, $224 billion for France, $213 billion for Great Britain, $82 billion for Italy, and $77 billion for Japan. See Ruth L. Sivard, *World Military and Social Indicators* (Washington, D.C.: World Priorities, 1983); and Japan, Ministry of Foreign Affairs, *Sekai no ugoki*, No. 398 (1982).

3. *Nihon keizai shimbun*, May 31, 1984.

4. For a recent example of this argument, see C. Steven Solarz, 'America and Japan: A Search for Balance'. *Foreign Policy*, No. 49 (Winter 1982-83), pp. 74-79.

5. For Reagan's foreign policy strategy, see Takashi Inoguchi, 'Daini kakumei no taigai senryaku' (The international strategy of the second revolution), *Ekonomisuto*, Apr. 16, 1985, pp. 12-22; reprinted in idem, *Kokusai kankei no seijikeizaigaku: Nihon no yakuwari to sentaku* (The political economy of international relations: Japan's roles and choices) (Tokyo:

University of Tokyo Press, 1985), pp. 124–49. See also Kenneth A. Oye, 'International System Structure and American Foreign Policy', in idem et al., eds., *Eagle Defiant: United States Foreign Policy in the* 1980s (Boston: Little, Brown & Co., 1983), pp. 3–32; and Mike Davis, 'Reaganomics' Magical Mystery Tour', *New Left Review*, No. 149 (Jan.–Feb. 1985), pp. 45–65.

6. In 1984, Japan's ODA was $4.3 billion, and the United States' was $8.7 billion. In terms of ratios to GNP and total grants, both Japan and the United States register lower figures than other major members of the OECD Development Assistance Committee. *Asahi shimbun*, June 27, 1985, evening ed.

7. For this argument, see Ken Matsui, *Keizai kyoryoku* (Economic cooperation) (Tokyo: Yuhikaku, 1983); and Shimin no Kaigai Kyoryoku o Kangaerukai, ed., *Shimin no kaigai kyoryoku hakusho* (Citizens' white book on foreign aid) (Tokyo: Nihon Hyoronsha, 1985). See also Japan, Ministry of International Trade and Industry (MITI), *Keizai kyoryoku no genjo to mondaiten* (Economic cooperation and its problems) (Tokyo: Tsusho Sangyo Chosakai, 1983); Denis T. Yamamoto, *Japan and the Asian Development Bank* (New York: Praeger, 1983); Alan Rix, *Japan's Economic Aid: Policymaking and Policy* (New York: St. Martin's Press, 1980); and Sukehiro Hasegawa, *Japan's Foreign Aid: Policy Practices* (New York: Praeger, 1975).

8. Japanese aid has now come to cover all these areas and to focus on human and social development in poorer countries. See William L. Brooks and Robert M. Orr, Jr., 'Japan's Foreign Economic Assistance', *Asian Survey*, Vol. 25, No. 3 (Mar. 1985), pp. 322–40. A most informative book on the subject is Asahi Shimbun, 'Enjo' Shuzaihan, ed., *Enjo tojokoku Nihon* (Japan as a developing aid-donor country) (Tokyo: Asahi Shimbunsha, 1985).

9. Needless to say, Japan is not the only self-seeking actor in the world: every country is.

10. See, e.g., Marvin Wolf, *Japanese Conspiracy: The Plot to Dominate Industry Worldwide and How to Deal with It* (New York: Empire Books, 1983). For the Yellow Peril image, see William Wetherall, 'Paranoia Invents the Rebirth of the Yellow Peril', *Far Eastern Economic Review*, Aug. 1, 1985; pp. 41–42.

11. Immanuel Wallerstein, 'Friends as Foes', *Foreign Policy*, No. 40 (Fall 1980), pp. 119–31.

12. Quoted in Steven Schlossstein, *Trade War: Greed, Power, Industrial Policy on the Opposite Side of the Pacific* (New York: Congan & Weed, 1984), pp. 201–2.

13. Winston William, 'Japanese Investment: A New Worry', New York Times, May 6, 1984, p. F1.

14. Ibid. See also 'Beikoku sangyo seisaku ni hirogaru Pentagon no kage' (The shadow of the Pentagon over US industrial policy), *Nihon keizai shimbun*, May 22–24, 1984.

15. Stephen Bronte, 'This Is the Decade of the Conquering Yen', *Euromoney*, Mar. 1982, pp. 71–81.
16. Zaisei Seisaku Kenkykai, ed., *Korekara no zaisei to kokusai hakko* (Finance and bond issues in the future) (Tokyo: Okurazaimu Kyokai, 1985), p. 112.
17. International Institute for Strategic Studies, *Military Balance, 1984–1985* (London, 1985).
18. Johan Galtung's structural theory predicts such an outcome. See his 'A Structural Theory of Imperialism', *Journal of Peace Research*, Vol. 8, No. 2 (1971), pp. 81–117. See also Immanuel Wallerstein, 'North Altanticism in Decline, *SAIS Review*, No. 4 (Summer 1982), pp. 21–26.
19. MITI, *Keizai kyoryoku*.
20. See Brooks and Orr, 'Economic Assistance'.
21. Yamamoto, *Japan*, gives such an impression. For a contrasting view, see Stephen Krasner, 'Power Structure and Regional Development Banks', *International Organization*, Vol. 35, No. 2 (Spring 1981), pp. 303–28. For the overall relationship between Japan and the Western Pacific countries, see Herbert S. Yee, 'Japan's Relations with ASEAN and South Korea: From Dependence to Interdependence?', *Journal of Northeast Asian Studies*, Vol. 2, No. 2 (June 1983), pp. 29–44.
22. *Euromoney*, May 1980, pp. 64–65; Apr. 1983, pp. 24–25; Oct. 1983, pp. 166–82; Mar. 1987, pp. 14, 18. At the end of 1986, Japan's outstanding net external assets reached $1,804 billion, higher than the peak figure the United States registered in 1982, i.e., $1,495 billion. *Nihon keizai shimbun*, May 26, 1987, evening edition.
23. Japan External Trade Organization, ed., *Sekai to Nihon no kaigai chokusetsu tōshi* (The world's and Japan's direct overseas investment) (Tokyo, 1985), and *Nihon keizai shimbun*, May 29, 1987.
24. Ibid. See also Davis Bobrow, 'Playing for Safety: Japan's Security Policy', *Japan Quarterly*, Vol. 31, No. 1 (Jan.–Mar. 1984), pp. 33–43; and J.W.M. Chapman, 'Dependence', in idem, R. Drifte, and I.T.M. Gow, *Japan's Quest for Comprehensive Security: Defense, Diplomacy and Dependence* (London: Frances Pinter, 1983).
25. Japan, Defense Agency, *Boei hakusho, 1985* (Defense white paper) (Tokyo, 1985).
26. See, e.g., Shinichiro Asao, 'Japan's Defense Policy', *New York Times*, Feb. 29, 1984.
27. David Calleo, *The German Problem Reconsidered: Germany and the World Order, 1970 to the Present* (Cambridge, Eng.: Cambridge University Press, 1978), p. 202.
28. Takashi Inoguchi, *Gaiko taiyo no hikaku kenkyu: Chugoku, Eikoku, Nihon* (A comparative study of diplomatic styles: China, Britain, Japan) (Tokyo: Gannando Shoten, 1978), esp. pp. 297–308; and James Crowley, *Japan's Quest for Autonomy: National Security and Foreign Policy, 1930–1938* (Princeton: Princeton University Press, 1966).
29. See Hajime Shinohara, *Keizai taikoku no seisui* (The rise and decline of

economic powers) (Tokyo: Toyo Keizai Shimposha, 1981); Walt W. Rostow, *The World Economy: History and Prospect* (London: Macmillan, 1978); and Joshua S. Goldstein, 'Kondratieff Waves as War Cycles', *International Studies Quarterly*, Vol. 29, No. 4 (Dec. 1985), pp. 411–44.

30. Kazushi Ohkawa and Henry Rosovsky, *Japanese Economic Growth: Trend Acceleration in the Twentieth Century* (Stanford: Stanford University Press, 1973); Takafusa Nakamura, *Senzenki Nihon keizai seicho no bunseki* (An analysis of prewar Japanese economic growth) (Tokyo: Iwanami Shoten, 1971); *Nihon keizai* (The Japanese economy) (Tokyo: University of Tokyo Press, 1978); and James W. Morley, ed., *Dilemmas of Growth in Prewar Japan* (Princeton: Princeton University Press, 1971).

31. For industrial structure, see Nakamura, *Senzenki Nihon*; Ryoshin Minami, *Nihon no keizai seicho* (Japanese economic growth) (Tokyo: Toyo Keizai Shimposha, 1981); and Hugh Patrick, ed., *Japanese Industrialization and Its Social Consequences* (Berkeley: University of California Press, 1976). For political authoritarianism, see Junnosuke Masumi, *Nihon seito shiron* (A treatise on Japanese political parties), vols. 6–8 (Tokyo: University of Tokyo Press, 1980); and Gordon M. Berger, *Parties out of Power in Japan, 1931–1941* (Princeton: Princeton University Press, 1978).

32. Alexander Gershenkron, *Economic Backwardness in Historical Perspective* (Cambridge, Mass.: Harvard University Press, 1962).

33. For Japanese technology policy, see e.g., Masanori Yoshimi, *Nihon no sangyo gijutsu seisaku: Kokusai kyosoryoku to gijutsu kakushin no kenkyu* (Japan's technology policy: A study of international competitiveness and technological innovation) (Tokyo: Toyo Keizai Shimposha, 1985).

34. It is interesting that Britain was a rapidly declining hegemon and Germany, Japan, and the United States were all regarded as potential challengers. It may be speculated that a challenger-state that initiates a hegemonic war tends to lose and a supporter-country that allies with a hegemon tends to win. In World War II, Germany and Japan challenged and lost, whereas the United States took over hegemonic legitimacy by allying with Britain. Britain did the same when France challenged the Dutch preponderance in the seventeenth century and then established the first Pax Britannica. On this point, see Kuniko Inoguchi, 'Haken no junkan to Pax Americana no ikue' (Hegemonic cycles and prospects for the Pax Americana), *Sekai*, Nov. 1985, pp. 168–83. This view differs from the hegemonic cycle model of Robert Gilpin, *War and Change in World Politics* (Cambridge, Eng.: Cambridge University Press, 1981).

35. Christopher Thorne, *Allies of a Kind: The United States, Britain, and the War Against Japan, 1941–1945* (London: Macmillan, 1978).

36. For the contrasts, see Nobuhiko Ushiba, Graham T. Allison, and Thierry de Montbrial, *Sharing International Responsibilities Among the Trilateral Countries* (New York: Trilateral Commission, 1983).

37. For US hegemony and its relative weakening in nuclear and nonnuclear areas, see Lawrence Freedman, *The Evolution of Nuclear Strategy* (London: Macmillan, 1981); and Fred L. Block, *The Origins of International Economic*

Disorder: A Study of United States International Monetary Policy from World War II to the Present (Berkeley: University of California Press, 1977). See also Franz Schurman, *The Logic of World Power* (New York: Pantheon Books, 1974); Stanley Hoffman, *Primacy or World Order: American Foreign Policy Since the Cold War* (New York: McGraw-Hill, 1978); and Fred Halliday, *The Making of the Second Cold War* (London: Verso & NLB, 1983). For an emphasis on US cultural hegemony despite some erosion in economic and military areas, see Russett 'US Hegemony: Gone or Merely Diminished, and How Does it Matter', in Takashi Inoguchi and Daniel Okimoto (eds), *The Political Economy of Japan Vol. 2: the Changing International Context* (Stanford, Stanford University Press, 1988). The most economic conflicts), *Chuo koron*, Nov. 1985, pp. 68–69. See also K. Inoguchi, 'Haken no junkan'.

38. The meaning of the US umbrella over Japan in such forms as the US occupation, the US-Japan Mutual Security Treaty, and high economic interdependence have been topics of high interest in Japan. See, e.g., Makoto Iokibe, *Beikoku no Nihon senryo seisaku* (The US occupation of Japan) (Tokyo: Chuo Koronsha, 1985); Kazuhisa Ogawa, *Zai-Nichi Beigun* (US forces in Japan) (Tokyo: Kodansha, 1984); PHP Institute, ed., *Shin Nichi-Bei kankeiron* (Japan-US relations) (Kyoto, 1983); Hiroshi Kitamura et al., *Nichi-Bei o toitsumeru* (Inquiring into US-Japan relations) (Tokyo: Sekai no Ugokisha, 1983); and Stephen D. Cohen, *Uneasy Partnership: Competition and Conflict in US-Japanese Trade Relations* (Baltimore: Johns Hopkins University Press, 1985).

39. OECD, *Historical Statistics, 1960–1980* (Paris, 1982).

40. I am referring to the debates on the 'Japanese model'. See, e.g., Tsuneo Iida, *Nihon chikarazuyosa no saihakken* (Rediscovery of Japanese strength) (Tokyo: Nihon Keizai Shimbunsha, 1979). On the debate, see the paper by Kenneth B. Pyle in 'Japan, the World, and the Twenty-first Century,' Takashi Inoguchi and Daniel I. Okimoto, eds., *The Political Economy of Japan Vol. 2: The Changing International Context*, (Stanford: Stanford University Press, 1988), pp. 446–86, 547–51; and Kozo Yamamura, 'Success That Soured: Administrative Guidance and Cartels in Japan', in idem, ed., *Policy and Trade Issues of the Japanese Economy* (Seattle: University of Washington Press, 1982), pp. 77–112.

41. The most noteworthy recent example is Theodore White, 'The Danger from Japan', *New York Times Magazine*, July 28, 1985, pp. 19–44.

42. Takashi Inoguchi, 'Western Europe and the Western Pacific: A Comparative Assessment', in National Institute for Research Advancement, ed., *The Future of the Asia-Pacific Region* (Tokyo, 1986), pp. 107–13.

43. Shumpei Kumon, 'Administrative Reform Requires New National Goals', *Economic Eye*, Vol. 3, No. 3 (1982), pp. 4–7.

44. Davis, 'Reaganomics' Magical Mystery Tour'. See also the references cited in note 37.

45. Ronald McKinnon, *An International Standard of Monetary Stabilization*

(Cambridge, Mass.: MIT Press for the Institute for International Economics, 1984).

46. These and other problems are touched on in such works as C. Fred Bergsten, *The Dilemmas of the Dollar* (New York: New York University Press, 1975); Block, *International Economic Disorder*; and Joanne Gowa, *Closing the Gold Window: Domestic Politics and the End of Bretton Woods* (Ithaca, N.Y.: Cornell University Press, 1983).

47. See, e.g., *Nihon keizai shimbun*, May 28, 1984.

48. See ibid., May 30, 1984.

49. Kent Calder, 'Opening Japan'. *Foreign Policy*, No. 47 (Summer 1982), pp. 82–87; and Bobrow, 'Playing for Safety'. See also Raymond Vernon, *Two Hungry Giants: The United States and Japan in the Quest for Oil and Ore* (Cambridge, Mass.: Harvard University Press, 1983).

50. The most useful book on trade policies in the 1980s is William R. Cline, *Trade Policy in the 1980's* (Cambridge, Mass.: MIT Press for the Institute for International Economics, 1984). See also Robert E. Baldwin and Anne O. Krueger, eds., *The Structure and Evolution of Recent U.S. Trade Policy* (Chicago: University of Chicago Press, 1984). For Japan's trade policy, see Ryutaro Komiya and Motoshige Itoh, 'Japan's International Trade and Trade Policy, 1955-1984', in Takashi Inoguchi and Daniel I. Okimoto, *op. cit.*, and Kiyohiko Fukushima, 'Japan's Real Trade Policy', *Foreign Policy*, No. 59 (Summer 1985), pp. 22–39.

51. On Japan, see Yamamura, *Policy and Trade Issues*; and Hugh Patrick and Henry Rosovsky, eds., *Asia's New Giant* (Washington, D.C.: Brookings Institution, 1976). On NICs, see OECD, *The Impact of Newly Industrializing Countries on Production and Trade in Manufactures* (Paris, 1979); Louis Turner et al., *Living with the Newly Industrializing Countries* (London: Royal Institute for International Affairs, 1980); William R. Cline, *Exports of Manufactures from from Developing Countries* (Washington, D.C.: Brookings Institution, 1984); and David B. Yoffie, *Power and Protectionism: Strategies of the Newly Industrializing Countries* (New York: Columbia University Press, 1983).

52. Illuminating these processes with some exaggeration is Mancur Olsen, *The Rise and Decline of Nations: Economic Growth, Stagflation, and Social Rigidities* (New Haven: Yale University Press, 1982). See also Robert Gilpin, *War and Change in World Politics* (Cambridge, Eng.: Cambridge University Press, 1981).

53. William R. Cline, 'Reciprocity': A New Approach to World Trade Policy?', in idem, *Trade Policy*; according to another estimate, more than 50 per cent of total world trade is 'controlled trade'. See Japan External Trade Organization, *JETRO hakusho boeki hen* (JETRO white paper on trade) (Tokyo, 1985). See also Robert O. Keohane, 'Reciprocity as a Principle of Governance in International Relations', *International Organization*, Vol. 40, No. 1 (Winter 1986), pp. 1–27.

54. Bronte, 'Conquering Yen'.

55. These perspectives are presented in such works as Robert Keohane, *After Hegemony: Cooperation and Discord in the World Economy* (Princeton: Princeton University Press, 1984); and Wolfgang Hager, 'Protectionism and Autonomy: How to Preserve Trade in Europe', *International Affairs*, Vol. 58, No. 3 (Summer 1982), pp. 412-28.

56. See MTI, *Tsusho hakusho*. See also 'NICs in a Twist', *Far Eastern Economic Review*, Sept. 26, 1985, pp. 99-106; Ippei Yamazawa and Takashi Nozawa, eds., *Ajia Taiheiyo shokoku no boeki to sangyo chosei* (Trade and industrial adjustment in Asian-Pacific countries) (Tokyo: Institute of Developing Economies, 1985); and Toshio Watanabe, *Seicho no Ajia, teitai no Ajia* (Growing Asia, stagnant Asia) (Tokyo: Toyo Keizai Shimposha, 1985).

57. MITI, *Tsusho hakusho*; and idem, *Keizai kyoryoku*.

58. *Nihon keizai shimbun*, May 31, 1984.

59. Ibid., Sept. 13, 1985, evening ed.

60. Yasusuke Murakami, 'Toward a Sociopolitical Explanation of Japan's Economic Performance', in Yamamura, *Trade and Policy Issues*, pp. 3-46; and Yasusuke Murakami, 'The Japanese Model of Political Economy,' in Kozo Yamamura and Yasuba Yasukichi, eds., *The Political Economy of Japan Vol. 1: the Domestic Transformation* (Stanford: Stanford University Press, 1987), pp. 33-90, 595-8. See also Yoshio Suzuki, *Money and Banking in Contemporary Japan* (New Haven: Yale University Press, 1980).

61. Yoshio Suzuki, *Nihon keizai to kin'yu* (The Japanese economy and finance) (Tokyo: Toyo Keizai Shimposha, 1981); Yoshio Suzuki, *Nihon kin'yu keizai ron* (Japanese monetary economics) (Tokyo: Toyo Keizai Shimposha, 1983) and Akiyoshi Horiuchi and Koichi Hamada, 'The Political Economy of the Financial Market,' Kozo Yamamura and Yasuba Yasukichi, *op. cit.*, pp. 223-60, 618-21.

62. For the politics of government revenues and deficits, see Yukio Noguchi, *Zaisei kiki no kozo* (The structure of the financial crisis) (Tokyo: Toyo Keizai Shimposha, 1980); and Yukio Noguchi, 'Public Finance,' in Kozo Yamamura and Yasuba Yasukichi, *op. cit.*, pp. 186-22, 613-8.

63. On saving, see Kazuo Sato, 'Japan's Savings and Internal and External Macroeconomic Balance', in Yamamura, *Trade and Policy Issues*, pp. 143-72; and Kazuo Sato, 'Saving and Investment,' in Kozo Yamamura and Yasuba Yasukichi, *op. cit.*, pp. 137-85, 601-13.

64. See, e.g., Takashi Inoguchi, *Gendai Nihon seiji keizai no kozu* (The contemporary Japanese political economy) (Tokyo: Toyo Keizai Shimposha, 1983), pp. 169-97.

65. On the US regulation and capital outflows for balance-of-payments reasons during the latter half of the 1960s, see Janet Kelley, *Bankers and Brokers: The Case of American Banks in Britain* (Cambridge, Mass.: Ballinger, 1977); on the US deregulation since 1974 because of the transition to the floating exchange rate regime, see, e.g., M. S. Mendelsohn, *Money on the Move: The Modern International Market* (New York: McGraw-Hill, 1980).

See also 'A New Awakening: A Survey of Banking', *The Economist*, Mar. 24, 1984, insert pp. 1-80.

66. *Nihon keizai shimbun*, May 30, 1984.

67. See Raymond Vernon, *Sovereignty at Bay: The Multinational Spread of US Enterprises* (New York: Basic Books, 1971); and Mendelsohn, *Money on the Move*.

68. See Barry Bluestone and Bennett Harrison, *The Deindustrialization of America* (New York: Basic Books, 1982). For a contrasting view, see Robert Z. Lawrence, *Can America Compete?* (Washington, D.C.: Brookings Institution, 1984).

69. See Wilkinson, 'Hopes'; and Samuel Brittan, 'Remedies Worse than the Disease', *The Financial Times*, Sept. 16, 1985.

70. Samuel Huntington, 'Renewed Hostility', in Joseph Nye, ed., *The Making of America's Soviet Policy* (New Haven: Yale University Press, 1984), pp. 265–89; Noam Chomsky, *Towards a New Cold War* (New York: Pantheon Books, 1982); Fred Halliday, *The Making of the New Second Cold War* (London: Verso & NLB, 1983); Adam Ulam, *Dangerous Relations: the Soviet Union in World Politics, 1970-1982* (New York: Oxford University Press, 1983). Hideo Otake, *Nihon no boei to kokunai seiji* (Japanese defense and domestic politics) (Tokyo: San'ichi Shobo, 1983); and Raymond L. Garthoff, *Detente and Confrontation* (Washington, D.C.: Brookings Institution, 1985).

71. Quoted in Huntington,'Renewed Hostility'.

72. Ibid.; and Halliday, *Post Conservative America: People, Politics and Ideology in a Time of Crisis* (New York: Random Books; 1982); and Silviu Brucan, *Post Brezhnev Era: An Insider's View* (New York: Praeger, 1984).

73. See, e.g., Jiri Valenta, 'The Explosive Soviet Periphery', *Foreign Policy*, No. 51 (Summer 1983), pp. 84-100; and Zalmy Kalizad, 'Soviet-Occupied Afghanistan', *Problems of Communism*, Vol. 29, No. 6 (Nov.-Dec. 1980), pp. 23-40.

74. Pierre Hassner, 'The Shifting Foundation', *Foreign Policy*, No. 48 (Fall 1982), pp. 3-20; Immanuel Wallerstein, 'North Atlanticism in Decline'; Nathaniel Thayer, 'The Emerging East Asian Order', *SATS Review*, Vol. 4, No. 1 (Winter-Spring 1984), pp. 1-41; and Calder, 'Opening Japan'.

75. See Halliday, *Second Cold War*; and Otake, *Nihon no boei*.

76. See Otake, *Nihon no boei*, for a detailed discussion of this trend.

77. See the symposium on Japan's defense policy, *Voice*. June 1984. See also Mike Mochizuki, 'Japan's Search for Strategy', *International Security*, Vol. 8, No. 3 (Winter 1983-84), pp. 152-79; and Ronald Morse, 'Japan's Search for an Independent Foreign Policy: An American Perspective', *Journal of Northeast Asian Studies*, Vol. 3, No. 2 (Summer 1986), pp. 27-44.

78. Prime Minister Ohira's Study Group, *Sogo anzen hosho senryaku* (Comprehensive national security strategy) (Tokyo: Okurasho, 1980).

79. Japan, MITI, *Keizai anzen hosho no kakuritsu o megutte* (Toward achieving economic security) (Tokyo: Tsusho Sangyo Chosakai, 1982); and Yoichi

Funabashi, *Keizai anzen hosho ron* (Economic security) (Tokyo: Toyo Keizai Shimposha, 1978).

80. But despite the advent of the second cold war, Japan's basic defense posture is still based on a set of assumptions associated with the heydey of détente. It is in that respect similar to West Germany's 'oasis of détente' assumption.

81. This argument is best articulated by the opposition parties, especially the Socialists and the Communists, but it is held by the government as well.

82. See Otake, *Nihon no boei*, for an excellent description of domestic trends.

83. Prime Minister Ohira's Study Group, *Sogo anzen hosho senryaku*. For a different view, see Morse, 'Japan's Search'.

84. Agitation by what are called 'Japan's Gaullists' is thus considered as complicating the government's task. See Tetsuya Kataoka, *Waiting for Pearl Harbor* (Stanford: Hoover Institution Press, 1980); and Yatsuhiro Nakagawa, 'The WEPTO Option: Japan's New Role in East-Asia/Pacific Collective Security', *Asian Survey*, Vol. 24, No. 8 (August 1984), pp. 828–39.

85. See note 77.

86. For the perspective that focuses on domestic structures to explain foreign policy strategy, see Peter J. Katzenstein, ed., *Between Power and Plenty: Foreign Policies of Advanced Industrial Countries* (Madison: University of Wisconsin Press, 1978); idem, *Small States in World Markets: Industrial Policy in Europe* (Ithaca, N.Y.: Cornell University Press, 1985); and idem, *Corporatism and Change: Australia, Switzerland, and the Politics of Industry* (Ithaca, N.Y.: Cornell University Press, 1984). See also John Zysman, *Governments, Markets, and Growth: Financial Systems and the Politics of Industrial Change* (Ithaca, N.Y.: Cornell University Press, 1983).

87. See the 39 annual maps of world conflicts for 1945–83 in Takashi Hirose, *Clausewitz no himitsu kodo* (Clausewitz's secret code) (Tokyo: Shinchosha, 1984), pp. 24–101.

88. See J. David Singer and Melvin Small, *The Wages of War, 1816–1965* (New York: Wiley, 1972).

89. Ben-Ami Shilloni, '1945 nen natsu: Truman saidai no guko' (Summer 1945: Truman's folly), *Jiyu*, Aug. 1985, pp. 21–25; and Roger Buckley, *Occupation Diplomacy: Britain, the United States, and Japan, 1945–1952* (Cambridge, Eng.: Cambridge University Press, 1982).

90. See Iokibe, *Beikoku no Nihon senryo*; Takafusa Nakamura, ed., *Senryoki Nihon no keizai to seiji* (The economics and politics of Japan during the Occupation) (Tokyo: University of Tokyo Press, 1979); and Shinjiro Sodei, ed., *Sekaishi no naka no Nihon senryo* (The occupation of Japan in world history) (Tokyo: Nihon hyoronsha, 1985).

91. It is well known that what is called the conservative mainstream's policy line is dependent heavily on the US provision of national security to Japan. See Masataka Kosaka, *Saisho Yoshida Shigeru* (Prime Minister Shigeru Yoshida) (Tokyo: Chuo Koronsha, 1968); and Yonosuke Nagai, *Gendai to senryaku* (The contemporary age and strategy) (Tokyo: Bungei

Shunjusha, 1985). See Michio Muramatsu and Ellis Krauss, 'The Conservative Policy Line and the Development of Patterned Pluralism', in Kozo Yamamura and Yasukichi Yasuba, *op. cit.*, pp.516–54, 645–8.

92. In a recent opinion poll on the Self-Defense Forces, 63.0 per cent said that its primary role was national security; 17.2 per cent said internal security; and 13.6 per cent said disaster relief. Japan, Office of the Cabinet, Public Relations Office, ed., *Gekkan yoron chosa*, Aug. 1985, pp. 71–120.

93. See Noguchi, *op. cit.* and Martin Bronfenbrenner and Yasukichi Yasuba, *op. cit.*

94. See Margaret A. McKean, *Environmental Protest and Citizen Politics in Japan* (Berkeley: University of California Press, 1981).

95. Kiyofuku Chuma, *Saigunbi no seijigaku* (The politics of rearmament) (Tokyo: Chishikisha, 1985).

96. See National Institute for Research Advancement, *Seikatsu suijun no rekishiteki suii* (Historical evolution of living standards) (Tokyo, 1985), for a detailed delineation of health, education, employment, income, physical environment, security, family, community life, and social stratification and mobility during the past century.

97. For the 1950s–1960s, see, e.g., Kozo Yamamura, *Economic Policy in Postwar Japan: Growth Versus Economic Democracy* (Berkeley: University of California Press, 1967). For the 1970s–1980s, see, e.g., Nagaharu Hayabusa, 'Kakegaeno nai jugonen: Shakaishihon jujitsu no kokî' (A crucial 15 years for social capital consolidation), *Asahi shimbun*, Sept. 1, 1985; Katsuhiko Suetsugu, 'Semarareru uchinaru fukinko zesei' (Rectification of internal disequilibrium urged), *Nihon keizai shimbun*, Sept. 29, 1985; and Davis, 'Reaganomics' Magical Mystery Tour'. See also Susan Chira, 'In Japan, Progress Eludes Many Among the Masses', *International Herald Tribune*, Nov. 1, 1985.

98. See, e.g., Masaru Yoshitomi, *Gendai Nihon keizai ron* (Contemporary Japanese economics) (Tokyo: Toyo Keizai Shimposha, 1977); Masaru Yoshitomi, *Nihon keizai* (The Japanese economy) (Tokyo: Toyo Keizai Shimposha, 1981); and Takeo Komine, *Sekiyu to Nihon keizai* (Petroleum and the Japanese economy) (Tokyo: Toyo Keizai Shimposha, 1982). See also Peter J. Katzenstein, ed., *Between Power and Plenty*; and Wilfred L. Kohl, ed., *After the Second Oil Crisis: Energy Policies in Europe, America, and Japan* (Lexington, Mass.: D. C. Heath, 1982).

99. Bank of Japan, *Nihon o chushin to shita kokusai tokei* (Japan in comparative international statistics) (Tokyo, 1985).

100. See, e.g., Yoshio Suzuki, *Nihon kin'yu keizai ron* (Japanese financial economics) (Tokyo: Toyo Keizai Shimposha, 1983); Yoichi Shinkai, *Gendai makuro keizaigaku* (Contemporary macroeconomics) (Tokyo: Toyo Keizai Shimposha, 1982); Seiji Shimpo, *Bunseki Nihon keizai* (The Japanese economy: An analysis) (Tokyo: Toyo Keizai Shimposha, 1985); and idem, *Gendai Nihon keizai no kaimei* (Anatomy of the Japanese economy) (Tokyo: Toyo Keizai Shimposha, 1979).

101 The Japanese definition of M2 + CD is cash currency in circulation + deposit money + quasi money + certificates of deposit. See Bank of Japan, *Nihon o chushin to shita kokusai tokei*, 1986 ed., p. 206.

102. Noguchi, *Zaisei*; Naohiro Yatsuhiro, ed., *Gyozaisei kaikaku no kenkyu* (Studies in administrative and financial reform) (Tokyo: Toyo Keizai Shimposha, 1982); Hiromitsu Ishi, *Zaisei kaikaku no ronri* (The logic of the financial reform) (Tokyo: Nihon Keizai Shimbunsha, 1982); Yukio Noguchi, 'Nihon de Keinzu seisaku wa okonawareta ka' (Has Keynesian policy ever been implemented in Japan?), *Kikan gendai keizaigaku*, No. 52 (1983), pp. 163–83.

103. Zaisei Seisaku Kenkyukai, ed., *Korekara no zaisei to kokusai hakko*, p. 46.

104. Noguchi, 'Nihon de Keinzu seisaku'.

105. Bank of Japan, *Nihon keizai*, p. 86.

106. See Noguchi, *op. cit.*

107. OECD, *Historical Statistics, 1960–1980* (Paris, 1982).

108. *Yomiuri shimbun*, Aug. 2, 1985.

109. For Japanese trade policy, see the paper by Komiya and Itoh in this volume. See also Gary Saxonhouse, 'The Micro- and Macroeconomics of Foreign Sales for Japan', in Cline, *Trade Policies*; idem, 'Evolving Comparative Advantage and Japan's Imports of Manufacturers', in Yamamura, *Policy and Trade Issues*, pp. 239–69; and see also Gary Saxonhouse, 'Comparative Advantage, Structural Adaptation, and Japanese Performance,' in Takashi Inoguchi and Daniel Okimoto, *op. cit.*, pp. 225–48, 521–4, n. 126 See Noguchi, *op. cit.*

110. For the restoration of self-confidence of the conservatives in Japanese politics toward the end of the 1970s, see T. Inoguchi, *Gendai Nihon*, esp. pp. 199–245; and the paper by Muramatsu and Krauss *op. cit.*

111. For the poll results, see Jiji Tsushinsha, ed., *Sengo Nihon no seitu to naikaku* (Postwar Japanese political parties and cabinets) (Tokyo, 1981), which provides monthly data complied by the Office of the Prime Minister up to June 1981. Since Aug. 1978, the *Yomiuri shimbun* has published another series of monthly data. For a first-rate historical narrative, see Junnosuke Masumi, *Gendai seiji* (Contemporary politics) (Tokyo: University of Tokyo Press, 1983), 2 vols.; and idem, *Sengo seiji* (Postwar politics) (Tokyo: University of Tokyo Press, 1985), 2 vols. On the LDP's victory, see Takashi Inoguchi, 'The Japanese Double Election of July 6, 1986', *Electoral Studies*, Vol. 6, No. 1 (April 1987), pp. 63–70.

112. For the mechanisms of these controversies, which permeate politics, see T. Inoguchi, *Gendai Nihon*, pp. 199–245.

113. Economic factors as well as policy and campaign factors do explain major portions of the increase in voter support for the LDP. See ibid.; and Takashi Inoguchi, 'Keizai jokyo to seisaku kadai' (Economic conditions and policy tasks), in Joji Watanuki et al., *Nihonjin no senkyo kodo* (Japanese electoral behavior) (Tokyo: University of Tokyo Press, 1985), pp. 203–36.

114. T. Inoguchi, *Gendai Nihon*, pp. 199–245.

115. Ibid.

116. Ibid.

117. On welfare, see Bronfenbrenner and Yasuba *op. cit.*; and Stephen J. Anderson, 'Nihon shakai fukushi no seisaku keisei katei' (The policy information process of Japanese social welfare), *Jurisuto*, No. 41 (Dec. 1985), pp. 172-76.

118. T. Inoguchi, *Gendai Nihon*, pp. 199-245; on the opposition governments at the local level, see Ellis Krauss et al., eds., *Political Opposition and Local Politics in Japan* (Princeton: Princeton University Press, 1980).

119. Funabashi, *Keizai anzen*; Nobutoshi Akao, ed., *Japan's Economic Security* (New York: St. Martin's Press, 1983); Chapman et al., *Japan's Quest*; and Edward Morse, ed., *The Politics of Japan's Energy Strategy* (Berkeley, Calif.: Institute of East Asian Studies, 1981). A telling indication of Japanese preoccupation with the economic dimension of global change during this period was Prime Minister Fukuda's revelation, in a conversation with Chancellor Helmut Schmidt, of his ignorance of the SS-20s.

120. Sogo Ansen Hosho Kenkyu Gurupu, *Sogo anzen*. See also Otake, *Nihon no boei*.

121. See Japan, Defense Agency, *Boei hakusho*, 1979-85.

122. See Otake, *Nihon no boei*.

123. Prime Minister Ohira's Study Group reports.

124. Rinji Gyosei Chosakai, *Rincho kihon teigan* (Basic proposals of the Provisional Council [on Administrative Reform]) (Tokyo: Gyosei Kanri Kenkyu Senta, 1982).

125. See T. Inoguchi, *Gendai Nihon*.

126. See Noguchi *op. cit.*

127. For the Action Program, see Shijo Kaiho Mondai Kenkyukai, ed., *Kodo keikaku* (The Action Program) (Tokyo: Gyosei, 1985).

128. See, e.g., Keizai Seisaku Kenkyukai, *Korekara no keizai seisaku* (Future economic policy) (Tokyo: Government Printing Bureau, 1985). See also *Asahi shimbun*, Sept. 1, 1985.

129. *Nihon keizai shimbun*, Aug. 29, 1985. Like the US government, the Japanese government avoids making necessary economic reforms and blames the other side while taking advantage of the other side's policy contradictions. See also David Hale, 'US and Japan Reach Historical Crossroads', *Far Eastern Economic Review*, Aug. 2, 1985; Suetsugu, 'Semarareru uchinaru fukinko zesei'; and R. Morse, 'Japan's Search'.

130. Japan, Ministry of Foreign Affairs, *Gaiko seisho* (Diplomatic blue book) (Tokyo, 1985), points out that the two major goals of Japanese foreign policy are to consolidate Japan's roles as a member of the industrialized countries and of the Asia-Pacific region.

131. See Hager, 'Protectionism and Autonomy'.

132. *Nihon keizai shimbun*, Feb. 3 and 10, 1984; and *New York Times*, Feb. 21, 1984.

133. Barry Buzan, 'Economic Structure and International Security',

International Organizations, Vol. 38, No. 4 (Autumn 1984), pp. 597–624.
134. For US commerical policy, see Baldwin and Krueger, *Structure and Evolution*. See also John Zysman and Laura Tyson, eds., *American Industry in International Competition: Government Policies and Corporate Strategies* (Ithaca, N.Y.: Cornell University Press, 1983).
135. For a justification of such a US policy strategy, see Keohane, *After Hegemony*.
136. Prime Minister Ohira's Policy Study Group, *Kantaiheiyo rentai no koso* (The idea of Pan-Pacific solidarity) (Tokyo: Government Printing Bureau, 1980).
137. See, e.g., William E. Griffith, *The Ostpolitik of the Federal Republic of Germany* (Cambridge, Mass.: MIT Press, 1978); and David Calleo, *The German Problem Reconsidered*.
138. Bruce Cummings, 'The Northeast Asian Political Economy', *International Organisation*, Vol. 38, No. 1 (Summer 1984), pp. 1–40.
139. Takahashi Inoguchi, 'The China-Japan Relationship in Perspective' (Paper presented at the Workshop on Australia, China, Japan, Canberra, Sept. 19, 1986). See also 'China's Economy: How Far? How Fast?' *Far Eastern Economic Review*, Aug. 29, 1985, pp. 50–56; and 'The Readjustment in the Chinese Economy', *China Quarterly*, No. 100 (Dec. 1984), pp. 691–865.
140. See OECD, *Interfutures: Facing the Future. Mastering the Probable and Managing the Unpredictable* (Paris, 1979); and Japan, Economic Planning Agency, *Nisen nen no Nihon* (Japan in the year 2000) (Tokyo: Government Printing Bureau, 1983).
141. See Mochizuki, 'Japan's Search'.
142. See Nakagawa, 'The WEPTO Option'.
143. See R. Morse, 'Japan's Search'.
144. Quoted in Pierre Hassner, 'Recurrent Stresses, Resilient Structures', in Robert Tucker and Linda Wrigley, eds., *The Atlantic Alliance and Its Critics* (New York: Praeger, 1983), pp. 61–94.
145. Bank of Japan, *Nihon keizai*.
146. International Bank for Reconstruction and Development, *World Development Report, 1985* (Washington, D.C., 1985). The Report acknowledges the benefits for developing countries of Japan's financial contributions and development loans.
147. Hayabusa, 'Kakegaeno nai jugonen'; and Davis, 'Reaganomics' Magical Mystery Tour'.
148. One can no less strongly argue that the United States has been much more disquieting and disorganizing than has Japan in the 1980s.
149. Bruce Roscoe, 'Against the Grain: Japan's Sudden Shift to Chinese Corn Has the US Worried', *Far Eastern Economic Review*, Oct. 3, 1985, p. 60.
150. Clyde Haberman, 'Japan: Uneasy on World Stage', *International Herald Tribune*, Aug. 3–4, 1985.

2

Japan's uncertainty and unease with itself: international structure and international role

Japan as supporter

How is a country's international role determined? Customarily, it is addressed on three levels: the international system, the national state, and individuals.[1] In this chapter I would like to take up primarily the international systemic explanation: Japan's role is somehow determined to a significant extent by how it is placed in the international system in terms of its economy, security, and memory.

A good starting-point is David Lake's typology of international roles: leader, supporter, spoiler, and free rider, as measured by the relative size and relative productivity of an economy.[2] A leader is an actor who shapes and sustains the framework for international economic interactions. A supporter is an actor who helps to support and sustain such a framework. A spoiler is an actor who benefits from such a framework but whose behaviour often has a negative effect on such a framework. A free rider is an actor who benefits from such a framework but who does not dare to shoulder the costs for the framework in any systematic manner. According to Lake, the role of a country is fairly well determined by its position in the world economy in terms of its size and productivity in relation to other major economies. Thus, according to Lake, how the United States moved from free rider through spoiler and supporter to leader in the international economic sphere between the late nineteenth century and the present can be well explained by looking at its relative size and relative productivity.[3]

Using this perspective, I have argued elsewhere that Japan is perhaps a supporter, although other images are no less widely held.[4] As long as one looks at its relative economic size and its relative productivity, Japan is not number one; it occupies the number two position following the United States. If the European Economic Community (EEC) is considered to be one integrated entity, then Japan is number three after the EEC and the United States. Nor is Japan's relative productivity number one. Despite its sometimes dazzling competitiveness in many manufacturing sectors, its overall labor productivity is not as high as some like to believe, in large part because of significantly longer working hours and accommodation of such less competitive sectors as defense, finance, and service. Seen in this way, Japan's international role is closer to supporter than to the other roles. Yet given the intense counterarguments that Japan is either free rider or spoiler or challenger, let me examine this point more specifically in some other areas that determine Japan's international role: trade, money, technology, security, and memory.

Japan's international role in selected areas

Trade

It is arguable that Japan is a supporter in trade given the immense stakes it has in a well-functioning world economy. Lacking huge natural resource endowments, Japan must utilize resources abroad to keep up its economy, either in the form of trade or investment. It is not surprising to find out that Japan's imports are largely in the areas of food and energy. On the other hand, Japan's exports tend to focus on manufactured products. These are massively exported to many countries, in part because as Japan's direct investment in manufacturing goes up, then imports of parts also increase from Japan. Thus this pattern of Japan's trade and especially the trade imbalance thus created have tended to encourage many to place Japan in the categories of free rider, spoiler, or challenger rather than supporter. Some call it Japan's unequal trade.[5]

Such arguments are enhanced by Japan's somewhat tactless emphasis on domestic imperatives in such areas as agriculture, distribution, financial service, and aerospace.[6] Agriculture is electorally and politically sensitive to the governing Liberal Democratic Party because the party has long been reliant on farmers' support and because a majority of the Japanese people do not wish to see 100 per cent of their major staple, rice, imported from abroad. Japan's position on agricultural trade in the Uruguay Round of GATT negotiations has been fairly clumsy, and Japan is becoming an easy target for criticism despite the fact that its position is no more protectionist than that of the EEC or the United States. Distribution is another area where the governing party feels electorally and politically sensitive, and it has thus accommodated small shops and factories by granting them fairly large tax exemptions and the privilege of excluding large retail stores from their neighborhoods. Talks on the Structural Impediments Initiative between Japan and the United States seem to have made some major breakthroughs toward further market liberalization, but the image of Japan as a discriminatory protectionist was enhanced during the talks because of its tenacious adherence to the position prescribed by bureaucratic-political sectoral interests until the eleventh hour.[7] Financial sectors have been relatively adept at handling liberalization pressure from abroad in part because the Ministry of Finance sees the benefit of some deregulation and liberalization in order not to 'lose' everything.[8] Aerospace will continue to be a market battlefield between Japan's fledgling space sector and the United States until another major breakthrough is made in Japan-US negotiations evolving around the threat of unilateral US action against Japan in the area of satellites. Japan's scientific-business sectoral interests want to advance space-related innovations endogenously, even if they must start from scratch and at immense cost, so that the present overdependence on US technology can be mitigated. Others have argued that Japan cannot and had better not attempt to achieve a competitive position in every area including those in which the United States has maintained a competitive position until now.

Despite these and other kinds of roles Japan plays to the detriment of its image as a supporter, Japan's stakes in world trade have been and will continue to be very great. It is this perception of self-interest that has led Japan to achieve the doubling of its imports from abroad and the remarkable reduction of the export dependency of the economy during the last half of the 1980s. By 1990 Japan's ratio of foreign trade to GNP was 9 per cent, in contrast to the US figure of 6 per cent and figures of 20–35 per cent in major West European countries.

Money

The area of international money seems to give a clearer picture than that of international trade. US dollars play a primordial and predominant role in the international monetary system which has been evolving especially since the breakdown of dollar-gold convertibility in 1971.[9] The termination of dollar-gold convertibility meant that the US dollar became quasi-gold and that, given no feasible alternative to the dollar-dominant system, the monetary authorities of each country accumulated US dollar reserves at the high rate of 16.9 per cent from 1970, as contrasted with 6.3 per cent for 1950–70.[10] In this dollar-predominant system, the Japanese yen plays a secondary or tertiary role.

The picture was steadily modified to give greater emphasis to the role of the Japanese yen during the last half of the 1980s, during which the Plaza Accord of the Group of Five (G5) was executed largely to support a cheaper dollar and the value of the Japanese yen was elevated to record highs. It was during this period that Japanese capital steadily penetrated the world with its high value *vis-à-vis* other currencies. During this period also Japan became a target of criticism for its possible ambition to become the global financial leader. The greater role of key currencies such as the Japanese yen and the German mark does not mean, however, that they can play a role as important as that which the US dollar has held since 1971. The Japanese yen in particular can play its structurally determined role only under the dollar-dominant system. The yen's fall in early 1990 made it clear that the yen is not as strong as some wish to believe. It is weak because 'the net outflow of long-term capital (bonds, equities, and direct investment) from Japan has been even greater than its current-account surplus'.[11] Both heavy overseas investment (1.1. per cent of GNP in 1989) and an overvalued yen in terms of purchasing power parity have tended to pull the Japanese yen further down as a backlash to the excessive policy of the late 1980s.

The problem is of course that the current dollar-predominant system tends to undermine the position of the US dollar and the US economy as the United States accumulates such huge deficits, with other countries accumulating dollar reserves steadily. This will be true as long as US monetary authorities stick to the position that the US dollar is the key currency not reliant on gold convertibility. The external position of the US dollar has ceased to be registered in US government documents since 1975.[12] The result is that whatever discipline the United States may have had has been diluted with the, on the whole, steady expansion of US trade deficits since 1976 and US current account deficits since 1982,[13] making the United States the largest deficit country of the world before the end of the 1980s.

The great amount of trade surplus and foreign reserves enjoyed or perhaps shouldered by Japan, West Germany, Taiwan, and other nations is the other side of the coin. That is, in the dollar-predominant system the United States does not see it necessary to impose discipline on its own use of US dollars. The astonishing speed with which these countries have accumulated money, especially during the period when the Plaza Accord was executed, more or less cooperatively, has alarmed the United States, particularly in response to the country perceived as most threatening, that is, Japan. Yet the fact remains that as long as the United States registers large current account deficits, capital is bound to be pumped into deficit-ridden countries such as the United States and some Third World countries. Here the role of Japan's financial leadership is sometimes argued for, especially in the areas of debt relief in the forms of rescheduling and government bond purchase and developmental assistance of many kinds.[14] It is important, however, to stress the difference between the role the United States plays and the role countries like Japan play. The former is that of leader, whereas the latter is that of supporter. Needless to say, if the US economy continues to deteriorate in terms of deficit accumulation and competitiveness, then the whole international monetary system may start to metamorphose and one or two key currencies might emerge to partially replace US dollars in some nebulous future. But even if such a future comes, it will be a much messier order than the at least superficially unified order of the US dollar's predominance.

Needless to say, Japan has much to improve if it wishes to enhance its role of supporter. Japan's dominant preoccupation with inflation and other considerations has tended to lessen its support of a high Japanese yen as was evident during 1988–9 when very low interest rates were maintained.[15] These and other factors have tended to give Japan an image of spoiler or free rider or challenger instead of supporter. Yet the basic picture of Japan as supporter will continue into the 1990s.

Technology

Japan has long been a free rider in technology and has been very protectionist until recently. Only in the last few years has Japan's expected role become that of supporter; its technological and manufacturing prowess combined with its marketing adroitness have encouraged some countries such as the United States to make use of Japan's technological capability. Japan's technology exports in comparison to imports have started to grow much more vigorously than before. Japan's scientists have begun to invite and cooperate with colleagues from abroad much more vigorously. The works of Japanese scientists are now often cited in such areas as biochemistry, material sciences, and electronics. Yet the basic picture is that of an emergent supporter.

Japan's supporter role in this area has been somewhat related to security in the United States. It is after all the Strategic Defense Initiative project that has led Japan to amend some technological cooperation agreements with the United States to accommodate the US request to tap Japanese technological prowess for the enhancement of its security position.[16] The recent co-development project between Japan and the United States over the next fighter plane for Japan's Self-Defense Forces, the FS-X, has been tentatively settled in its terms of collaboration. As the agreement now stands, Japanese companies must give away to their counterparts whatever developments they may come up with, whereas US companies can withhold the transfer of technologies to Japanese counterparts if deemed necessary for security reasons.

If US technological supremacy was attained by government-led spending in defense sectors which in turn went to civilian sectors in the form of spin-offs, it is not difficult for the United States to think that Japan's technological advance in its civilian sectors can be tapped for defense purposes as well in the form of spin-ons. But the picture does not seem to be so neat. There have not been many instances in which Japanese firms have collaborated with US counterparts in the SDI project so far. The Japanese firms on the FS-X co-development project do not seem enthusiastic about terms that seem to them too asymmetrical. More recently, the main Japanese firm, Mitsubishi Heavy Industries, has together with other firms of its *keiretsu* struck a deal with the German firm group Daimler Benz which has firms specializing in engines and aircraft as well.

Japan's recent concessions in the area of aerospace, in response to the US government's threat of unilateral protectionist measures unless Japan proceeded with more vigorous market liberalization in some key areas, may be taken as Japan's greater interest in conciliation and collaboration than in confrontation and competition when it comes to high technology areas where the United States has been a forerunner. The overall framework in this area is again that of the United States. Although Japan has been catching up quite admirably, its status is that of a supporter, not that of a challenger. In order to retain the overall hegemonic position it has enjoyed for so long, the United States does not seem to tolerate the development of a challenger. Needless to say, technological protectionism cannot be maintained forever as discovery and innovation will spring up once a certain set of conditions develop, including the technological level and enormous needs and efforts, in other countries.[17]

Security

Japan is, like Germany, a semi-sovereign country in the area of security in the sense that its autonomous role in security is denied by arrangements made immediately after its defeat in World War II.[18] Japan's Self-Defense Forces can act only together with the US Armed Forces and only when Japan must act for strictly defensive purposes. The United States initially wanted Japanese military potential, including its strong industrial base, to be completely eradicated. With the onset of the Cold War, however, it sought instead to transform Japan into a country with a stable and friendly government and a strong economic foundation so that the United States could station its armed forces in Japan to confront communism on the continent as well as in Pacific rim countries. Japan's Self-Defense Forces were created to supplement the weakened US military presence in Japan when a large bulk of it had to wage war in the Korean peninsula. Since then the Self-Defense Forces' role has been auxiliary and supplementary to the US Armed Forces in the region. Despite its important role supporting the

United States, the legitimacy of the Self-Defense Forces at home has been less than what it has wanted to see. The Constitution denies Japan's right to resort to war to resolve conflicts of interest among nations, and the Japan-US Security Treaty ensures that US Armed Forces stations in Japan will help Japan to enjoy peace and stability in case of armed attacks against Japan. Thus both domestic and international arrangements have reinforced each other to keep Japan a semi-sovereign country in the nineteenth-century sense of the word.

Problems with these arrangements have started to grow slowly in tandem with two international developments. One is the relative scaling down of the United States in terms of its economic competitiveness and its military commitment. The other is the development of the US-Soviet detente, which reduced the allies' perception of the Soviet military threat. Japan has not been affected by these global factors as much as Europe for three major reasons. First, the United States is determined to retain its hegemonic position in world-wide naval-air power, especially in the north Pacific. Second, the Soviet Union improved its naval and military capabilities in the north Pacific and in the Soviet Far East in disproportion to the substantial arms reduction in Soviet Europe and Eastern Europe. Third, with the prospect of the United States' withdrawal from South Korea and the Philippines in the intermediate-term future, Japan is vital for US Armed Forces in the entire region. Fourth, without the presence in Japan of US Armed Forces, Japan's neighbors are likely to grow more apprehensive about its military predominance.

Yet undeniable uncertainty has been growing in the region. To cope with this uncertainty the Japanese government has seemingly pursued the following policy lines: (1) the Soviet military threat was not declining in the Pacific, thus vigilance and military ties with the United States were more strongly called for; (2) without strong ties with the United States, Japan's relationship with all its neighbors including the United States would be more likely to deteriorate; (3) improvement of Russo-Japanese relations must be worked out without compromising the two major issues of naval arms reduction and territories.[19] These policies point clearly to Japan's favorite security role, that of supporter. The US government has also been trying to keep Japan as a supporter of the US-led international security network and seems determined to stay put, despite its growing need for fiscal retrenchment, as a leader convinced of its role, i.e., 'Bound to Lead'.[20] Thus, at least for the foreseeable future, it does not seem that the basic picture will undergo any drastic change that would reverse the two roles of leader and supporter in the Pacific. Needless to say, this depends on many complex factors such as the possibilities of American economic renewal,[21] North Korea's possession and diffusion of nuclear weapons, and Pacific naval arms reduction, although major potential parties—the United States, China, North and South Korea, Japan, and Taiwan—are not quite ready for the latter.[22]

Memory

By memory I mean the human remembrance of the past, especially in relation to Japanese misconduct in the 1930s and 1940s. It constrains significantly how Japan behaves and how Japan conceives its policy *vis-à-vis* its neighbors and friends. I call it the debt-of-history factor. The human memory of being victimized is not easy to eradicate. A lifetime is necessary for that, according to the late Hu Yaobang, former Secretary General of the Chinese Communist Party. He told Yamazaki Toyoko, a Japanese novelist, that the Boxer Rebellion of 1900–1 was forgotten but that the Second Sino-Japanese War of 1937–45 has not been forgotten by the Chinese.[23] Furthermore, the steady Japanese ascendance after World War II and Japan's salient economic presence in many parts of the world have made it easy for old memories to be revived and remolded in a new fashion, although the Japanese have been somewhat oblivious to this debt-of-history factor, especially at the mass level.

The Japanese difficulty in coming to terms with the debt-of-history issue lies in their search for the meaning of their modern history. Without experiencing the drastic discontinuity of history found in West Germany, where German history led to the Third Reich and ended with it,[24] the Japanese can see some basic continuity between the pre-1945 and post-1945 years, including fairly steady economic development and political democratization, while the 1930s and 1940s can be seen as unfortunate 'aberrations'. The Japanese difficulty increases when they differentiate, as they do, between two kinds of war: one against Pacific Asians, and the other against Americans and Europeans. Whenever the Japanese feel that the latter war was one of imperialist rivalry, they are, if unwittingly, making it more difficult for their case to be accepted by their friends and neighbors. Both Pacific Asians and Euro-Americans suffered from war with the Japanese, thus encouraging them to align with each other *de facto* whenever the Japanese issue comes up. Koreans, Chinese, other Pacific Asians, and Americans have been especially vocal in this respect. Under this circumstance, I can see only insanity in Japan's wish for a challenger status as it would simply undermine Japan's international status from the very beginning.

Yet with growing self-confidence in its economic power and with an increasingly critical perception of Japanese motivations circulated abroad, some Japanese have started to express somewhat more than mildly nationalistic reactions, although these have a low level of appeal. Thus the debt of history will continue to constrain the scope and method of the kind of role the Japanese assign to themselves.

Why do uncertainty and uneasiness abound?

I have so far examined, if briefly, how Japan's international role is fairly well determined by the international structure. Using Lake's insight into the relationship between economic position and international role, I have argued that Japan's role as prescribed by its economic position in the world economy is that of supporter. I have augmented the argument by looking at selective areas of importance: trade, money, technology, security, and memory. Although there are often significant differences in Japan's position in each of these areas, the basic role of Japan as supporter in the international system seems to be affirmed. What remains to be done is to explain why there continues to be so much uncertainty and uneasiness about Japan's expected role of supporter. One reason is Japan's extremely steady and sometimes rapid rise in the international system. When an object changes dramatically and drastically, then one's perception tends to be revised accordingly. Yet when the object changes incrementally and without *dramatis personae*, one tends to be slow to modify the picture of the object. The latter applies to Japan's change. One can detect some justifiable frustration about Japan when such phrases as 'slow change' and 'lack of decisive leadership' are heard.

Underlying the uncertainty and uneasiness about Japan's role is globalization and two features of it: a series of structural adjustments at home and a spate of heavy investment abroad. By globalization I mean the growing difficulty of differentiating between narrowly defined national interests and what may be called the global common interest for Japan. Two mutually reinforcing factors can be noted. First, the economic interactions of Japan have become highly globalized. With such large economic stakes in virtually every corner of the world, Japan cannot afford to define its national interest separately from what might be called the global common interest. The latter obviously includes the security interest most broadly defined. Thus Japan's national interest as traditionally conceived is becoming increasingly obsolete and collides with the role expected of Japan by the international structure.

A second, more universal factor is that both economic and security interactions of the world are now enhancing the concept of one global community. Technological progress has made possible instant transactions of money of astronomical proportions with the aid of advanced telecommunication technologies. Perhaps the world economy in the most literal definition seems to be just emerging after a long nascent period of five centuries. Technological progress has also made it possible to construct balanced arms reductions with the aid of advanced detection technologies. Instead of measuring the adversary's strength on the battlefield, the time seems not too far away when adversaries can measure each other's strength and possibly intentions as well, thus creating the scheme of conceptualizing what may be called common and cooperative security through pre-battle political interaction. Although this is perhaps a little too futuristic, it cannot be denied that technology is increasingly narrowing the globe into one common entity.

When globalization is taking place so steadily and when so much in common is being shared across borders, the kind of distinctions Lake has made between leader, supporter, free rider, spoiler, and challenger may be getting more difficult to make. Rather, sharper lines tend to be drawn sometimes between relatively competitive sectors and relatively less competitive sectors across borders. Globalization thus first means structural adjustments everywhere. Whether fast or slow, whether prolonged by backward protectionism or smoothed by visionary policies, it is taking place everywhere. Japan has been very steady in making structural adjustments in the broad sense of the words, especially in the 1970s and 1980s. This fact means that protectionist voices must be heard 'sincerely' by bureaucrats and politicians. Without attending to the less competitive and painful adjusting sectors that political weight has been placed on, it would be politically explosive to allow global forces to ignite structural adjustments too rapidly. Therefore it is no wonder that Japan has evinced such strong protectionist voices over time. Japan's image of protectionism has been enhanced, somewhat ironically, by a series of structural adjustments made at an almost breathless pace, although I must note that Japan did start from an excessively protectionist level toward market liberalization. It is essential to note that Japan's protectionist stars have been changing very steadily. They were textiles in the late 1960s, steel and petrochemicals in the 1970s, through automobiles in the 1980s, and agriculture and distribution into the 1990s. Japan's structural adjustments took place in three waves: (1) the first oil crisis in which energy costs forced business firms to become energy-efficient; (2) the high yen revolution of the first Reagan presidency which forced business firms to become labor-efficient; and (3) the Structural Impediments Initiative talks between Japan and the United States which will become a trigger to help make Japanese daily life more attuned to amenities.

While at home globalization means structural adjustments, globalization abroad means global economic expansion. In particular, when the United States wanted to keep the US dollar cheaper to reduce its trade deficit and raise its competitiveness, and when Japanese assets were on the whole dearer in part for its regulatory distortions, Japanese surplus capital went for massive overseas investment. Furthermore, Japan's policies of helping to keep the US dollar from falling and of boosting domestic demand in 1987-8 required an immense increase in money supply. The policy has also helped to raise share and property prices, thus further encouraging surplus capital to go abroad. Hence, the net outflow of long-term capital (bonds, equities, and direct investment) from Japan has been bigger than its current account surplus.[25] These outflows have invited heavy criticism from abroad of a Japanese take-over or buy-up of the world. It has raised the level of apprehension over Japan's ambition in the rest of the world. Hence Japan's image of challenger has risen rapdily. Yet Japan's position, like its currency, seems basically weak, presuming leadership by the United States, as the policy of 1987-8 and its consequences now being made visible have shown.

I have tried in this brief chapter to explain why Japan's international role so often gives the sense of uncertainty and uneasiness to many, sometimes even to itself. Using Lake's framework, I have examined area-specific roles of Japan to conclude that Japan's role is that of supporter. Yet to explain the uncertainty and uneasiness, I have concluded that one must examine the extent to which structural adjustments at home and global expansion abroad have been proceeding at an almost breathless pace. If the time horizon is stretched to 10-50 years, then an entirely different set of questions must be asked and examined. I have already considered those questions elsewhere.[26]

Notes

1. Kenneth Waltz, *Man, the State, and War: A Theoretical Analysis* (New York: Columbia University Press, 1959).
2. David Lake, 'International economic structure and American foreign economic policy, 1887-1934', *World Politics*, Vol. 35, No. 4, 1983, pp. 517-43.
3. David Lake, *Power, Protection, and Free Trade: International Sources of US Commercial Strategy, 1887-1939* (Ithaca: Cornell University Press, 1988).
4. Takashi Inoguchi, 'Japan's images and options: not a challenger, but a supporter', *Journal of Japanese Studies*, Vol. 12, No. 1, 1986, pp. 95-119, and 'Looking ahead with caution', in Takashi Inoguchi and Daniel Okimoto (eds), *The Political Economy of Japan, Volume 2: The Changing International Context* (Stanford: Stanford University Press, 1988).
5. Edward Lincoln, *Japan's Unequal Trade* (Washington: Brookings Institution, 1990).
6. Cf. Kent Calder, 'Japanese foreign economic policy formation: explaining the reactive state', *World Politics*, Vol. 40, No. 4, 1988.

7. Takashi Inoguchi and Tomoaki Iwai, *Zoku giin no kenkyu* (A study of policy tribes-parliamentarians) (Tokyo: Nihon Keizai Shimbunsha, 1987).
8. Frances McCall Rosenbluth, *Financial Politics in Contemporary Japan* (Ithaca: Cornell University Press, 1989).
9. Milton Gilbert, *The Quest for World Monetary Order: The Gold-Dollar System and Its Aftermath* (New York: Wiley, 1980).
10. Buntaro Tomizuka, *Doru taisei no mujun to kiketsu—tsuka kiki kara hogoshugi* (Contradictions and consequences of the dollar system: from monetary crises to protectionism) (Tokyo: Yomiuri Shimbunsha,1990).
11. 'The Japanese paradox', *The Economist*, 7-13 April 1990, p. 79.
12. Ushio Sakuma, 'Amerika no shin kokusai shushi hyoji ho' (A new US format for representing balance of payments), *Monthly Bulletin of the Bank of Tokyo*, November 1976, as cited in Tomizuka, *Doru taisei no mujun to kiketsu, op. cit.*
13. Tomizuka, *Doru taisei no mujun to kiketsu, op. cit.*
14. Shafiqul Islam, *Yen for Development* (New York: Council on Foreign Relations, 1991); Takashi Inoguchi, 'Four Japanese scenarios for the future', *International Affairs*, Vol. 65, No. 1, 1988-89, pp. 15-28.
15. Tomizuka, *Doru taisei no mujun to kiketsu, op. cit.*, pp. 244-6.
16. Takashi Inoguchi, 'Trade, technology and security: implications for East Asia and the West', *Adelphi Papers*, No. 218, Spring 1987, pp. 39-53; Richard Samuels and Benjamin Whipple, 'Defense production and industrial development: the case of Japanese aircraft', in Chalmers Johnson *et al.* (eds), *Politics and Productivity: How Japan's Development Strategy Works* (Cambridge: Ballinger, 1989), pp. 275-318.
17. Anne G. Keatley (ed.), *Technological Frontiers and International Relations* (Washington: National Academy Press, 1985).
18. Peter Katzenstein, *Politics and Policy in West Germany* (Philadelphia: Temple University Press, 1987).
19. Cf. Takashi Inoguchi, 'Change and response in Japan: international politics and strategy', in Stuart Harris and James Cotton (eds), *The End of the Cold War in Northeast Asia*, (Melbourne: Longman Cheshire, 1991, pp. 229-36).
20. Joseph S. Nye, *Bound to Lead: The Changing Nature of American Power* (New York: Basic Books, 1990).
21. Richard Rosecrance, *America's Economic Resurgence: A Bold New Strategy* (New York: Harper & Row, 1990).
22. Gerald Segal, *Rethinking the Pacific* (Oxford: Clarendon Press, 1990).
23. Inoguchi, 'Four Japanese scenarios for the future', *op. cit.*
24. Charles Maier, *The Unmasterable Past: History, Holocaust, and German National Identity* (Cambridge: Harvard University Press, 1989).
25. 'The Japanese paradox', *op. cit.*
26. Inoguchi, 'Four Japanese scenarios for the future', *op. cit.*

Part II:
Redirecting Japan's foreign policy

3

Japanese responses to Europe 1992: implications for the United States

The very rapidly evolving situation in Europe has taken the Japanese by surprise, and there is as yet no unified Japanese strategy towards Europe 1992. In this chapter, I will attempt to outline the main lines of the seemingly disjointed Japanese responses to Europe 1992 and discuss their implications for US policies.

The Reagan presidency: a watershed for Japanese and Europeans?

What did the Reagan period bring about? Besides infusing what may be called a new American vision into the minds of many Americans who had been soured by a series of events including the Vietnam war, the Watergate scandal, inflation, and the Iran crisis, it meant two things to Japanese and Europeans: first, an unprecedented military buildup in peacetime, subsequent detente with the Soviet Union, and the effect of reduced tension in the rest of the world; and second, large-scale tax reduction, wide-ranging deregulation and market liberalization, high deficits in government and foreign trade, and efforts toward enhancing competitiveness at home and pushing trade liberalization abroad.[1]

Detente made the Japanese (and Europeans) much more conscious of their constraints and maneuvering room. With the United States and the Soviet Union coming to terms, they found no reason to sacrifice what they thought were their legitimate interests if these could be pursued in harmony with American-defined Western global interests. In other words, they have become much more conscious of their ability to construct their own security environment, using a policy mix of three directions: reducing the burden of alliance with the United States, moderating their perception of threat from the Soviet Union, and enhancing their own military capabilities. In the light of the relative decline of the United States and the consequent need for reduction of US world leadership burdens, Japan had not only to promote burden-sharing schemes but also to bring about a less overloaded alliance relationship with the United States. This modified posture will inevitably lead Japan in the longer term to modify its policy stance toward the Soviet Union in order to decrease Soviet antagonism. Furthermore, it means that Japan must be much more capable of defending itself than its present structure allows.

The tide of market liberalization has made the Japanese more aware of the benefits and costs of retaining competitiveness while deepening inter-dependence. They are eager to benefit from liberalization on a national scale (as Thatcher and Nakasone among others did in the early and mid-1980s), as well as bilaterally (as the United States and Canada did in their bilateral free-trade agreement), regionally (as the European Community has done toward and beyond 1992), and globally (as the GATT Uruguay Round Talks have been trying to do). But the Japanese also have to retain and enhance their own competitiveness in the face of intensifying American pressure toward further liberalization and toward protectionism. American efforts to retain and enhance competitiveness tend to focus on 'backward-looking' protection of those sectors that have shown a relative decline in competitiveness, a policy that can only have negative long-term conse-quences for competitiveness. Conversely, the Japanese (and Pacific Asians) and West European efforts have two other major features, 'forward-looking' protection in nascent competitive sectors plus the retention of national and regional political, economic, and social structures and ways of life.[2] In other words, they have become more concerned about their own competitiveness and productivity precisely because they are now more exposed to the pene-tration of global market forces in both directions: liberalizing and regularizing. The Reagan presidency produced the unique mix of unilateralism, bilaterialism, and protectionism exemplified by the Super 301 clause of the Trade Act and the Structural Impediment Talks. This trend has been further enhanced during the Bush Administration.

One Japanese policy, in times of growing interdependence accompanied by protectionist reaction, is to enlarge and enhance economic activities on a regional scale. This would bring the benefit of liberalization on a larger scale than when applied to a single national economy while minimizing the negative effects of protectionism by other countries and regions. Thus the Europeans naturally conceive of enlargement and liberalization within the Community and, gradually, beyond. Similarly, the Japanese try to broaden their interaction with their neighbors in Pacific Asia. Needless to say, this global liberalizing trend has encouraged economic actors to act much more strongly than their sectoral, national, or regional inclinations would other-wise allow them, for they have all come to share an increasingly strong com-mon stake in global markets. This especially applies to three major economies, the North American, Japanese (and Pacific Asian), and West European, for which any policy sectorally, nationally, or regionally defined would have immediate and long-term global ramifications.

In these two senses the Reagan presidency was a watershed to both Europeans and Japanese, because it encouraged them to think about their own destiny in the light of changing US power and policy *vis-à-vis* its allies and partners. Needless to say, this kind of change is only slowly detectable. But it is important to understand the basic direction of change when our task is to see the longer-term implications for US policies.

Japanese policies during the Nakasone period

Before analyzing the Japanese responses to Europe 1992, let me look more closely at how Japanese policies were conceived and executed under Prime Minister Nakasone (1982–7), whose tenure in office largely coincided with that of President Reagan (1981–8). This will enable us to understand better why the Japanese are responding to Europe 1992 in the way they are.[3]

When Nakasone was appointed prime minister in November 1982, he faced two problems that had caused his predecessor, Zenko Suzuki, to resign: deteriorating Japan-US relations and Japan's budget deficit. When the governments of Japan and the United States issued a joint communiqué after the Suzuki-Reagan talks in 1982, many Japanese saw the use therein of the term 'alliance' to mean a greater Japanese commitment to increase its security efforts for the alliance. The US government did not hide its displeasure when Suzuki stated to Japanese journalists on his way home from the talks that 'alliance' did not mean 'military alliance'. In 1982, one may recall, the US economy was experiencing a very painful deflation whereas US defense expenditures were rapidly expanding. Thus, the US mood was not favorable to what was perceived as Suzuki's apparent lack of sincerity. To remedy this situation, LDP leaders chose Nakasone as prime minister.

Nakasone thought American security demands provided a golden opportunity to overhaul what he labeled the post-war system, i.e., the semi-sovereign international status of Japan and all those associated with it. Instead of taking issue with the United States over its treatment of Japan as a quasi-vassal state, Nakasone decided that his extension of the fullest possible support to the United States would help establish Japan's equal partnership with it. Thus the prime minister who had a record of anti-American nationalism in his earlier political life promoted the most pro-American policies at home and abroad. To justify opening the Japanese market and increasing Japan-US military cooperation, he exploited fledgling Japanese nationalism. With the steady rise of their country's economic clout, the Japanese searched for a political equivalent. Though the pressures from abroad on both trade and defense were strong, Nakasone believed they produced beneficial effects. Pressure for economic liberalization made Japanese industries more competitive and strengthened the horizontal interdependence of the Japanese economy with other economies. Pressure for strategic integration made Japan 'an ordinary country' (meaning a sovereign state, thus implying that Japan had not been) and thus less vulnerable to accusations of inadequate defense expenditures from the United States.

Thus there were three Japanese responses under Nakasone leadership. First, the defense buildup was prosecuted vigorously in concert with the United States. Without agreeing to the American call for burden-sharing, it would have been difficult for Japan to maintain its friendship with the United States when it was frustrated in its economic and security policies. Japan's defense buildup was so steadily pursued that by the end of the 1980s Japan had become the third largest military spender in the world.[4]

Second, market liberalization also continued steadily. Because the United States was suffering from economic troubles at home and abroad, it would have been very difficult for Japan to carry out market liberalization more slowly than it did in the 1980s. As a result, 'in 1988, Japanese imports were 25.3 per cent higher than those in 1987, including a 33.3 per cent increase in imports from the United States. . . Investments from the United States total[ed] $940 million in fiscal 1987—a 92 per cent increase in value over the previous year'.[5] According to a survey of 434 top world business managers conducted jointly by leading business newspapers such as the *Nihon keizai shimbun* (the *Japan Economic Journal*) and the *Wall Street Journal*, Japan is seen as the market with the fewest policy barriers to access and the highest profitability.[6] As a matter of fact, liberalization was so steady during this period—some perceptions notwithstanding—that it undermined severely the economic bases of some core supporters of the governing party in the Upper House election of July 1989. Notably, farmers all over Japan, especially in dominantly agricultural districts, overwhelmingly voted socialist in protest at the government's liberalization policy on farm products.

Third, regionalist initiatives were largely left to other countries such as Australia (Prime Minister Bob Hawke's initial proposal on the Asia-Pacific group, without the United States), South Korea (enthusiastic about the Australian initiative on the Asia-Pacific group), the United States (a network of bilateral free-trade arrangements), the Soviet Union (the Vladivostok and Krasnoyarsk initiatives on greater Pacific Asian interaction), and ASEAN (ASEAN consolidation). Japan opted for a loose networking approach on the basis of its own economic, financial, and technological advantage over its regional neighbors, despite what may be called its debt of history to Pacific Asians. Its major policy instruments are credits, technology transfers, grants, foreign direct investment, and cultural exchanges.[7] Needless to say, these policy initiatives were accompanied by efforts to assuage Japanese public opinion's heavily pacifist sentiments and strong proclivity to retain the structural features embedded in Japanese traditions and way of life. The effort has thus brought alive nationalist sentiments, which have grown steadily with increasing self-confidence in Japanese affluence and influence and the 'rough-and-tough' American policy on economic disputes.

It is very important to stress that in doing all this, the overall thrust of Japanese foreign policy is to play the role of supporting the US-led international system, be it in security, economic, or regional matters. The Nakasone period was noteworthy for Japan's efforts to overcome its image as a free rider with respect to defense burden-sharing and as a spoiler with respect to its external economic activities and its internal barriers against foreign economic actors. As Japan's external policy evolved—and has been evolving—the Japanese conception of their nation's role in global affairs was formed largely with respect to Japan's relations with the United States.[8]

Looking to Japan's future: scenarios

While still focusing on its relationship with the United States, Japan none the less has started to look ahead with varying scenarios in mind as the global economic and security configurations change steadily and as Japan enhances its profile in both these areas. To determine options for future policies, Japanese leaders have to solve a complex set of equations involving at least three major variables: (1) economic and technological dynamism of major countries and regions; (2) prospects for dominant military technology or the possibility of nullification of nuclear arsenals either through US-Soviet detente or through revolutionary breakthroughs similar to the Strategic Defense Initiative; and (3) the burden of Japanese history as a constraining factor. Japanese policy-makers envision four major scenarios possible for the future: Pax Americana Phase II (the world largely led by the United States), Bigemony (the world largely shaped by the two co-supremos, the United States and Japan), Pax Consortis (the world organized by various policy-related consortia), and Pax Nipponica (the world largely shaped by Japan).[9]

Briefly stated, Pax Americana Phase II is a scenario involving the revival of American power, if in a somewhat reduced form, brought about with major assistance from Japan's economic power. Bigemony is the joint dominion of the United States and Japan in economic and security arenas. Pax Consortis envisages loosely and flexibly aligned sets of major countries concerned with particular, important issue areas, where no one is predominant. Finally, Pax Nipponica is a world where Japan enjoys a pre-eminent economic position and nuclear arsenals are somehow nullified.

The scenario I see as most probable is a combination of the above: whereas in the intermediate term of a quarter century, Pax Americana Phase II and Bigemony are feasible, in the longer term of a half century, Pax Consortis and Pax Nipponica may become more feasible. Economic and technological dynamism are very important in differentiating Pax Americana Phase II and Pax Nipponica. The improbability of the user of nuclear arsenals is crucial in making feasible both Pax Consortis and Pax Nipponica because without them the two superpowers cannot remain the dominant actors. The debt of history is crucial in differentiating Pax Americana Phase II and Bigemony since only without it can Japan become a fully fledged global military power along with the United States.

Along with such long-term scenarios, there are short-term policy-oriented calculations. More concretely, two pairs of short-term options differentiate the four major, long-term foreign policy orientations: those options are (1) favoring alliance with the United States versus opposing alliance with it; and (2) trilateralism versus Asianism. The first concerns how closely Japan should align its positions with the United States while the second concerns how much weight Japan should give to Pacific Asia. In other words, the first has to do with the degree of distance that Japan should keep from the United States while the second has to do with the interest Japan should give to Western Europe, one of the three pillars of the industrialized world.

In the discussion of these short-term options, four schools of thought have emerged on Japan's major policy alternatives: (1) the thinking that emphasizes the bigemonic integration of Japan with the United States and the disinclination to institute some form of Pacific Asian community; (2) the inclination to keep distant from the United States in security affairs but to enhance basic bi(tri)lateral economic relations; (3) the policy line of retaining and even enhancing security ties with the United States while giving Pacific Asia much more emphasis in economic matters than Western Europe or sometimes even North America; and (4) the thinking that de-emphasizes the Japan-US alliance and upgrades economic ties with Pacific Asia.

The first school of thought is sometimes called the bigemonic scenario. The place of Europe is somewhat murky in this scenario, because it envisages a greater Pacific economic-financial-technological-security complex which encompasses not only the United States and Japan but also Pacific Asia. The second is often termed the Gaullist scenario in that it seeks to defend Japan's autonomous security interests while advancing ever-expanding global economic interdependence. If the Gaullist scenario is remolded in a co-operative and conciliatory spirit, it becomes more compatible with Pax Consortis—a scenario in which various actors in each policy area coordinate and cooperate to bring about policy adjustments in an increasingly multipolar world.

The third school of thought is sometimes called the Pax Americana Phase II scenario, one which is taken as a basic continuation of Japan's present policy direction. The fourth is termed the Pacific Asian scenario. It envisages the steady emergence of Pacific Asia as a critical determining factor in the world economy and international relations over the long term, with Japan naturally playing the leading role although its predominance will be mitigated somewhat by the increasingly regional relationship. If the Pacific Asian scenario is globalized, then it becomes more compatible with Pax Nipponica, in which Japan is envisaged as a key actor deftly making use of its economic, financial, and technological predominance and its arbitrating influence in a way not so different from England in the nineteenth century.

It is important to note that while they have added three future alternatives for the international system (Bigemony, Pax Consortis, and Pax Nipponica) to the still-predominant image of the US-led international system (Pax Americana Phase II), the majority of responsible Japanese leaders consider the pillar of Japan-US friendship and the Western alliance for freedom and democracy as the key to any Japanese role in the international system. No less important to note is that Japanese thinking about the nation's future is largely positive, whether or not Japan will be assigned to manage the international system. The many difficulties involved with a transition from one international system to another do not seem to come up very explicitly in discussion about future alternatives except as the result of the Japanese tendency to make somewhat compulsive precautions and preparations for emergencies.

Japanese responses to Europe 1992

Responses of the Japanese to Europe 1992 are part of their broader adaptation to the changed international environment of the 1980s. For the Japanese Europe 1992 does not require any direct or immediate responses unlike those demands from the United States to Japan which do require immediate and concrete responses to demonstrate Japan's openess and fairness. Instead, at least viewed from Japan, the challenge of 1992 is primarily a question of Japan's long-term economic and security strategy. That is not to say that the American demands do not compel the Japanese to think about their long-term strategy. The point is that because of overall distance in terms of economic relations and security arrangements, and because of the overwhelming scope of Japan-US relations, Europe 1992 is seen in Japan as something that requires more strategic thinking. I will examine three dimensions of Japanese thinking on 1992: economic, security, and regional.

First, it is very important to recognize the prevalent Japanese view that Japan's economic relations with Europe need to be enhanced in the light of Japan's overdependence on the United States; this lumping together of trade, technology, and security in the same basket is increasingly perceived as a liability for Japan.[10] 'Europe 1992' is thus 'a chance to lessen their dependence on the American market. . . They [the Japanese] hope that in [the] case of a slow-down in the US economy or renewed protectionism in the US Congress, Europe will provide an alternative market'.[11] As long as Europe is the largest regional market in the world, Japan's external economic policy toward Europe should be based on that fact. As long as the yen remains high, the Japanese must establish inroads in Europe before its walls are built. Finally, as internal market rules regulating such areas as standards, rules of origin, and reciprocity are enhanced, the Japanese must learn to cope with them.[12]

The Japanese discussion is overwhelmingly centered on the problem of access, be it for trade or investment. Thus the key question for the Japanese to ask is, to what extent will Europe 1992 be discriminatory to non-members? And, related to this, how might such discrimination be skirted or mitigated or at least be best handled? It may come as a surprise to Europeans to hear that the Japanese catch-phrase these days is how to become 'good corporate Europeans'. As a matter of fact, Japanese firms have been received much more favorably in Western Europe than in North America[13] and have often registered higher labor productivity than they do in Japan.

Here it will be useful to briefly summarize some of the key aspects of Japan-EC economic relations. In trade, the European Community has restricted Japanese exports through the following kinds of regulations:[14] (1) rules of origin requiring elements of local content; (2) the reciprocity concept, which could be used by the Commission to close EC markets to foreign competitors; (3) the harmonization of standards in ways that make it more difficult for Japanese companies to produce for the European market; (4) national quantitative restrictions which may become Community-wide, reflecting the restrictions of the most protectionist EC states; and (5) proposals involving transitional rules designed to give 'temporary' protection to industries that need to be nurtured before they are exposed to international competition.

In addition to these trade regulations, the newly drafted rules of origin are much more restrictive. Those dealing with semiconductors, for instance, require that 'the process of diffusion take place in the European Community if semiconductors are to qualify as European'. Since there is the possibility that quantitative restrictions placed by member states on imports of Japanese products will be replaced by EC-wide quotas, 'Japanese automobile manufacturers are hedging against European protectionism by establishing production facilities in Europe'. Thus, there has been a surge in Japanese investment: the number of manufacturing facilities in Europe jumped from 282 in 1987 to 411 in January 1989. Japanese direct investment in Europe was estimated to be $33.3 billion by the end of 1989. 'The average European investment by a Japanese company is $11 million, generating annual sales of $136 million and employing an average of 347 Europeans and 8 Japanese'. Thus, 'the mixed feelings of many Europeans toward Japanese investment have been overridden by the recognition that such investment creates badly needed jobs—Europe still faces a 10 per cent unemployment rate'. 'In terms of manufacturing facilities, Britain, West Germany, and Spain appear to be the favorites of Japanese corporate leaders.' As headquarters, marketing bases, and R&D facilities, West Germany and Britain are favored, with France taking a strong third. Because the Community has said that it would not apply any reciprocity test to banks established prior to 31 December 1992, 'Japanese banks are moving now to establish themselves in Europe before EC banking directives go into effect. Large amounts of Japanese capital appear to be flowing into Luxembourg and Paris'. As West Germany recently gained entry into the Nikkei stock exchange, Japan obtained reciprocal rights in the FRG. 'As a result, Japanese investments are pouring into Frankfurt'.

By 1989, the initially exaggerated fear of Fortress Europe had subsided somewhat in Japan. The recent Bank of Japan report about the effects of Europe 1992 on discrimination against non-members seems to confirm this changed perception.[15] Still more recently, the Japanese government expressed a positive view of Europe 1992, having abandoned the hitherto dominant view of Fortress Europe.[16] This new perception seems to be enhanced by the following three factors.

First, the trend toward increasing global interdependence cannot be reversed. Second, within the Community such relatively free-trade countries as West Germany, the Netherlands, Denmark, and the United Kingdom seem to have a strong say *vis-à-vis* those less free-trade countries such as France, Italy, Spain, Portugal, and Greece. Third, internal rivalry within the Community seems to be manifested in part in the competition among EC members to receive more direct foreign investment than other Community countries. As French Industry Minister Roger Fauroux stated, 'It is better to have Japanese investment in France than unemployed people'.[17]

However, the overall Japanese optimism remains tempered by caution and vigilance backed up by high-level economic intelligence efforts.[18] Although the Japanese now believe that Europe 1992 presents an opportunity, many of them are very well aware of the fact that 'the EC won't be like an orchard where everyone can run in and snatch all the fruit from the trees'.[19] The Japanese are also not oblivious to the possibility that any global economic depression, whether originating from a US 'hard landing' or from a precarious transition from Yalta to a post-Yalta international system, could only encourage a closed, inward-looking European Community. Japan and the United States therefore have every reason to encourage the European Community to become freer, more open, and more prosperous. Otherwise, Japan and the United States could find themselves fighting over each other's marketing much more fiercely.[20]

Furthermore, although Europe 1992 in the security arena does not pose any immediate problems for Japan, it does encourage Japan to think about its own strategy. Japanese security thinking is based on the recognition that Europe has been trying to secure peace and stability in its own way, if not necessarily on its own terms. This tendency, combined with US-Soviet detente, has accelerated the Japanese re-examination of security strategies. This re-evaluation has not manifested itself in any dramatically overt manner. It has, however, surfaced in two ways. First, it is strengthening the kind of thinking in Japan that does not wholly embrace the wishes and whims of the United States. Although the recently well-publicized volume by Akio Morita and Shintaro Ishihara, *Japan that Can Say No*, may come immediately to mind, much more important than this extreme stance is the dominant view in Japan that US trade deficits may be rooted in too much spending, too little saving, and too little investment, and the view that US unilateralism (like application of the Super 301 clause) and bilateralism (like Structural Impediments Talks) may not be very harmonious with GATT rules.[21] Needless to say, the vast majority of Japanese leaders do not conceive of a foreign policy direction that in any way excludes the component of the alliance with the United States. But they recognize the necessity of lessening Japan's swollen security dependence on the United States because the American president and Congress (if not public opinion) want Japan to shoulder more of the defense burden and because decreased military spending would help the United States to revitalize its economy.

Second, Japan has attempted to begin discreetly the diversification of its technological cooperation from the currently predominant form with the United States to that with Europe. One recent small example of this is the Japanese Self-Defense Force purchase of military aircraft from British Aerospace. The Japanese SDF had previously purchased solely US-made weapons and equipment. The stringent requirements placed on US-Japanese co-development of Japan's next fighter aircraft, FSX, in order to protect US-made technologies compared to EC willingness to sell advanced equipment to Japan testifies to the intense struggle between the United States and the European Community to capture the rapidly expanding weapons market in Pacific Asia.[22] Another example is the recent announcement by the Japanese government that the institutional body that administers the Human Frontier

Project launched by the Japanese government for enhanced technological, especially biotechnological, cooperation with leading industrial countries will be located in Strasbourg.[23]

All this is to say that Europe 1992 has provided Japan with food for thought in the security arena. Japan has been laggard in terms of recognizing the trend of detente between the two superpowers. Until quite recently the Ministry of Foreign Affairs refused to recognize the fact that detente was evolving between the two superpowers. The ministry stated that there was no such thing as detente in its dictionary, if only because it apparently thought that the recognition of detente would compel the Japanese government to modify some of the basic corner-stones of its foreign policy, i.e., its antagonism toward the Soviet Union with regard to the Northern Territories and the absolute necessity of the Japan-US security treaty.

In this connection, one might ask, why is it that the Northern Territories issue has been so salient as to almost determine Japan's Soviet policy? It seems that there are deep-seated fears that were Japan to suddenly relax its position on the Northern Territories and its Soviet policy in general, it might start to unravel the major arrangements made during 1945–52, such as the Constitution and the Japan-US Security Treaty, which in turn would be very destabilizing to other Japanese political and security arrangements. Also, were Japan to modify its position toward the Soviet Union, the government would find it difficult to justify the strongly anti-Soviet defense buildup to the Japanese electorate while the United States pushes arms control and consolidates detente with the Soviet Union. Fortunately, however, more than two-thirds of the public has supported the Japanese government's position on the territories. Furthermore, the mere thought that any Japanese flirtation with the Soviet Union—whether concerning territories, technology transfer, direct investment, or a disarmament co-initiative—would provide every reason for the United States to increase its suspicions of Japan's intentions seems to dissuade the Japanese government from taking such a course.

Until recently, the small likelihood that the Soviet Union would return the Northern Territories to Japan, given the vexing Soviet nationalities problem and the not-so-strong political base of Mikhail Gorbachev, enabled the Japanese government to be rigid and completely unwavering in its Soviet policy. But the evolution of superpower detente, the incredibly fast pace of East European change, the growing self-confidence of Western Europe toward 1992, the intensifying demands of the United States to Japan concerning burden-sharing and market liberalization, and, no less important, the Japanese perception of the lax economic management by the United States have all contributed to the modification of the Japanese government's view toward detente and Japan-US relations. In other words,

Japan has started to probe its way toward peace and stability in the, for it, somewhat frightening evolution of global change. It is again important to stress that the Japanese reorientation does not imply any fundamental change in the Japan-US security relationship, given the fact that Japan and the United States—two very dynamic economies—find their common global interests (interests related not just to defense and security but also to global economic stability and prosperity, freedom and democracy, and such global problems as the environment and energy) increasingly more important than any bilateral friction.

Japanese reorientation would entail the following three components.[24] The first involves the gradual reduction of overdependence on the United States, whether in trade, technology, or security. Europe is obviously one of the areas with which Japan hopes to enhance its ties, given the high level of income, the large population, the high technological level, and the spirit of accommodation with the Soviet Union. Although an enhanced Japanese-European relationship has been encumbered by trade deficits, the European Community as a whole has started to decrease its trade deficits *vis-à-vis* Japan. Some countries such as Italy and Denmark, for instance, have recently registered trade surpluses *vis-à-vis* Japan. Most impressive of all, Italy has doubled its exports to Japan in three years.

The second component involves the reduction of tension with the Soviet Union. Even with the territorial issue and traditional hostility, it is not prudent for Japan to continue its hostility toward the Soviet Union with the resultant heavy defense burden, provided that the United States would not be likely to come to Japan's defense were the Soviet Union to attack. Although the growing perception in the United States that Japan rather than the Soviet Union poses the primary threat—a development revealed in various opinion polls in the United States—tends to be toned down in Japan, such opinion polls and articles reflecting a similar line have encouraged some Japanese leaders seriously to consider reducing tension with the Soviet Union over the longer term. Some mode of limited detente seems to be encouraged. The visit of Secretary General Mikhail Gorbachev to Japan in 1991 and Aleksandr Yakovlev's visit to Japan in November 1989—as well as a series of meetings on scientific and academic cooperation, cultural exchanges, economic and technological cooperation, trade, and investment prior to Gorbachev's visit in April 1991—may signal the advent of limited detente, Japanese style, with the Soviet Union.[25] The two aforementioned negative factors, along with the presumably negative reaction of the United States to any suggestion from Japan to cooperate with the Soviet Union, would limit the Japanese change of style. Not surprisingly, the 1989 White Paper on Defense (Japan's Defense Agency) portrays the Soviet military threat as very strong—in fact, much stronger than the US Defense Department's recent analysis of Soviet military power.

In my opinion, the chance of the Soviet Union's returning the four northern islands to Japan is not very high, despite its burning desire to obtain Japanese capital and technology in order to help *perestroika*—and thus extend the tenure of Mikhail Gorbachev. At the same time, the prospects for larger Japanese involvement in the Soviet Union are improving, although not on as large a scale as the Japanese economic participation in China since 1978. Foreign financial lending, of which Japan was the largest source, provided as much as 6 per cent of Chinese government expenditures in 1988. The suspension of Japanese loans to China due to the brutal suppression of demonstrators in June 1989 has thus caused the Chinese government grave difficulties.[26]

The final component of a Japanese reorientation is the enlargement and enhancement of Japan's ties with Pacific Asia. Of course, this is at least in part both a Japanese reaction to Europe 1992 as well as to the US-Canadian bilateral free-trade agreement—and to protectionism of all kinds in these regions. But it would be incorrect to view this process only in these terms. An equally important motive for Japan's enhanced ties in Pacific Asia is what many Japanese see as the lax economic management of the United States and the possible unreliability of Japan-US security arrangements, given the deepening distrust displayed on both sides.[27]

By conceiving Pacific Asia as a region Japan could fall back upon, Japan is not unaware of the contrast between West Germany and Japan: Germany is divided while Japan is not; West Germany anchors itself in the European Community and NATO while Japan does not belong to any such regional organizations (organizations such as the Asian Pacific Economic Cooperation Conference and the Asian Pacific Economic Ministers Conference are quite different); West Germany is considered a 'repentant' country atoning for its past misconduct, despite the Bitburg incident, as if all of German history led to and ended with Nazi Germany. Japan, on the other hand, is sometimes suspected of political continuity with the past, as is evidenced by Prime Minister Nakasone's official visit to the Yasukuni Shrine, as if one imperial lineage of ten thousand reigns were still believed. Thus Japanese leaders are well aware of the need to anchor the nation firmly within the Japan-US security alliance and to exercise humility and modesty in their interactions with Pacific Asia.

Pacific Asia is increasingly attracting Japanese attention in the light of Europe 1992. It is useful to summarize briefly the basic profile of Pacific Asia as seen from Japan. Pacific Asia is composed of roughly three layers: (1) the Asian NICs (South Korea, Taiwan, Hong Kong, and Singapore); (2) ASEAN (Thailand, Malaysia, the Philippines, Indonesia, and Brunei) and Burma; and (3) socialist states (China, Vietnam, Laos, Cambodia, Outer Mongolia, North Korea, and the Soviet Union). In the economic realm, Thailand and the Philippines are the current foci of Japanese investment, while Indonesia and China are the two major recipients of Japanese official

development assistance. The horizontal trade relationship (exports of manufactured goods) between Japan and the Asian NICs has been steadily consolidated; and ASEAN members' trade relationship with Japan has been following
a path similar to that of the NICs.

Regarding security arrangements, South Korea and the Philippines do
have a similar security alliance with the United States. Yet they differ from
Japan in that both see future prospects for substantially reducing or termi-
nating the US military presence. Like Japan, Thailand and Taiwan have
friendly relations with the United States, especially in terms of arms
supplies, but both have very different security pictures from those of the
United States or Japan. Malaysia and Indonesia lean toward non-alignment
and neutrality. China sees the Soviet Union as not a danger at present. All of
these countries have different threat perceptions from Japan.

More importantly, the Japanese seem to be well aware that Pacific Asia is
a region not bereft of pitfalls. Two of the most important of these are (1) that
this region is the area where Japanese past misconduct is well remembered
and (2) that the region is the area where US military predominance is still
quite strongly felt. For these reasons, the Japanese approach to the region
has to be quiet and low-key. The Asian Pacific Economic Cooperation Conference (APEC) in November 1989 was held in Canberra at Prime Minister
Bob Hawke's initiative, and was enthusiastically supported by South Korea.
Japan did not move actively until the United States, which had not been
included in the initial Australian scheme, decided to join it. Also, Japan was
concerned that the ASEAN countries should not feel 'slighted' by the obvious
leadership of Australia, the United States, and Japan in holding the APEC.[28]

The following three components of the Japanese approach in Pacific Asia
should be noted. First, it is overwhelmingly economic and technological,
reflecting the Japanese comparative advantage. It is not just government
policy, but more importantly involves market forces that have been pushing
Japanese economic influence in the region. Trade, aid, investment, and
international monetary policies directly bear on Japanese influence. Second,
the Japanese approach focuses on institutional networks, reflecting the
intense need for them in the light of ever-increasing business and policy
interactions. Japan has made steady progress in building and creating
telecommunication networks and new monetary markets rather than first
trying to reduce trade barriers. The Japanese business sector and bureaucracy
have also been assiduous in creating personnel networks through training
and secondment programs across borders. Lacking fully encompassing
organizations in the region, Japan has been busy in making the best of
existing organizations such as the Asian Development Bank, the Pacific
Economic Cooperation Conference, and its bilateral ties.[29]

What is emerging from all of this is an increasingly manifest asymmetry in terms of freedom of choice between Japan and the rest of Pacific Asia. It is somewhat analogous to the ability of West Germany to pull the rest of the European Community members into alignment with the German mark and with the German version of a European Central Bank as well as to penetrate East European markets with trade, aid, and investment. This is obviously an oversimplification of both German and Japanese influence. But the point is simply that economic regionalization without regional demarcation or regional organization is in the offing in both cases, despite problems in other areas such as security, politics, and culture. The fact that Pacific Asia has been one of the most dynamic areas in the world allows Japan to be less concerned with formal institutional set-ups. Rather, it is the majority view in Japan that any effort toward creating closed and binding institutional bodies in Pacific Asia is counter-productive.

In view of this, the Japanese are trying to create a boundary-less region of dynamism that could become a region of last resort when America and Europe fall into protectionism and malevolent regionalism and therefore Pacific Asia must stand on its own feet of free trade. The recently inaugurated APEC (including ASEAN, South Korea, Japan, Australia, New Zealand, Canada, the United States, but not China, Taiwan or Hong Kong, although they are likely to join sooner or later, nor the Soviet Union, Vietnam, North Korea, or Outer Mongolia) has the following features: (1) it retains an open character; (2) it keeps as its major roles information-gathering and policy study as well as communication, consultation, coordination, and cooperation; (3) its major purpose is to facilitate freer economic interaction within the region, thus boosting economic development.

Implications for the United States

The implications of the Japanese responses to Europe 1992 for the United States need to be explored further for three major reasons. First, US–EC economic relations are bound to intensify as Europe moves toward 1992. As trade relations are roughly balanced between them, unlike Japanese trade relations with United States or with the European Community, the competition between the United States and the European Community will focus more on who plays the predominant role in setting and reshaping the rules of trade, including those directly related to the GATT Uruguay Round talks. In particular, the United States' emphasis on bilateralism and its structural impediment reduction approach collide head-on with the European Community. The European Community is somewhat apprehensive about the possibility of Japanese surrender to American bilateralism, or their provoking the United States to apply the Super 302 clause to Japan, thus giving way to American unilateral protectionism.

The European Community's policy of transforming EC rules of origin, reciprocity, and standards into those of the GATT has met resistance from the United States and Japan. Japan has ot been able to play a positive role in trade rule-making. Japan has neither the ability nor the will to make its own preferred trade rules into international unified rules. One can argue that structural impediment negotiations could be utilized to facilitate the Asians NICs' market liberalization. But Japan has been not only reluctant to execute swiftly its liberalization in agriculture, distribution, construction, or securities, but also unaware that Japan could use its roles to facilitate the Asian NICs' liberalization. Japan's pet notion of food security has not been received well except by a very few countries such as Switzerland.[30] In the mean time, Japan has expanded its niches within the EC market. The rate of increase in Japanese technological co-development for 1988 over 1987 demonstrates that it is the highest for Western Europe, 30.4 per cent compared to 25.1 per cent for the United States and 15.7 per cent for Asia.[31] Local content rules or rumors thereof encourage Japanese firms to put their parts factories and not just assembly lines in the EC market.[32] Intra-European rivalry enables Japanese firms to invest not only in the United Kingdom, which was called by some the Trojan Horse of Japan in Europe, but also Italy and France, both of which have accused Japanese firms of trying to colonize Europe but which more recently have come to appreciate the benefits of receiving Japanese direct investment.

A second reason for exploring Japanese responses to Europe 1992 is that the overall convergence between the enlargement of the European Community (including the EFTA and the Comecon as quasi-members) and the Soviet 'common European house' approach encouraged Japanese firms to strengthen their ties with EFTA and East European Comecon countries because this would enable Japan to achieve two aims: first, it would provide Japan with a market from which to penetrate the European Community. The EFTA and Comecon countries' enthusiasm for Japanese economic participation in their economies is a big factor Japanese firms can count on. Japan's economic vigor and anti-Russian (anti-Soviet) and non-colonialist past in the region seem to make it a very popular nation in some of the East European countries. For instance, in Poland Japan is ranked at the top of all nations of the world in terms of its favorable image.[33] Needless to say, their enthusiasm is somewhat tempered by what seems to them as the excessive cautiousness of Japanese business. Yet now in progress in Hungary are a joint venture of Suzuki Automobiles and Ikals (a bus manufacturer) and the transfer of Nissan diesel engine technology to the Laba Railway, and, in Poland, Daihatsu Engine's technology transfer to FSO (an automobile manufacturer). In addition about a dozen economic-technological cooperative projects between Japanese business and Eastern Europe are already in progress.[34] Not surprisingly, the Japanese are the second largest lender to Eastern Europe, following West Germany.

Second, enhanced ties with Comecon attract the Soviet Union to closer economic ties with Japan by means of its demonstration effects. Japanese assistance in Eastern Europe will also somewhat lessen Soviet suspicion of Japan and enable Japan to participate in the global detente process in which Japan has been only a marginal player, without arousing unnecessary American suspicion of Japan.[35] The second is much harder to achieve. Japanese experts do not seem to have a very high opinion of East European economic prospects. But it is not far-fetched to think that active Japanese help along with the strong economic pull of the European Community might bring about positive economic effects in the region, especially because European economic integration has permeated gradually from the core to the peripheries, from six to twelve, from the European Community to the EFTA, and from the EC/EFTA to Comecon.

Most recently, in November 1989, negotiations began on integration of the European Community and EFTA.[36] For the longer term one can predict that Japanese participation in Eastern Europe on a large scale would produce the same kind of effect on the globalization of economies there, linking the Atlantic, inter-European, and Pacific regions much more closely, as was produced by Japanese financial lending to American banks burdened with Latin America's debt (in this instance, Pacific and inter-American economic coupling has occurred). The US offer of economic assistance to Poland and Hungary in July 1989 and the Western package that followed it, including significant aid from Japan, will trigger such a process in the longer term. In the immediate future, Japan's assistance to Eastern Europe will begin with teaching management know-how and training workers in running manu-facturing factories. Japan will also transfer technology, attendant on direct investment and official development assistance, and make immediate food deliveries for those who face a hard winter.[37]

A third reason is that increasing Japanese economic interactions with Europeans toward Europe 1992 and beyond will also lessen the currently predominant dependence of Japan on its security ties with the United States, and for that matter of all Pacific Asia's American allies and friends, through technological cooperation. It is somewhat ironic to see that not only Japanese but also South Koreans and Taiwanese want to build their own fighter aircraft but that they have been somehow persuaded to co-develop their aircraft with Americans despite the fact that US criticism as well as criticism from within these countries against co-development seems to be on the rise. The purchase of European military weapons and joint manufacturing of hi-tech products, including civilian aircraft, should gradually reduce the weight of American weapons and facilities in Pacific Asia. This process will not become salient in 1992, or throughout the 1990s, but will grow beyond 2000.

All of these implications may be summed up as follows: Japanese responses to Europe 1992 will have far-reaching effects on US policy toward not only Europe but also Japan and Pacific Asia in general by gradually reshaping the economic and security maps of the world. It will have effects that will globalize and multilateralize Atlantic, Pacific, and intra-European relations in the longer term. Needless to say, Europe 1992 is not the sole factor causing these changes, but it is certainly accelerating the globalization and multilateralization of economic, security, and regional processes pertaining to US policies toward the rest of the world.

Notes

1. As to the evolution of Japan's foreign policy in the early and mid-1980s, see Takashi Inoguchi, 'The ideas and structures of foreign policy: looking ahead with caution', in Takashi Inoguchi and Daniel Okimoto (eds), *The Political Economy of Japan, Vol. 2: The Changing International Context* (Stanford: Stanford University Press, 1988), pp. 23–63, 490–500; Takashi Inoguchi, 'Japan's images and options: not a challenger, but a supporter', *Journal of Japanese Studies*, Vol. 12, No. 1 (Winter 1986), pp. 95–119.
2. See 'America's Japanophobia', *The Economist*, 18–24 November 1989, pp. 17–18. See also John Zysman, *Governments, Markets and Growth* (Ithaca: Cornell University Press, 1982); John Zysman and Laura Tyson (eds), *American Industry in International Competition* (Ithaca: Cornell University Press, 1984); Chalmers Johnson *et al.*, (eds), *Politics and Productivity: How Japan's Development Strategy Works* (Cambridge: Ballinger, 1989); Richard Samuels, *The Business of the Japanese State* (Ithaca: Cornell University Press, 1987); Benjamin Lee Miller, 'The political economy of Japan's tariff policy', unpublished Ph.D. dissertation, Australian National University, 1987. Also see the recent report of the Economic Planning Agency's Economic Research Institute on distribution, which demonstrates that the distribution costs over total retail sales are lowest in the United States while Japan is on par with the United Kingdom, France, and West Germany. The figures are 49.7, 57.6, 55.6, 55.3, and 58.9 per cent, respectively. *Nihon keizai shimbun*, 7 November 1989.
3. See Takashi Inoguchi, 'The legacy of a weathercock prime minister', *Japan Quarterly*, Vol. XXXIV, No. 4 (Oct.–Dec. 1987), pp. 363–70; Takashi Inoguchi, 'The political economy of Pacific dynamism', in Susumu Awanohara (ed.), *Japan's Growing External Assets: A Medium for Regional Growth?* (Hong Kong: Centre for Asian Pacific Studies, Linnan College, 1989), pp. 67–77; Takashi Inoguchi, 'Shaping and sharing Pacific dynamism', in *The Annals of the American Academy of Social and Political Science*, Vol. 504 (September 1989), pp. 46–55, a special issue on 'The

Pacific region: challenges to policy and theory'. Portions of this and the next sections are adapted from the latter.

4. International Institute for Strategic Studies, *Strategic Survey, 1989-1990* (London: IISS, 1989); Research Institute for Peace and Security, *Asian Security, 1989-1990* (Tokyo: RIPS, 1989).
5. Saburo Okita, 'Japan's quiet strength', *Foreign Policy*, No. 75 (Summer 1989), pp. 128-45.
6. *Nihon keizai shimbun*, 22 September 1989.
7. See Inoguchi, 'Shaping and sharing Pacific dynamism', *op. cit.*
8. See sources cited in note 1 and Takashi Inoguchi, 'Nichi-Bei kankei no rinen to kozo' (The ideas and structures of Japan-US relations), *Leviathan: The Japanese Journal of Political Science*, No. 5 (October 1989), pp. 7-33.
9. Takashi Inoguchi, 'Four Japanese scenarios for the future', *International Affairs*, Vol. 65, No. 1 (Winter 1988-89), pp. 15-28.
10. Murray Sayle, 'The powers that might be: Japan is no sure bet as the next global top dog', *Far Eastern Economic Review*, 4 August 1988, pp. 38-44.
11. Jay Collins, 'EC-Japan relationship—crucial to US business', *Euro-Market Digest*, Vol. II, No. 6 (June 1989), pp. 8-11. (I am grateful to Jay Collins for enabling me to use this article.)
12. 'A survey of Europe's internal market', *The Economist*, 8-14 July 1989, pp. 1-52; Andreas Van Agt, 'Japanese perception of Europe 1992', speech delivered at CEPS, Brussels, 1 June 1989 (I am grateful to Andreas Van Agt for making this speech available to me); Toshiro Tanaka, 'The European Community and Japan: countdown to 1992', *Japan Review of International Affairs*, Vol. 3, No. 2 (Fall/Winter 1989), pp. 213-27 (I am grateful to Toshiro Tanaka for drawing my attention to this article); Karl-Rudolf Korte, 'Japan and the Single European Market', *Aussenpolitik*, Vol. VI (1989), pp. 397-407 (I am grateful to William Griffith for making this article available to me).
13. On this point, I am indebted to Elizabeth Jager's comments at the workshop of 4-6 October 1989. See Kozo Yamamura (ed.), *Japanese Investment in the United States: Should We Be Concerned?* (Seattle: Society for Japanese Studies, 1989); and 'Japan and Europe 1992: battleground', and '1992 schizophrenia', *Newsweek*, 2 October 1989, pp. 10-15.
14. This quotation and others following it on Japan-EC economic relations are all from Collins, *op. cit.*
15. '1992-nen EC ikinai shijo togo o meguru ugoki ni tsuite' (On moves toward 1992 EC internal market integration), *Chosa geppo*, Bank of Japan, Vol. 40, No. 1 (January 1989).
16. *Yomiuri shimbun*, 14 August 1989.
17. Collins, *op. cit.*
18. *Nihon keizai shimbun*, 9 October 1988.
19. Andreas Van Agt, 'Japan and the EC Single Market 1992', *EC News* (Tokyo) PR 8/88(E), April 1988, p. 11, cited in Tanaka, *op. cit.*
20. Collins, *op. cit.*
21. Okita, *op. cit.*

22. I owe this point to William Griffith, to whom I am grateful. On US-Asian competition on arms production, see Susumu Awanohara, 'Sorcerer's apprentices', *Far Eastern Economic Review*, 30 November 1989, pp. 24-6.
23. *Asahi shimbun*, 13 June 1989 (evening edition), and 20 November 1989.
24. See Inoguchi, 'Nichi-Bei kankei no rinen no kozo', *op. cit.*; '1990 nendai no Nihon gaiko no kadai to tembo' (Tasks of and prospects for Japan's diplomacy in the 1990s), *Nihon keizai shimbun*, 18 March 1989; 'Bush seiken no anzen hosho seisaku' (US security policy under President Bush), *Keizai semina zokan*, May 1989, pp. 46-58; 'Europe shijo togo no kokusai rikigaku' (International dynamics of European market integration), *Ekonomisuto zokan*, 20 March 1989, pp. 96-103.
25. *Asahi shimbun*, 28 September 1989.
26. *Asahi shimbun*, 29 September 1989. Also see Takashi Inoguchi, 'Sino-Japanese relations: problems and prospects', manuscript prepared for the International Institute for Strategic Studies, London, October 1989.
27. Morita Akio and Ishihara Shintaro, *No to ieru Nihon* (Japan that can say no) (Tokyo: Bungei Shunju-sha, 1989); James Fallows, *More Like Us* (New York: Harper and Row, 1989).
28. See *Far Eastern Economic Review*, 16 November 1989, pp. 10-19.
29. Sadako Ogata, 'Shifting power relations in multilateral development banks', *Journal of International Studies* (Sophia University, Tokyo), No. 22 (January 1989), pp. 1-26.
30. Hideo Tamura, 'Kokusai ruru o tsukurenai Nihon' (Japan that cannot create international rules), *Nihon keizai shimbun*, 15 November 1989.
31. *Asahi shimbun*, 8 August 1989.
32. *Nihon keizai shimbun*, 14 July and 4 August 1989.
33. *Nihon keizai shimbun*, 16 November 1989 (evening edition). The Polish State News Agency reported on the results of the opinion poll conducted in November 1989. The poll also showed that Germans ranked no higher than in the past.
34. For further details, see *Asahi shimbun*, 6 November 1989.
35. *Nihon keizai shimbun*, 31 July 1989.
36. *Asahi shimbun*, 24 November 1989.
37. *Yomiuri shimbun*, 16 October and 17 November 1989.

4

Change and response in Japan's international politics and strategy

It is a cliche to say that Japanese foreign policy has been evolving around the Japan-US relationship for the nearly forty years since Japan regained its independence in 1952 (Inoguchi & Okimoto 1988; Inoguchi 1988–89; Drifte 1990). Virtually no official statement by the Japanese government has failed to reiterate the pivotal and primordial importance of Japan-US relations in the foreign relations of Japan. Those statements normally emphasis two aspects of the relationship: the Western alliance; and economic interdependence.

This emphasis was most apparent during the Nakasone era of 1982–1987 when Nakasone prosecuted his policy of internationalisation, by which he meant the steady anti-Soviet defence build-up in concert with the United States and market liberalisation, again in harmony with that of the United States (Inoguchi 1987). Market liberalisation would, according to his calculation, enhance Japanese industrial competitiveness while the defence build-up would enable Japan to be accepted as a fully fledged member of the alliance. While Nakasone was in office this policy approach manifested no glaring negative consequences. Now, however, both market liberalisation and the defence build-up would seem to pose some basic problems were they to be pursued without Japan's foreign policy tenets being redirected in the light of its own growing politico-economic weight and the rapid changes evidenced in the strategic and economic map of the world.

First, Japan's weight in the world economy and international relations has been growing so steadily that it is critical for it to articulate its own foreign policy tenets much more clearly than it has yet done in terms of what Japan should and would do toward attaining common global purposes (Inoguchi 1989a, 1989b; Inoguchi et al 1990). This applies whether it is concerned with international monetary stability, multilateral and liberal trade and development assistance, or whether it is concerned with its objectives of freedom and democracy, regional stability and global peace-keeping. It is not sufficient to think about Japanese foreign policy only in the bilateral

terms of Japan-US relations, whether it is trade deficits, technological cooperation, market liberalisation, defence cooperation, academic exchanges or
structural impediments. Yet the sad fact is that when both countries talk to
each other, they spend much of their time and energy on bilateral issues
rather than global issues. The Structural Impediments Initiative talks
between the United States and Japan held in April 1990 are a case in point.

Second, the rapid changes in the international environment—most
importantly, the relative scaling down of the two superpowers and the
detente between them, the changes in Eastern Europe and the reunification
of Germany, the tighter integration of the European Community as 1992
approaches, the steady enhancement of the Asia-Pacific economies and the
movement towards a regional economic grouping without building a fortress
on the Pacific Ocean—are pointing to the need for Japan to think about its
foreign policy directions in a manner more liberated from the legacy of
bilateral parochialism and euphemism. Most symbolically, the collapse of
the Berlin Wall in November 1989 and the US-Soviet summit in Malta in
December 1989 have provided the Japanese with considerable food for
thought. These, and subsequent events, are making it more difficult than
before to argue brusquely and bluntly for Japan's policy not to resume talks
with the Soviet Union without the return of the Northern Territories and for
Japan's steady anti-Soviet build-up and security cooperation with the US.

This being said, I would like to speculate on the direction in which Japan
might fruitfully redirect its policy in this rapidly changing world with the
enlarged profile of Japan being one major component. In my view, there
are three pillars of such a redirection and I discuss each one in turn.

Metamorphosis in Japan-US relations

The Japan-US relationship is of fundamental importance, not just for those
two countries but for many other countries as well as, indeed, for global
stability. Nevertheless, Japan-US relations need to be recast less in bilateral
terms, and more in terms of resolving common global issues. It would be
detrimental for both countries as well as the rest of the world for the relationship to bog down in the whole process of bilateral parochialisms manifested
in the various forms of Japan-bashing and America-bashing. In order to
defend Japan against the accusation often made against it that it is a free
rider, it would be best for Japan to set out its foreign policy tenets in global
terms and to execute them as vigorously as possible.

Such an elaboration of policy would demonstrate to the rest of the world
that Japan is ready to undertake things not only for itself but also for the
global community, even at the sacrifice of its own immediate national interests.

It would also have the positive merit of disciplining itself by publicly committing itself to such values as freedom and democracy, fairness and openness, much more strongly than before. More concretely, the Japan-US friendship should become the major stabilising factor in terms of global economic management, the attainment of peace and the encouragement of freedom and democracy. If the two governments and peoples are prudent and wise enough in handling these bilateral relations, the two most dynamic and largest economies are bound to stick closely to each other with increasing economic interdependence and interpenetration despite occasional government interventions and regulations working against them.

Were the two economies to become part of two separate blocs, that would make the world economy much less flexible in resolving major global economic and environmental issues. If the two countries do not achieve such a positive and constructive relationship, but place themselves instead in a relationship characterised by intermittent political and economic mud-slinging, that would make the international system unbearably unstable. Speaking of Sino-Japanese relations, Deng Xiaoping said 'that if Japan and China cooperate they can support half of heaven'. The corollary, according to Laura Newby, is 'that if China and Japan fail to cooperate in this endeavour half of heaven may well come crashing down upon them' (Newby 1981). Speaking of US-Japan relations, I would say that if the United States and Japan do not cooperate, the entire heaven may well fall down upon the world.

Japan and the United States, in cooperation with each other and the rest of the world, need to tackle head on such global issues as peace and stability, demographic growth and economic development, environment and energy, and equality between social groups. For instance, Japan should take initiatives, and provide leadership, in the area of developmental aid, especially in education, health, agriculture, telecommunications, electricity generation and distribution, manufacturing technologies and factory management, environmental control, and peaceful conflict resolution associated with the offer of economic recovery assistance.

This is not to be critical of the Japan-US security alliance. Rather it is to suggest that it be recast in a form which might be called the global alliance for peace and progress. It should be transformed gradually into the alliance for global stability and human progress. In the near future it could also play the role of assuring stability in the Asia-Pacific region which includes such potentially destabilising areas as the Korean Peninsula, the Philippines, Cambodia and Burma, China and Vietnam, and the Soviet Union.

Tension reduction with the Soviet Union

The reduction of tension with the Soviet Union must take place if Japan is to take greater responsibility for its own territorial defence. Japan's Self Defence Forces could not realistically aim at defending Japan against a totally antagonistic Soviet Union. Such an objective would lead Japan to spend too much on defence, and its neighbours to react negatively against Japan. Some form of limited detente with the Soviet Union is preferable here. Needless to say, such knotty issues as territories and naval reductions stand as major hindrances to tension reduction even of a very limited scale. Yet quite significantly, the governing party of Japan, the Liberal Democratic Party, included among its electoral pledges in the last general election of February 1990 'to make efforts toward a genuine improvement of Japan-Soviet relations', the first time such a pledge has been made since the foundation of the LDP in 1955 (*Mainichi Shimbun* 25 January 1990). Also prior to the general election, two major leaders of each country, Messrs Yakovlev and Abe exchanged visits in December 1989 and January 1990. Already, talks between Japan and the Soviet Union on such matters as economic, technological, cultural and academic cooperation are planned for 1990 and 1991 before President Mikhail Gorbachev's visit to Japan, scheduled to take place some time in 1991.

Much has been changing in Eastern Europe as well as in the Soviet Union. Although the basic difference in economic systems makes it hard to do much in terms of trade and direct investment in Eastern European countries, even a relatively small involvement in financial and other resource terms from the Japanese point of view would make a large difference there because of the small size of their GNPs. It is Japan's task to extend a helping hand to assure political stability and to instil economic vigour. If that involvement is at least partially successful, that would become a useful demonstration of Japanese aid to Communist countries. That also might encourage the Soviet Union to show a greater interest in having vigorous economic exchanges with Japan. Such a heightened interest would encourage the Soviet Union to take a less harsh attitude towards Japan. Furthermore, Japan's economic presence in Eastern Europe is already substantial; its presence is second to that of Western Germany in terms of financial lending. Its sustained involvement there would be a positive factor in avoiding the conversion of Eastern Europe into an economic area singularly dominated by West Germany, and for aiding the process of European integration towards 1992 and extending European integration eventually beyond the current twelve members of the European Community (Inoguchi 1990).

Enhanced ties with the rest of the world

The enhancement of ties with the rest of the world is an absolute necessity for Japan at a time when the United States is tightening its managed trade stance and thus limiting access to its market. The first response that Japan can make to the increased restrictions on access to the US market is naturally the expansion of its own domestic demand. This has been substantially in progress since 1986 but the process needs to be extended further. A second response is to explore and enlarge Japan's markets elsewhere. Most immediately, the Asia-Pacific region has been growing steadily in economic terms (Inoguchi 1989; Drysdale 1988; Garnaut 1989). Not only the newly industrialising economies (NIEs) of Asia but also some ASEAN countries have been strengthening rapidly their economic links (particularly in the expansion of manufactured goods exports) with the US and Japan. Furthermore, despite their many problems, China and especially India have been registering respectable growth rates. Already, populations of around two hundred million in each country, those in China's coastal economies and those in India's urban industrial economies, are considered to be moving towards comparability with those of the Asian NIEs. It may be significant to note that the Japan Economic Research Centre, a think-tank of the *Nihon Keizai Shimbun*, included South Asia in its latest report on the economic prospects for Asia (1990). Reports of this kind have tended in the past to exclude the Indian sub-continent from their coverage of the Asia-Pacific region. Not coincidentally, Prime Minister Toshiki Kaifu made an official visit to South Asian countries in April-May 1990.

Western Europe is no less an important area with its invigorated prospects arising from Europe 1992. It is imperative for Japanese business firms to be accepted as good corporate Europeans, to become insiders before the wall against outsiders is built, assuming such a wall is to be built (Inoguchi 1990). Of the trilateral economic transactions among industrial democracies, the Japan-European Community link is regrettably much weaker than the US-European Community link and the link between Japan and the US. Needless to say, the other side of the coin is to make the Japanese market more attractive and accessible to the rest of the world. Furthermore, the ties that bind originate not only from business, but also from non-economic exchanges, and most importantly from participating in common endeavours at the global level, whether it is cultural attainment, academic progress, or global environment protection. Prime Minister Toshiki Kaifu's visit to Western and Eastern Europe in Janaury 1990 indicates the major importance Japan attaches to development in Europe. No less importantly, the non-Pacific-Asian world, South Asia, the Middle East, Africa and Latin America are all areas where no Japanese colonial and militaristic pasts have left negative legacies. In these areas, the Japanese efforts to promote the global alliance for progress would be most effective.

On these three fronts, Japanese foreign policy redirection will take place sooner or later as the present rigidities fixed by the bilateral provincialism of Japan's foreign policy since 1952 slowly unravel themselves. Underneath the oft-seen Japanese caution and slowness to move, as is evidenced by its responses to Gorbachev's *perestroika* and the US-Soviet detente, one can occasionally find such rethinking surfacing. The irony is that, in attempting to redirect itself and to diversify its foreign relations, Japan-US relations again come to the forefront of the problem-set in Japanese thinking and this discourages Japan from making its policy redirection more explicit than otherwise. Hence it is easy to understand why the catchwords of the Japanese government are caution, careful watchfulness, vigilance, prudence, and steady transition. Meanwhile, the Japanese political-economic weight in the world economy and international relations will slowly grow. At first its growth will often be unnoticed, but at a later stage its growth is likely to be somewhat exaggerated. This would reinforce the sense of surprise and uneasiness among the rest of the world and make Japan's proper global role more difficult to play.

References

Baggage, Ross, 1989, *The Soviets in the Pacific in the 1990s*, Brassey's Australia, Rushcutters Bay, NSW.

Drifte, R., 1990, *Japan's Foreign Policy*, Routledge, London.

Drysdale, P., 1988, *International Economic Pluralism: Economic Policy in East Asia and the Pacific*, Allen & Unwin, Sydney.

Garnaut, R., 1989, *Australia and the Northeast Asian Ascendancy*, Australian Government Publishing Service, Canberra.

Inoguchi, T., 1987, 'The Legacy of a Weathercock Prime Minister', *Japan Quarterly*, Vol. 34, No. 4, pp. 363–70.

Inoguchi, T., 1988–89, 'Four Japanese Scenarios for the Future', in *International Affairs*, Vol. 65, No. 1, pp. 15–28.

Inoguchi, T., 1989a, 'Shaping and Sharing Pacific Dynamism', in *The Annals of the American Academy of Political and Social Science*, special issue P. Gourevitch (ed.), *The Pacific Region: Challenges to Policy and Theory*, Vol. 505, pp. 46–55.

Inoguchi, T., 1989b, 'Nichi-Bei Kankei no rinen to kozo' ('The Ideas and Structures of Japan–US Relations'), *Leviathan: Japanese Journal of Political Science*, Vol. 5, Autumn, pp. 7–33.

Inoguchi, T., 1993, 'Japanese responses to Europe 1992: Implications for the United States', in this volume pp. 71–90.

Inoguchi, T. and D. Okimoto (eds), 1988, *The Political Economy of Japan Vol. 2: The Changing International Context*, Stanford University Press, Stanford.

Inoguchi, T., Ikuo Kabashima, David Rapkin and Tamotsu Asami, 1990, *Policy Recommendations on Japan, the United States and Global Responsibilities*, Japan Forum on International Relations, Tokyo, April.

Japan Economic Research Centre, 1990, *Sekai no nakano Ajia: Ajia keizai no tenbo* (Asia in the World: Prospects for the Asian Economies), Tokyo.

Newby, L., 1988, *Sino-Japanese Relations: China's Perspective*, Routledge, London, p. 91.

Wada, H., 1990, *Hoppo ryodo o kangaeru* (Thinking about the Northern Territories), Iwanami shoten, Tokyo.

5

Japan's response to the Gulf crisis: an analytic overview

Like a bolt from out of the blue

The Middle East has long been considered a remote region by most Japanese. No doubt, one can recount in considerable detail the Persian and, to a lesser extent, Turkic and Arabic influence on Japanese history and culture through China, most notably during the T'ang dynasty.[1] Yet, there were no direct encounters between the Middle East and Japan until the late twentieth century. Japan's first major encounters with the Middle East were occasioned by the oil crisis of 1973, triggered by the fourth Arab-Israeli war and the OPEC oil embargo, and by the second oil crisis of 1980, triggered by the Iranian Revolution and the Iran-Iraq war. These two crises, however, did not involve Japan in any substantial way other than their negative impact on the Japanese economy. The Gulf crisis is different. Since August 2, 1990, it has forced Japan to be an indispensable part of the war efforts led by the United States. Thus, of the three recent crises emanating from the Middle East, the Gulf crisis has presented a novel challenge to Japan. This article will describe and analyze how Japan's historically molded psyche and institutional structures influenced its response to this crisis and how its response was forged as part and parcel of political competition over systemic restructuring at home.

August 2 came literally like a bolt from out of the blue to the Japanese government, which was surprised by Iraq's bold move into Kuwait. This was in part because it lacks a sufficiently competent political and military intelligence apparatus in the region. It was also a surprise because the US government had not give a consistent, unambiguous signal to Iraq and the rest of the world.[2] But Japan was unusually quick in responding to the Iraqi invasion by issuing its own economic embargo even prior to its participation in the United Nations-sponsored economic embargo. Japan's rapid response to the Iraqi invasion of Kuwait was natural, given the strong position it has taken against military aggression such as Vietnam vis-à-vis Cambodia since 1979, and given the relatively strong position it had developed since 1973 through its program of diversifying its oil supply rather than relying on any one oil supplier. Japan's quick implementation of an economic embargo stands in sharp contrast to its slow and spasmodic response to contributing to the military operations of the anti-Iraqi multinational forces.[3]

After the UN resolution calling for Iraq to pull out of Kuwait was approved by an overwhelming majority of nations including Japan, Japan moved surprisingly slowly. Before the Iraqi invasion of Kuwait took place, Prime Minister Kaifu Toshiki planned to visit the Middle East, but his trip was cancelled immediately upon news of the invasion. After the US government called on its allies to demonstrate solidarity and contribute to the multinational effort in any possible form, the Japanese government was to stumble almost continuously. Within a few days after pledging $100 million as a contribution to the multinational forces and those allied countries suffering from the crisis in the Middle East, the government increased its pledge to $4 billion. A natural reaction of many was why not $4 billion from the beginning? A United Nations Peace Cooperation bill was first drafted largely by the Ministry of Foreign Affairs in August and September. Its thrust was to make non-military contributions to the multilateral forces and not to send Japan's Self-Defense Forces (SDF) to the Middle East. This period coincided with the intense lobbying by US Ambassador Michael Armacost of LDP leaders, including Secretary General Ozawa Ichiro, and also with the previously postponed visit to the Middle East by Prime Minister Kaifu. A first draft of the bill was forced to undergo drastic revision in order to incorporate the 'forward-looking' policy orientation (meaning pro-deployment of SDF in response to the US government's call) of party leaders such as Ozawa Ichiro and Nicshioka Takeo, chairman of the LDP's Party General Council. Once the special National Diet session started, the government exhibited an unusual degree of incompetence in its handling of criticism and questions raised against the bill. The debate on the bill aroused the entire nation to an unprecedented degree. Public opinion was polarized with those opposing the bill constituting more than two-thirds of the nation. The government backed down from passing the bill at the end of the autumn 1990 Diet session. The new emperor's enthronement ritual took place as planned immediately thereafter. Then the heat of public opinion apparently subsided with the busy weeks toward and after the end of the year, which was filled by budget-making and cabinet reshuffling.

Immediately before the United States opened fire against Iraq on January 17, 1991, the mood in Japan was one of eagerly awaiting and optimistically expecting peace to prevail. Once the war began, the Japanese government exhibited a kind of reactiveness similar to that of August and September

1990. This time its response was much quicker, in part because this response came not from the Ministry of Foreign Affairs, but from the Ministry of Finance for financial contributions and from the Defense Agency for SDF operations. Once prodded by the US government, the Japanese government pledged $9 billion to the United States. It also announced that SDF aircraft would be used to help refugees return to their home countries in Asia. Debate on what Japan's response to the crisis should be was resumed inside and outside the Diet by those critical of the government's position on revenue sources for the $9 billion and on the use of SDF aircraft for overseas operations. The Japanese government had to obtain the approval of both houses of the National Diet for new taxation and bond issuing. It bypassed the National Diet, however, on SDF operations by resorting to an 'administrative directive'. In order to secure the approval of the two smaller opposition parties, especially the Clean Government Party whose support was necessary in the opposition-controlled Upper House, for the $9 billion contribution to the multinational forces, the government incorporated some of the policy preferences of the Clean Government Party. It agreed not to increase taxes on tobacco and somewhat reduced the defense budget. In turn, the Clean Government Party pledged to accept the government's policy on SDF operations despite the resistance of rank-and-file members of the party. The LDP also agreed to endorse a new candidate in the spring 1991 election for the Metropolitan Tokyo governor, a candidate acceptable to the Clean Government Party instead of the current governor backed by Tokyo-based Dietmen and Metropolitan Assembly members from the LDP. The supplemental budget bill enabling the $9 billion contribution was passed in the National Diet on March 6, 1991. The problem of whether the government may have gone beyond the constitution and the SDF law remains disputed and will not be resolved for some time. Japan's response to the Gulf crisis may be characterized as follows. At the government level, support was extended to the US-led multinational forces' war efforts. Yet its decision and implementation tended to be on the whole slow and spasmodic. At the popular level, more than two-thirds of the Japanese were basically unhappy about the government's support for the US-led war efforts. They were somewhat skeptical of whether use of military power could help achieve war aims and mildly suspicious of the US government's war aims and the Japanese government's motivation in using foreign pressure for its own political purposes. Looking at the interactions between the government and the masses, namely, the final decision on financial contributions and SDF operations, it seems safe to say that the democratic mechanism of feedback has worked to bring the government to take a centrist position.[4]

Factors shaping Japan's response to the Gulf crisis

Three major factors depict Japan's response to the crisis: They are (1) uncertainty and anxiety; (2) historical learning; and (3) self-confidence. They point to the primary importance of historically molded psyche and institutional structures of Japanese society.

Uncertainty and anxiety. First, the Japanese government has been cautious in adapting to the post-Cold War order because it has not found the post-Cold War reality so comfortable: removal of the East-West schism from the configuration of world politics means that the Japan-US Security Treaty, the key device for Japan's foreign policy line, has a lessened significance.[5] The Japanese government thus kept refusing to acknowledge the advent of detente until as late as spring 1990 by saying that there is no such word as detente in its dictionary. It has two strong reasons for not quickly adapting to post-Cold War conditions. One is the unresolved territorial issue with the Soviet Union. Furthermore, the refusal of the US Navy to enter a full arms control agreement with the Soviet Union with respect to nuclear submarines and vessels, especially in the Northwest Pacific region, also provides a good excuse for the Japanese government not to change its direction in any way. Yet the unexpectedly fast unfolding of global detente and dismantling of the Cold War institutions throughout 1989 and 1990 made the Japanese government apprehensive about new realities. Able neither to chart its own independent and autonomous line nor to embed itself within some new international institutional framework except the Japan-US Security Treaty, Japan is in many ways apprehensive about the evolution of the post-Cold War international system.[6]

A second reason for adapting only slowly to post-Cold War conditions is that the Japanese government has been somewhat apprehensive about the course the United States may take, especially in light of the overwhelming rigidities of its fiscal and energy policies and the increasing signs of losing its manufacturing competitiveness vis-à-vis the Japanese and other difficulties in its manufacturing and financial sectors. It is concerned about the United States declining too early and too fast as no other candidate seems ready to take up the kind of major international leadership role the United States has so far played. It is clearly not in the interest of Japan to see the United States prematurely decline.[7] Yet, what the Japanese government has seen in the United States for the last decade or two is not very reassuring. First, US fiscal policy has been so rigid in the face of its twin major deficits in government spending and trade that no bright prospect is yet to be seen. Japan's concern has been repeatedly expressed in joint declarations of the Western economic summits since the mid-1980s, which called on the United States to reduce its deficits, along with the call for Japan to expand its domestic demand and for Germany to enhance its supply capacity. The Japanese government's concern is sometimes transformed into indignation vis-à-vis the United States as Japan doubled its domestic demand dutifully between 1985 and 1989 while the United States did not 'do its homework' at all and continued to press Japan for further concessions.

A second signal Japan has received from the United States is that while many competitive US firms have been doing well at home and abroad, the increasing call for protectionist measures in less competitive sectors at home has encouraged Japanese firms to seek other outlets. There have been three stages in this process: US criticism against Japanese export-oriented growth in the decade after the first oil crisis encouraged Japanese firms to seek direct investment in the United States. The steady expansion of their presence in the United States through setting up new manufacturing facilities and purchasing US companies and properties has aroused a fear that the United States is gradually being bought up by Japan. Second, these purchases have been prompted not only by the consideration of averting trade friction but also by the simple fact that many Japanese firms have had huge financial surpluses, largely from their inflated assets in the form of land holdings in Tokyo and its vicinity. At the third stage, Japanese investment has been steadily turning away from the United States. This is not only due to lower US interest rates as the US economy entered a recession, which discourages Japanese companies from retaining their US investment portfolio, but also because of growing uncertainty in the international business environment, which has led them to diversify their assets in other regions, namely, Western Europe and Pacific Asia. This phenomenon took place much more steadily than many thought in the late 1980s.[8]

Most important of all is the vague angst about Japan's position and role in the world. Long accustomed to the virtual absence of a major global security role in its foreign policy agenda, Japan is apprehensive about what it sees as the imposition on it of unwanted roles by the United States. Whether or not Japan should take on more global responsibilities is not subject to much dispute, as many opinion polls have indicated. More than two-thirds of those surveyed in Japan are of the view that Japan should enhance its contributions to the global community, but that such contributions should be restricted to a non-military role in conformity with its pacifist constitution.[9] The most popular notions of what Japan's role should be in the world are predictably a 'trading state' and a 'global social welfare state'.[10] In other words, it is advocated that Japan should continue to prosper by focusing on commercial activities and endeavor to make financial, technological, and scientific contributions to keep the world safe from hunger and war.

The very position and power Japan has acquired through economic means for the last two decades, however, has also been forcing Japan to take on new global political responsibilities. By falling short of these responsibilities, or at least doing 'too little, too late' in many cases, Japan has been intermittently exposed to barrages of criticism from abroad. The very fact that Japan is exposed to such criticism has led many Japanese to react in an increasingly negative manner to calls for it to play a more global political role. They are being attracted to pacifism, rejectionism, and isolationism. Pacifism wants to see the spirit of Japan's pacifist constitution spread to the rest of the world in terms of peaceful conflict resolution. Rejectionism arises from anti-American nationalistic feelings and calls for refusing to act in concert with US-led military actions. Isolationism preaches the virtue of distance from politico-military involvement in the Gulf war. These three threads of response come not only from the left but also from the right and the center.[11] Aside from these refusals, economic signs have started to point to a decline in Japan's surplus that could be used for global contributions. The Japanese current account surplus in relation to its GNP has been steadily shrinking from 4.5 per cent in 1986 at its peak through 1.9 per cent in 1989 to a predicted 0.8 per cent in 1992.[12] In tandem with the steady increase in the non-productive population, tax revenue has started to stagnate and social welfare expenditures have begun to increase steadily. The Ministry of Finance's attempts at increasing taxes have met staunch resistance, as did the introduction of the consumption tax in 1989, and it has become much more cautious to introduce new taxes. This revenue-collecting difficulty seems to enhance uncertainty about the new role expected of Japan.

Historical learning. The most salient aspect of Japanese learning from history is deep skepticism about the utility of military power, especially as projected onto foreign terrain for a prolonged period of time. A century of striving as an ambitious newcomer for a 'venerable place in the world' ended in complete failure in 1945. In contrast to this failure, concentration on economic activities for nearly half a century since then has brought about both peace and prosperity.[13] Some recent major events in the world have simply reinforced this belief. The most cogent examples include the American war in Vietnam and the Soviet war in Afghanistan, in both of which the interventionist powers were not able to impose their will for a period considerably longer than military presence. The guess of many Japanese is that even if the United States has won militarily in the Gulf war, more enduring regional factors will diminish the long-term impact of the outcome of the war to a marginal extent. For Japanese, lessons of history inform them that military supremacy in foreign terrain will be short-lived and that military action begets counter-actions, which tends to nullify whatever thrust interventionist powers' military action may be intended to have. With this lesson of history, it is very natural that the Japanese are basically skeptical of the effectiveness of military action to attain political goals in the longer term. Further reinforcing this skepticism is what they see as the growing importance of economic interdependence in the world economy. Although somewhat shaken by the Gulf war, the basic tenet of this dogma has been retained so that Japan can envisage a kind of world where international finance—not military power—will be the key to influence.[14]

Another thread of Japanese learning is the debt of history. By debt of history, I mean the legacy of Japanese misconduct in the prewar and war-time years as constraints on Japanese diplomacy. It became evident that, once the Gulf crisis led the Japanese government in autumn 1990 to move toward using the Self-Defense Forces for the purpose of creating the appearance of solidarity with other nations, Pacific Asians, especially the Chinese, manifested their concern about the direction of Japan's drive.[15] Is Japan really grudgingly following the US call for military participation in the Gulf war? Or is it adroitly using this opportunity to send the SDF abroad in wartime for the first time since its inception in 1954 in order to pave the path for future SDF activities outside Japan? The instinct of those nations who suffered from Japanese aggression has been to revive the memory of the past. As a result, they criticize Japan's attempt to dispatch the SDF abroad in a preventive fashion and call for a US military presence in order to mitigate the already fairly predominant Japanese economic influence in the region.

From a different angle, the debt of history can be seen as an excuse for reluctant Japanese not to shoulder such security-related burdens. When the Japanese government cited the debt of history as a reason for its hesitancy to dispatch the SDF to the Gulf, some saw this as an attempt at self-contrived sabotage. At any rate, the debt of history has operated as a constraint on Japanese diplomacy. Whether Japan is constrained happily or unhappily is somewhat difficult to tell.[16]

The third strand of Japanese learning from history is anti-colonialism. It may sound somewhat strange to mention Japanese anti-colonialism as Japan itself was a colonial power until 1945 and might be categorized as a neocolonialist in the world today by commentators of radical leftist persuasion. But deep in the Japanese mind, Japanese colonialism was portrayed largely as the result of Japanese counter-action vis-à-vis Western colonialism. It was meant as anti-colonialism, however awkward its justification may sound to many. Since relinquishing its militarist past in 1945, Japan has been more anti-colonialist and may be called anti-expansionist. Postwar Japanese anti-colonialism or anti-expansionism overlaps with its having a very close relation-ship with the United States. Anti-colonialism was revived by the US occupation of Japan and has been retained as the US armed forces have kept their bases and other kinds of presence in Japan and its vicinity. Thus, whenever the United States uses high-handed pressure during negotiations on issues of trade, the economy, market liberalization, and burden sharing, this sentiment is awakened among many Japanese. They have no difficulty, for instance, in finding quasi-evidence in Ambassador Armacost's energetic pressure for Japan to liberalize its market or contribute more to the maintenance of international order in recent years.

Given such coercion already experienced by the Japanese themselves, or at least seen as such by them, it is not difficult to understand why many Japanese have felt that the Iraqis were punished by the Americans somewhat out of proportion to their misconduct in Kuwait, which most Japanese strongly condemn. Although the Middle East is not an area with which most Japanese are familiar, a sizable proportion of them do have a modicum of historical knowledge about the region, especially since the first oil crisis of 1973. Conflicts of interest among OPEC members like Iraq versus states in the Gulf Cooperation Council, rivalries between Iran and Iraq and between Palestinians (Arabs) and Israelis, and their historical origins constitute such knowledge. In US diplomacy toward both Japan and the Middle East, many educated Japanese see traces of colonialism in a modern form. However unjustifiable and brutal Iraqi conduct may be, this aspect of the Gulf war is not missed by many Japanese, or for that matter by many Asians.[17]

Self-confidence. It may be paradoxical to juxtapose anxiety and self-confidence as two factors shaping Japan's response to the Gulf war. But it would miss a great deal if one dropped self-confidence as a factor shaping Japan's response. Japanese are confident in their ability to make structural adjustments as they did successfully in the two previous oil crises.[18] When Americans were citing the Japanese oil dependence on the Gulf oil-producing states as a reason for Japan to become more involved in the Gulf crisis, Japanese felt that they could secure petroleum through markets. This was confirmed by seeing neither drastic oil-related price hikes nor a deterioration in the Japanese yen's exchange rate vis-à-vis the dollar at least in the short term. The first oil crisis forced Japan to minimize energy consumption fairly drastically while the second oil crisis forced Japan to substantially reduce the relative weight of labor costs in manufacturing. The present oil crisis seems to have accelerated the diversification of Japanese money away from the United States to other areas, most notably to Japan, Pacific Asia, and Western Europe. With land prices in Tokyo stabilizing, Japanese spending has become less flamboyant. Yet the large-scale recycling of surplus capital by the Saudis, Japanese, and others to the United States in the form of international contributions to the multinational forces' war expenses is expected to activate the US and world economies.[19]

Japanese self-confidence is also very clear with respect to economic competitiveness. Although Japanese competitiveness is not overwhelming in many respects, the fact that Japan along with some Pacific Asian countries has been further enhancing its competitiveness in many areas underlies its self-confidence. Irrespective of whether such self-confidence is well founded or not, it very much shapes their attitude. Even though some short-term and intermediate-term disturbances from the Gulf war may turn out to be far more serious than they want to see, Japanese self-confidence when combined with a large degree of uncertainty about the evolution of the international system seems to encourage them to 'watch and wait' rather than 'go and get it'. Needless to say, self-confidence encourages cost-sharing and sacrifice. That would be an absolute necessity for those who want to minimize the negative consequences of the Gulf war. Thus from this angle also, it is fairly clear why the Japanese government has opted for the policy of non-military contributions instead of the two extremes of 'watch and wait' and 'go and get it'.

Japanese self-confidence is also based more generally on nationalistic sentiments originating from the combination of enlarged self-esteem and growing criticism from abroad.[20] As a result of their economic achievements, Japanese self-esteem has already become high. In general, the Japanese are secretly or openly proud of themselves and want to see their achievements appreciated and acknowledged, if not necessarily applauded. But what they often see abroad is that their achievements are criticized for being callous to others. No doubt, jealousy and enmity do play an important part in such criticism. As Carlo Cipolla has written of first- and second-generation empire builders, many Japanese tend to take such criticism as personally directed at themselves.[21] According to Cipolla, first-generation achievers, so preoccupied with their task, cannot enjoy life with others. They do not know how to relax. Second-generation achievers tend to look down on others, not necessarily aware that their achievements were a result of the first generation's exertions. Third-generation achievers relax and associate with others and know how to laugh at themselves. Many Japanese resemble Cipolla's first- and second-generation achievers. This being the case, there is no wonder that nationalistic sentiments tend to grow in tandem with Japanese economic success and foreign criticism typified by Japan-bashing. With nationalistic sentiments ever-growing underneath the surface of Japan's politeness, it is no wonder that public opinion has reacted very negatively to the US call for greater Japanese contributions to the Gulf war.[22]

Larger political competition over systemic restructuring

Looking at the Japanese response to the Gulf crisis, it is immediately clear that how to frame the response is part and parcel of a larger political competition over how to restructure the Japanese political system. It has been called the 'overall settlement of the postwar era' (*sengo so kessan*) by former Prime Minister Nakasone Yasuhiro. The competition has become intense because a number of forces have been leading Japan to tackle the issue head on. This competition is best understood when seen from three main angles: the traditional ideological cleavage between the right and the left, Japan's changing position in the international system, and private-sector strength.

Traditional ideological cleavage. The intense right-left cleavage in Japanese politics has led many observers to call it 'divided politics' or 'cultural politics'.[23] The cleavage was strong from the immediate postwar years to the early 1970s. The right-wing policy platform tended to stress the following four lines of policy positions: (1) alliance with the United States, greater expenditures and role for Self-Defense Forces, and anti-communism; (2) national identity, traditional morality, and the emperor; (3) production, efficiency, and innovation; and (4) protection of and subsidies to socially weak sectors. The left-wing policy platform emphasized four different lines of policy positions; (1) neutrality or non-alignment, light defense posture, and anti-hegemony nationalism; (2) civil freedom, egalitarian norms, and democracy; (3) a better working and living environment and protection of consumers; and (4) social welfare, education, and public expenditure. These are more or less similar to right-left cleavages in many other countries.[24]

The cleavage seemed to be mitigated somewhat during the post-oil crisis period when distributive issues in an era of lower economic growth placed both the left and the right on more or less pragmatic grounds concerning social and economic policy issues. Most symbolically, wage increases were somewhat restrained more or less cooperatively by labor during the post-oil crisis recessionary periods. Even those two core areas where the right-left cleavage used to be most intensely observed, that is, defense and diplomacy and the emperor and national identity, seemed to be watered down substantially in the 1970s and 1980s. On defense and diplomacy, the positions of the non-Communist opposition parties have moved to, or at least toward, de facto approval of the Japan-US Security Treaty and the Self-Defense Forces as the Cold War has waned. On national identity and the emperor also, their positions have seemingly moderated, perhaps helped by the increasingly nationalistic stances taken by many Japanese on what they see as Japan-bashing. Yet, it has turned out that the pacifist position on the constitution has been no less divisive now than before as demonstrated by the division in public opinion over the SDF's military participation and financial contributions to the multinational forces including for the supply of weapons. Moreover, pacifism has permeated large portions of the right wing as well on these issues. It is not exactly the expression of traditional ideological cleavage but does revive and amplify it.

Japan's changing position in the international system. In tandem with the growth of Japan's profile in the international system, the voice for a more proactive rather than reactive diplomacy has become increasingly strong. Reactive diplomacy has been noted as the hallmark of Japan's diplomacy during the postwar era, especially for the last two decades.[25] It has a number of origins. Consensual decision making is often depicted as a factor slowing down Japan's diplomatic responses. Another reason is that Japan's prime ministers during the last 18 years have come from smaller factions of the governing party and offered weak political leadership; two exceptions are Nakasone Yasuhiro, who overcame this weakness by other means, and Takeshita Noboru, who was a member of the largest faction. Weak leadership has tended to stifle any bold initiatives coming from the bureaucracy or the party as the cabinets have become an arena for competing interests to meet without being resolved rather than being a strong actor to aggregate various voices into one national policy action. Third, Japanese diplomacy has been largely preoccupied with what has been traditionally called low politics, i.e., politics of commerce, where coordination and consultation with the private sector is essential and where market forces are the key variable often overriding the policy preference of the government, hence all the reactiveness. Fourth, and most relevant to the Gulf crisis, the security shyness of Japan has to be stressed. Given the legacy of its failed militarist past, institutionalized constraints within the constitution against using force for resolving international disputes, and constraints arising from the Japan-US Security Treaty on adopting any autonomous defense policy, Japan's reactiveness is natural in most foreign policy crisis situations where war and peace are at stake.

Yet for those reasons summarized earlier, the voice calling for a proactive rather than reactive diplomacy has become stronger. This voice takes two forms. One calls for a greater political role in the world more or less in tandem with the United States. The second seeks an autonomous route, perhaps in loose concert with Pacific Asia and with the United Nations.[26] It is not necessary to emphasize that mainstream thinking has been of the passive type. But these two forms of proactive diplomacy are increasing in strength and have been further emboldened by the Gulf crisis.

The line of thought for a greater political role is roughly as follows: Given the institutionalized and psychological impediments against Japan assuming global security responsibilities and given the alleged political sterility of debate within the Diet and bureaucratic impasse, advocates of this approach try to make the best use of the demand for Japan's greater security roles in order to make a breakthrough in resolving the dilemma of Japan's security shyness. To accomplish this, they rely on a flexible interpretation of the Japan-US Security Treaty and Japanese law, which is less directly vulnerable to parliamentary scrutiny. Both the decision on Japan's financial contributions to the multinational forces and the use of SDF aircraft in rescuing refugees might be considered as small yet important steps in that direction. This diplomatic position is basically preoccupied with avoiding further deterioration in the Japan-US relationship before Japan can relinquish its semi-sovereign status. Needless to say, this voice for proactive diplomacy does not seem intent on turning Japan into a state with heavy armaments like the United States or the Soviet Union. Rather, along with those who advocate greater autonomy, it stresses the paramount importance of international finance over that of military and nuclear weapons.

The thinking of those who favor an autonomous route for Japan is roughly as follows: Given Japan's prominent stature, it ought to be able to act more independently of the US government and more in harmony with 'domestic demands'. This position reflects some negative sentiments toward the United States, not necessarily psychological but, more importantly, based on their forecast of the increasing economic vigor and weight of Japan (and no less importantly that of Pacific Asia) vis-à-vis that of the United States at the dawn of the next century.[27] Given the predominantly pacifist orientation of domestic opinion, this 'autonomous route' thinking advocates more use of what has been called 'soft power'[28] in the sense of forging, consolidating, and making the best use of the network of interdependence shaped largely through market forces and augmented by some loose and flexible institutional arrangements. An example would be the slowly emerging role of the Bank of Japan as a coordinating actor for monetary policy in Pacific Asia.[29] Furthermore, in this scheme of things, the international security apparatus will become much less salient than in the view of those pushing for a greater political role, and arms control will be an important agenda not only to make the world safe from war but also to make Japan's predominantly economics-oriented diplomacy more effective in an environment where weapons are not of overwhelming importance and are simply another form of power. An example would be Japan's initiative to participate in an international nuclear power generation/reprocessing scheme.

There is no clear-cut division between these two proactivist positions and one might see both positions as largely complementary. A greater political role is loosely represented by the views of politicians such as Secretary General Ozawa Ichiro and the members of the defense *zoku* (Diet defense specialists who are advocates of strong and often autonomous defense[30]), as well as the Defense Agency and defense contractors. Those supporting the autonomous role are loosely represented by big business, especially the finance sectors, as well as the economic ministries, most importantly the Ministry of Finance and the Ministry of International Trade and Industry. The Ministry of Foreign Affairs seems to be inhabited by both reactive and proactive schools fairly equally but dominated in practice by the reactive school with its domestic power base remaining feeble and shallow.[31] At any rate, the proactive schools are in ascendance in correlation with the slowly intensifying political competition over domestic systemic restructuring. What form their ascendance will take politically in terms of party reconfiguration remains to be seen as public opinion has not yet indicated a preferred direction in a convincingly clear-cut fashion.

Private sector strength. Corporate strength has become an undeniable key factor in Japanese politics. Growth in the strength of the private sector and decline in the strength of the public sector may capture a key aspect of Japanese politics in the 1980s.[32] The driving force is market liberalization. With the partial dismantling of bureaucratic regulations and restrictions so tenaciously guarded for so long, private sector strength has come to the fore in the 1980s. An important force sustaining market liberalization is the maturity of the Japanese economic society, which demanded freer economic activities and consolidated interdependence with the world economy, most notably with the US economy. Politically, the Japanese government wanted to act with the United States in giving support to the tide of market liberalization most vigorously initiated by the United States in the early 1980s. The Japanese government also wanted to see Japan's private sector become more competitive in a less protected market. When the economic society was loosened in many ways in the form of market liberalization, the bureaucratic instinct of the Japanese government led it to 'discipline' the society in another form.[33] This took the form of a renewed emphasis on national defense and identity. National defense received most privileged treatment in the budget along with foreign aid throughout the 1980s in terms of the continuously high expansion rate of budget. Since 1985, national identity has been officially stressed in public schools at primary and secondary levels in the form of raising the national flag and singing the national anthem.[34] These two policy areas are so closely enmeshed with the traditional political cleavage of Japanese politics that they are bound to arouse the somewhat semi-dormant opposition. They are also deemed necessary by the Japanese government precisely because Japan has to 'internationalize' itself much more vigorously and steadily and is bound to be exposed to the vagaries of international influences, be they security threats, migrants, or foreign ideas and religions.

Thus, these three forces—traditional ideological cleavage. Japan's changing international position, and private sector strength—have been further intertwined in shaping the Japanese response to the Gulf crisis, preparing the stage for intense political competition over the framework for systemic restructuring.

Prospects

Half a century after 1945, when Japan was heavily bombed by the Americans without mercy, the Japanese now watch the Gulf war with analogies drawn to the Japanese war in the 1940s.[35] Superimposed on the multinational forces' air attacks on Iraq seen on TV news programs are memories of US air raids on Japan. Suddenly Iraq becomes analogous historically to Japan: Wasn't Japan somewhat like Iraq when Japan conquered Manchuria? Didn't Japan recklessly plunge into confrontation with the United States at Pearl Harbor? Constrained significantly by their understanding of historical lessons about the utility of military power, the debt of history, and anti-colonialism, what makes distinctive the Japanese response to the Gulf crisis, including the public support for the multinational forces' military action in the Gulf, is the somewhat awkward mix of apprehension and self-confidence. With GATT and the Gulf suddenly clouding the blue sky of the first phase of the post-Cold War era and the second phase looking gloomy in many ways, Japan nonetheless will move on, based somewhat feebly at first but later more confidently on its own vision and dynamism. The Gulf war will be remembered by many Japanese in a somewhat strange way as a vindication of the Japanese wisdom based on the negation of the Pearl Habor complex since 1945. That would significantly affect the tone of the Japanese historical reflection on the fiftieth anniversary of Pearl Harbor in late 1991 and the course Japan will take into the next century. With its somewhat amorphous vision of how the world should be shaped and with its not necessarily overwhelming economic strength in the longer term, whether Japan can steer its course safely and live happily with the rest of the world remains to be seen.

Acknowledgement

I gratefully acknowledge Courtney Purrington's comments on an earlier draft of this article.

Notes

1. Yamada Nobuo, *Persia to To* (Tokyo: Heibonsha, 1971), and the five other volumes in the series *Tozai bunmei no koryu*, 6 vols. (Tokyo: Heibonsha, 1970–71).
2. See for example Ted Gup, 'A Man You Could Do Business with', *Time*, Feb. 27, 1991, pp. 50–54.
3. For descriptive details, see for instance Asahi Shimbun, *Wangan senso to Nihon* (Tokyo: Asahi Shimbun, 1991); Courtney Purrington and Akira Kato, 'Japanese Crisis Management During the Iraqi Crisis', *Asian Survey*, Vol. 31, No. 2 (April 1991).
4. Bruce Russett, *Controlling the Sword: The Democratic Governance of National Security* (Cambridge, Mass: Harvard University Press, 1990), especially pp. 146–69.
5. Takashi Inoguchi, 'Change and Response in Japan: Japan's Politics and Strategy', in Stuart Harris, ed., *Change in Northeast Asia* (London: Longman Cheshire, 1991); Takashi Inoguchi, 'Pacific Asia in a Post-Cold War Era', paper presented at the Yomiuri Symposium, Tokyo, October 11–12, 1990.
6. See for instance Sakaiya Taichi, 'Sekaishi no naka no Wangan senso', *Chuo koron*, April 1991, pp. 48–87. See also Takashi Inoguchi, 'Four Japanese Scenarios for the Future', *International Affairs*, Vol. 56, No. 1 (Winter 1988–89), pp. 15–28.
7. Inoguchi Takashi, 'Zen chikyu ampo kyoryoku kaigi no teisho', *Chuo koron*, March 1991, pp. 124–37.
8. See for example Kenneth B. Pyle, ed., *The Trade Crisis: How Will Japan Respond?* (Seattle: Society for Japanese Studies, 1987); Kozo Yamamura, ed., *Japanese Investment in the United States: Should We Be Concerned?* (Seattle: Society for Japanese Studies, 1989); and Kozo Yamamura, ed., *Japan's Economic Structure: Should It Change?* (Seattle: Society for Japanese Studies, 1990).
9. See for instance the following polls: *Tokyo shimbun*, Sept. 4, 1990; *Yomiuri shimbun*, Sept. 30, 1990; *Asahi shimbun*, Oct. 1, 1990; *Mainichi shimbun*, Oct. 15, Oct. 23, and Oct. 29, 1990; *Asahi shimbun*, Nov. 1 and Nov. 6, 1990; *Nihon keizai shimbun*, Nov. 21, 1990; *Yomiuri shimbun*, Dec. 26, 1990; *Asahi shimbun*, Jan. 1, 1991; *Tokyo shimbun*, Jan. 30, 1991.
10. Richard Rosecrance, *The Rise of the Trading State* (New York: Basic Books, 1987); Sasa Atsuyuki, 'Posuto Maruta ni okeru Nihon no chii', *Chuo koron*, March 1991, pp. 48–59.
11. On these three strands of response, see for instance Komiya Ryutaro, 'Nihon higunjiteki koken o', *Nihon keizai shimbun*, Oct. 8, 1990; Koyama Shigeki, 'Nihon, dokuji no gaiko o', *Nihon keizai shimbun*, Sept. 24, 1990; Ishikawa Yoshimi, 'Wangan kiki, nanimo shinai, to iu daisan no sentaku', *Asahi shimbun*, Sept. 13, 1990, respectively.
12. Economic Planning Agency, *Keizai hakusho* (Tokyo: Okurasho Insatsukyoku, 1990).

13. Akira Iriye, *Shin Nihon no gaiko* (Tokyo: Chuo Koronsha, 1991).
14. See for instance the discussion on the Gulf war by Kato Koichi and Yamazaki Tasuku, both members of the Lower House and former Director Generals of the Defense Agency, and Koyama Shigeki, member of the Middle East Economic Research Institute, a think tank under the umbrella of the Economic Planning Agency, in 'Imakoso Pax Japonica no kakuritsu o', *Ekonomisuto*, Feb. 19, 1991, pp. 44–50.
15. See *Ajia no shimbun ga hojita Jieitai no 'kaigai hahei'* (Tokyo: Nashinokisha, 1991). On the mildly affirmative responses from many Asian leaders to the idea of SDF participation in UN Peace Keeping Operations, as occasioned by the tour of an LDP politician, Watanabe Michio, in East and Southeast Asia, see *Mainichi shimbun*, March 10, 1991.
16. On the debt of history, see Takashi Inoguchi, 'Four Japanese Scenarios for the Future', *International Affairs*, Vol. 65, No. 1 (Winter 1988–89); Takashi Inoguchi, *Japan's International Relations* (London: Pinter Publishers, 1991), especially Chapter Seven. 'Sino-Japanese Relations: Problems and Prospects'; Takashi Inoguchi, 'Asia and the Pacific since 1945: A Japanese Perspective', in Robert H. Taylor, ed., *Handbooks to the Modern World: Asia and the Pacific*, Vol. 2 (New York: Facts on File, 1991), pp. 903–20. With regard to Sino-Japanese relations, see also Laura Newby, *Sino-Japanese Relations: China's Perspective* (London: Routledge, 1988); Nakajima Mineo, *Chugoku ni jubakusareta Nihon* (Tokyo: Bungei Shunjusha, 1987); Tanaka Akihiko, *NitChu kankei* (Tokyo: University of Tokyo Press, 1991).
17. 'Asia Asks: War for What?', *Far Eastern Economic Review*, Jan. 24, 1991, pp. 10–14; 'Impact on Asia: Once This Lousy War is Over', *Far Eastern Economic Review*, March 7, 1991, pp. 8–12.
18. See Kozo Yamamura and Yasukichi Yasuba, eds., *The Political Economy of Japan, Vol. 1: The Domestic Transformation* (Stanford: Stanford University Press, 1987); Edward Lincoln, *Japan: Facing Economic Maturity* (Washington: Brookings Institution, 1987); Yasuba Yasukichi and Inoki Takenori, eds., *Kodo seicho* (Tokyo: Iwanami Shoten, 1989); Takashi Inoguchi, 'Japan's Politics of Interdependence', *Government and Opposition*, Vol. 25, No. 4 (Autumn 1990), pp. 419–37.
19. Kikuchi Tetsuro, 'Nihon mane futatabi kaigai e', *Mainichi shimbun*, March 5, 1991.
20. One of the best-known examples is Morita Akio and Ishihara Shintaro, *'No' to ieru Nihon* (Tokyo: Kobunsha, 1989).
21. Carlo Cipolla, ed., *The Economic Decline of Empires* (London: Methuen, 1970), p. 12.
22. See the opinion polls referred to in note 9.
23. J.A.A. Stockwin, *Japan: Divided Politics in a Growth Economy* (London: Weidenfeld and Nicolson, 1975); Joji Watanuki, 'Pattern of Politics in Present-Day Japan', in Seymour Martin Lipset, ed., *Party Systems and Voter Alignments* (New York: Free Press, 1967).
24. Takashi Inoguchi, 'Japan 1960–1980: Party Election Pledges', in Ian

Budge et al., eds., *Ideology, Strategy and Party Change: Spatial Analayses of Postwar Election Programmes in 19 Democracies* (Cambridge: Cambridge University Press, 1986), pp. 369-87; Takashi Inoguchi, *Public Policies and Elections: An Empirical Analysis of Voters-Parties Relationship under One Party Dominance*, Papers in Japanese Studies, No. 2, Department of Japanese Studies, National University of Singapore, February 1989.

25. Kent Calder, 'Japanese Foreign Economic Policy Formation: Explaining the Reactive State'. *World Politics*, Vol. XL, No. 4 (July 1987), pp. 517-41; Takashi Inoguchi, 'The Nature and Functioning of Japanese Politics', *Government and Opposition*, Vol. 26, No. 2 (1991), pp. 185-98; Inoguchi, 'Japan's Politics of Interdependence'.

26. Takashi Inoguchi, 'Shaping and Sharing Pacific Dynamism', *The Annals of the American Academy of Political and Social Science*. Vol. 505 (September 1989), pp. 46-55; Inoguchi, 'Zen chikyu ampo kyoryoku kaigi no teisho'.

27. Iwata Kazumasa, for example, has sketched three scenarios of the world and regional economies in the 1990s, namely, Pacific optimism, Pacific pessimism, and Eurooptimism, as expounded at the conference on the political economy of international cooperation, Hakone, Japan, Jan. 12-13, 1991.

28. Joseph S. Nye, Jr., *Bound to Lead: The Changing Nature of American Power* (New York: Basic Books, 1990).

29. See Ashley Rowley, 'Shy Bloc Leader', *Far Eastern Economic Review*, Feb. 14, 1991, p. 42.

30. Inoguchi Takashi and Iwai Tomoaki, *Zoku giin no kenkyu* (Tokyo: Nihon Keizai Shimbunsha, 1987).

31. See for instance Daniel Okimoto, 'Political Inclusivity', in Takashi Inoguchi and Daniel Okimoto, eds., *The Political Economy of Japan, Vol. 2: The Changing International Context* (Stanford: Stanford University Press, 1988), pp. 305-44. See also a gossipy yet very informative series of articles on ministries and agencies of the Japanese government, 'Shiriizu gun Kanryo shinka ron', *Zaikai tembo*, Jan. 1990-March 1991.

32. Kent Calder, 'Japan's Public and Private Sector: Beyond the Revisionism Debate', *The JAMA Forum*, Vol. 9, no. 1 (Sept. 1990), pp. 3-7. On the increased influence of pressure groups and politicians, see Muramatsu Michio et al., *Sengo Nihon no atsuryoku dantai* (Tokyo: Toyo Keizai Shimposha, 1986); Inoguchi and Iwai, *Zoku giin*.

33. Inoguchi Takashi, *Kokka to shakai* (Tokyo: University of Tokyo Press, 1988), pp. 150-67; and Inoguchi, *Public Policies and Elections*.

34. *Yomiuri shimbun*, March 9, 1991.

35. See for instance, 'Tensei jingo', *Asahi shimbun*, March 8, 1991.

Part III
Envisioning Japan's foreign policy

6

Japan's foreign policy
in a time of global uncertainty

Japan is not enigmatic but iridescent.[1] It is not a dark and unfathomable entity but an opalescent one, offering differing perspectives as its colours shimmer and change. When Robert Scalapino and Junnosuke Masumi call the party system in Japan a 'one and a half party system', the observer is puzzled at first but on the whole persuaded when told that in Japan the dominant party endures without being replaced by the opposition whose seats in parliament are only one-half the number occupied by the ruling party.[2] Ronald Dore's characterization of industrial relations in Japan as 'flexible rigidities' provokes a similar reaction. Although Japanese industrial relations were once known for the rigid adherence to the life employment system, they have proved quite flexible in the 1980s.[3] My description of the contemporary Japanese political system as 'bureaucratically-led, mass-inclusionary pluralism' prompts much the same response. Although the Japanese bureaucracy is strong, takes initiatives in many ways, and is proud that it takes into account as many of the preferences of the masses as possible, it is also a bureaucracy which is fragmented into ministries and agencies and functions in a political system which does not ensure that the various interests of these bodies will be melded into policy by the cabinet and prime minister.[4] In a word, a seemingly contradictory phrase is often a most eloquent characterization of some aspect or other of Japanese society. It is in this way that Japan is iridescent. In one light it can appear to be fast-moving and flexible while in another it will seem slow-moving and rigid. Some recent developments in Japan's foreign affairs are illustrative.

For example, when the Japanese government was pressed by the Group of Seven (G–7) countries in 1979 to shoulder more of the burden attendant upon dealing with the Soviet intervention in Afghanistan, Japan's official development assistance to most South Asian countries was very limited. Japan was harangued over the next few years for not living up to the standard set by the other advanced countries for sharing the normal responsibilities of these nations with respect to the Third World. Even when the Japanese government expanded its assistance by approximately 5 per cent per annum, few were impressed. But by 1989 Japan had become the number one aid donor to all the South Asian countries. Needless to say, a number of factors can be identified as prompting this change. One is the Japanese desire to move in the same direction as other members of the Western alliance, to the extent that its constitutional and other constraints permit. Another is the maturing of many South Asian countries so that they now meet Japan's own criterion for assistance—the belief that aid should be a vehicle to help those Third World countries which help themselves ('jijo doryoku'), especially in the building of manufacturing industries and the social infrastructure they require.[5] A third arises from the substantial and increasing economic clout of Japan which naturally seeks to expand the network of inter-dependence.[6]

Or, to take another example. When the Japanese government was criticized at almost every Western summit for following a policy of export-led economic growth during the first decade of the fourth quarter of the century, Japan's domestic demand looked small and feeble. This was true even in 1985 when the Maekawa Report set out a new policy under which the market was to be liberalized and domestic demand expanded.[7] However by 1989 not only was Japan one of very few countries moving steadily in the direction of increased market liberalization, but it had doubled its imports in four years and transformed itself from an export-dependent to a domestic-demand-based economy.[8] Today Japan has the lowest tariffs of any country so far as manufactured commodities are concerned and, along with the United States, is one of the few industrialized countries to exhibit a low ratio of trade dependence to gross domestic product.[9]

A third example. When it was suggested that the Japanese government conduct minesweeping operations in the Red Sea in 1948, the proposal did not fare well in Japan and was turned down.[10] There was very little in the press because the Japanese government did not want to stir up public opinion on the issue. Then in 1987, when the Iran-Iraq War made it necessary for commercial powers like Japan to conduct minesweeping operations in the Gulf, the Japanese government took the proposal to the people for debate.[11] Public opinion was not particularly favourable to the idea of sending mine-sweepers to the Gulf, even though Prime Minister Yasuhiro Nakasone and the Foreign Ministry supported the proposal. The chief cabinet secretary, Masaharu Gotoda, was vehemently opposed, however, and Prime Minister Nakasone backed down. Then, in March 1991, when the Gulf War was over and some businesses with Middle East links were bringing strong pressure to bear on the government to provide ships for minesweeping operations in the Gulf, the government swiftly decided to participate in these operations immediately after the German government had decided to do so.[12] After

Iraq invaded Kuwait in August 1990, the Japanese government had not been able to play much of a role in the activities of the American-led coalition. Indeed, its United Nations Peace Co-operation bill died ignominiously because of the strong resistance of the public and the disarray within the government in autumn 1990. Therefore the swift decision to dispatch the Self-Defence Forces (SDF) in April 1991 was a distinct surprise to many observers.[13]

One can argue that policy-making in Japan is either slow-moving or fast-moving, reactive or proactive, depending on which time-span you choose to examine and which kind of lens you use. In this sense Japan is iridescent. But it is not an enigma. An exploration of the issues involved and of the process of decision-making on any particular policy make it easy to comprehend the reasons for selecting that policy without resort to the culture-based explanations that many Japanologists are fond of putting forward. With this caveat in mind, let us look at the central thrust of Japan's foreign policy direction.

The Gulf and Gorbachev

The post-Cold War world has been an unsettling one for Japan. With the deepening of détente since the mid-1980s, both the idea of a world of two opposing camps and the institutions based on that assumption have gradually been undermined. One of those institutions is the security treaty between Japan and the United States which has been the foundation of Japan's foreign policy since 1952.[14] The possibility that the United States might move in the direction of weakening its security ties with Japan in the context of its rapprochement with the Soviet Union has been a concern of many Japanese leaders in recent years. That is why sentences like 'There is no word like détente in my dictionary' were reiterated by Japanese foreign ministers until early in 1990. At the same time, however, many Japanese leaders welcomed the fact that the post-Cold War world seemed likely to be less governed by military power and competition and thus more comfortable for those nations, like Japan, which take pride in their economic competitiveness.

In the event, this new world has turned out to be more complex than either of these images suggests. Unlike the gradual weakening of the military structure created under the North Atlantic Treaty Organization, the security structure embodied in the Japanese-American treaty remains intact, largely because there has been little change in the basic configuration of Soviet-American naval competition in the North Pacific. Moreover, the Gulf War reminded the world of the predominant role of the United States in handling military aggression in the Third World as well as of the continuing importance of military power in international politics in general. Furthermore, Japan has found economic management in the post-Cold War world to be more troublesome than expected as it faces increasing criticism from the United States and, more recently, France.

The Gulf War posed a severe dilemma for Japan. How could it shoulder international security responsibilities in ways that were broadly compatible with the dominant view of the Japanese public that an expanded security role for Japan was undesirable. Pressed and prodded by the United States government to participate in the American-led coalition's military efforts in any way that was possible for Japan given its constitutional and political constraints, the Japanese government stumbled.[15] The government itself was divided on the issue of Japan's participation in the coalition's military activities. One camp headed by Ichiro Ozawa, secretary general of the ruling Liberal-Democratic party (LDP), wanted to go ahead and let the SDF participate in the multinational force, at least at the level of the non-combatant actions allowed by the 'broadened' interpretation of the constitution and the Self-Defence Forces Law. This camp included LDP politicians who had been former directors general of the Defence Agency and members of the party's defence committee and was supported by a small but steadily increasing segment of the public who believed generally in a stronger defence policy and particularly in the crucial need to respond to the evident wishes of the United States government by participating in the anti-Iraq alliance. The other camp was headed by Prime Minister Toshiki Kaifu and supported by many officials in the economic ministries, by major business leaders (with some significant exceptions), and, most importantly, by more than two-thirds of the public. This group wanted Japan's support to be confined to non-military activities such as financial contributions to the United States and the member-countries of the Gulf Co-operation Council as well as to those countries severely hit by the Gulf War like Jordan and Turkey. They also supported such activities as helping refugees in and from Iraq, assisting in bringing Asian refugees back to their home countries from Jordan and Egypt, and helping with the environmental clean-up of the contaminated Gulf region. This conflict ended with the defeat of the former camp when the United Nations Peace Co-operation bill was killed in the Diet in the autumn of 1990. After that, Japan pledged and has systematically implemented a variety of contributions to non-military activities related to the Gulf War.

Nonetheless, as noted above, when the German government decided to participate in minesweeping operations in the Gulf after the war, the Japanese government decided to follow suit. Since then the political mood in Japan has been steadily swinging towards support for a more active security role, with the gradual acceptance by the LDP and the two smaller opposition parties of the SDF's participation in the United Nations' peacekeeping operations. Even in the largest opposition party, the Japan Socialist party, the largest right-wing group has been moving in this direction. Although this basic dilemma about Japan's international security role remains unresolved, it would appear that Japan has started to move, in an incremental fashion, towards some changes in defining it. It is possible that this incrementalism could give way to more rapid change. Just as the German government with its pledge to revise its constitution seems to be working towards enabling its armed forces to participate in United Nations-sanctioned multinational forces, the Japanese government seems to be working towards enabling the SDF to participate in United Nations peacekeeping operations, a task which has tended in the past to be confined to small and/or neutralist-leaning Scandinavian countries, Canada, and Third World countries hungry for foreign reserves.[16]

If the Gulf War provoked a measure of rethinking about Japan's international security role, the visit of the Soviet president to Japan in April 1991 provided a reason for re-examining Japan's place in the détente process. Mikhail Gorbachev's visit had long been anticipated. Originally, it was to be the final step in the rapprochement which had been impeded for many years by the issue of the Northern Territories. But two major factors worked against the fulfilment of these expectations. First, the Soviet Union was in disarray, and Gorbachev was in no position to move boldly against domestic opponents (on both the left and the right) who were eager to take advantage of any possible concession Gorbachev might make to a foreign country. In consequence, the Japanese offer of an economic aid package in return for the territories and closer relations, the plan put forward by Ichiro Ozawa during his visit to Moscow in March 1991, was not taken up.[17] A second factor working against further Soviet-Japanese rapprochement was the apparent unhappiness of the United States government about the prospect of any dramatic improvement in Soviet-Japanese relations.[18] At a time when American public opinion was becoming steadily more critical of Japan, the United States government saw no merit in the Japanese government pursuing friendlier relations with third countries of major rank like the Soviet Union whose objectives are not necessarily in tune with those of the United States. (This stance on the part of the United States may have arisen from its view that there should be no application of major arms control measures to the North Pacific where its own navy is supreme, save for those linked to arms control centred on Europe's land-based armaments.) In the light of US and Soviet developments, the Japanese government appears to have decided that it was more beneficial to stick to its original position that the issue of the territories should be resolved first, to be followed by a 'gradual expansion of equilibrium', irrespective of the heightened expectations of the Japanese public.

This hardline position has been most closely associated with the Ministry of Foreign Affairs and had been strongly supported by the generally anti-Soviet feelings of the Japanese public. It was based on a concern within both the Ministry of Foreign Affairs and the Defence Agency that a settlement on the Northern Territories will bring an end to the Cold War and might possibly lead to the termination of the alliance with the United States. This apprehension arises not so much from reasons of bureaucratic politics (the loss of control over much foreign policy vis-à-vis the Soviet Union), but more importantly from a fear of the consequences of the loss of an alliance which provides a form of insurance as much against the actions of the United States as against those of the Soviet Union.[19] Fears that the deepening of détente in Europe might lead to Japan's increasing isolation had eventually led to a modification of the hardline position, however. A scheme for a 'gradual expansion of equilibrium' was advanced; under this proposal territorial reversion remained the prerequisite to any final rapprochement, but economic, technological, cultural, and academic exchanges and measures to expand and enhance trade could be undertaken without compromising the principle of the indivisibility of politics and economics ('seikei fukabun'). This position did not seem to change very much even after the ruling party issued a pledge (for the first time in its history) during the election campaign for the House of Councillors in March 1990 that it would 'strive towards genuine rapprochement with the Soviet Union'.[20]

The achievements of the Kaifu-Gorbachev summit meeting were not significant. Fifteen agreements dealing with more pragmatic issues have been signed and enacted. Given the major constraints placed on any dramatic Soviet-Japanese rapprochement and given the clear preference of the Japanese government to place utmost priority on its friendship with the United States, the outcome of the summit which offered no major breakthrough but the prospect of expanding and enhancing the very low-level transactions between the two countries does not seem to have been ill received in Japan. Because incrementalism has long been the hallmark of Japanese diplomacy, it probably seemed inappropriate to expect more rapid shifts in Soviet-Japanese relations.[21]

If Japan's handling of its participation in the Gulf War and its relations with Gorbachev may be taken as pointers towards the course Japan is likely to pursue in the area of international security during the 1990s, what will be the major components of that policy?

First of all, the primary importance the Japanese government has long attached to the alliance with the United States is not likely to change. As long as the United States remains the key to Japanese security, as long as it determines the global détente process, as long as it exercises control over regional conflict management in the Third World, and as long as the Japanese government fears the United States to some extent, Japan has no feasible alternative to working closely with the United States. That is not to say that Japan will inevitably follow the course the United States sets for the world, but that the idea of Japan actively seeking an alternative to the alliance relationship with the United States is difficult for any responsible Japanese leader to contemplate. The strenuous efforts in the United States to reduce budget deficits especially in relation to defence costs for overseas forces and the steady deterioration in the attitude of the American public towards Japan mean that the alliance relationship is likely to experience some setbacks over the next decade, but these will more likely arise from United States initiatives than from Japanese ones. Needless to say, Japan has its own complaints about the United States in relation to economic conflicts and burden-sharing, and the steady increase in its economic clout and competitiveness vis-à-vis the United States and other nations has naturally increased its self-esteem and self-confidence. In consequence, it is possible that Japan may show a greater disposition to independence and firmness in its policies. But it is very unlikely that the alliance relationship with the United States would be allowed to suffer from such actions because almost all responsible Japanese leaders consider that alliance essential to Japan's international well-being.

A second element of Japan's foreign policy, as long as it can be pursued without undermining this primary element, will be the attempt to enhance its relations with the rest of the world, if only to reduce the pressure on the overburdened Japanese-American relationship, for, as one observer has put it, Japan has 'far too many eggs' in the one basket called the United States.[22] This development has been encouraged in part by the recent pressure that the United States government has placed on its allies to take on a larger share of global responsibilities. Because the Japanese government desires to shoulder some of these responsibilities for other reasons as well, it has moved steadily to expand its links with other countries. In particular, the Japanese government, and especially the Ministry of International Trade and Industry (MITI), want to reduce the economic influence of the United States on Japan. The Japanese are uneasy with the current state of affairs which combines—as they see it—a relative decline in American competitiveness with an intransigent and high-handed attitude in the area of United States economic diplomacy. This perception of the United States has encouraged the Japanese to reduce their overdependence on the United States in the areas of trade, direct investment, technology, and security. Trade has been diversified fairly effectively since the mid-1980s thanks to two developments: the first was the move towards the united Europe of 1992 which prompted Japanese business to move into Europe before the wall became impenetrable and the second has been the remarkable economic expansion in Pacific Asia, whose regional gross national product is expected to match those of North America and western Europe by 2010.[23] Direct investment in the United States, which rose dramatically during the Reagan presidency, also began to decrease in the late 1980s and early 1990s with the remarkable expansion of domestic demand achieved in Japan in the latter half of the 1980s and the movement of Japanese investors into western Europe and Pacific Asia. There has also been an attempt to diversify in the area of technology.

This diversification of trade, investment, and technology does not mean that the unprecedented interdependence of the Japanese and American economies, so firmly and irreversibly interwoven at both the macro and micro levels, has been in any way watered down. But if one expects the solution to every problem will be found in the alliance and the interdependence between the two countries, then management of the relationship is not going to be easy. Each party will tend to blame the other partner in an unending zero-sum conflict over every problem which arises.[24] Thus, a reduction of the overload on the Japanese-American relationship, where possible, is likely to have beneficial effects in the long term.

International security is the area in which Japan is least able to do something to pursue this objective. All it could do in the short term was to shoulder the costs of maintaining United States bases in Japan and contribute its SDF to minesweeping activities in the Gulf and to United Nations peacekeeping operations in the short term. But in other areas Japan has taken modest political initiatives designed to improve its standing in the international community: renewing relationships with such countries as the Soviet Union and North Korea, helping to soften economic sanctions against China at the G–7 meeting in Washington early in 1991, and facilitating the pursuit of peace in Cambodia. Rapprochement with North Korea was desired by some parliamentarians led by Shin Kanemaru, a former LDP vice prime minister. Improved relations with the Soviet Union have been pursued by some parliamentarians such as Ichiro Ozawa. A lifting of the economic ban on China, which had been imposed in the wake of the Tiananmen massacre of 1989, during the G–7 meeting in 1991 was an initiative of Japan's finance minister, Ryutaro Hashimoto. The Tokyo conference on Cambodia in the summer of 1990 was engineered by the Japanese government although it did not succeed in persuading all the Cambodian parties to participate. Although some of the parliamentarians' activities were not welcomed either by the Foreign Ministry or by the United States government, they do seem to represent attempts (however premature or ill guided) to broaden Japan's role in the international community.

In short, there will be no fundamental change in the primary and primordial emphasis Japan places on the alliance with the United States. As Japanese economic interests spread out to every part of the world, and the United States remains the sole military superpower endowed with the ability and will to project power throughout the world, the Japanese view of international security tends increasingly to overlap with the Japanese conception of national security. Japan is nevertheless more and more self-confident about putting forward its own ideas on regional and global security interests.

GATT and G-7

The Uruguay Round of talks under the General Agreement on Tariffs and Trade (GATT) did not reach an accord by the deadline of December 1990. They collapsed because of the major conflict of interest with regard to agricultural liberalization among the three major trading blocs, North America, western Europe, and Japan, as well as over no less major conflicts of interest among various other groups of member-countries. The stubborn refusal of the United States and the European Community to compromise on the means for agricultural liberalization brought about this stalemate. While Japan, no less an agricultural protectionist, is basically ready to go ahead with the minimal scheme for liberalization of the rice market, it is not willing to take a unilateral initiative as long as the United States and the European Community show no signs of resolving their own conflict of interest. It is unfortunate that the Japanese government cannot take a leadership role in pursuit of liberalization of the global agricultural market because the benefit to Japan of retaining the world-wide free trade régime is far greater than any possible cost associated with any scheme for a minimal liberalization of the rice market. Yet, the Japanese government has not been able to persuade its strong domestic agricultural interests to allow such an initiative. The Ministry of Agriculture, Forestry and Fisheries, always mindful of the need to secure the food supply in the event of an emergency and supported by two-thirds of the general public, whether for environmental or autarkic reasons, does not want to see any increase in Japan's dependence on overseas food supplies, especially in light of the current astonishingly high level of those imports compared with those of most industrialized countries.[25]

Meanwhile, the future of the international trade régime is increasingly uncertain. Because the régime is like a bicycle which falls over without periodic attempts to liberalize the market, régime uncertainties have certainly been encouraging domestic protectionist interests all over the world. The basic reason why the primary thrust of the United States government in trade negotiations has been towards the further opening of foreign markets is its need to demonstrate to protectionist interests at home that trade liberalization can be of more benefit to the United States than protectionism.

Hence the very aggressive push by the American government—at the uni-lateral, bilateral, and multilateral levels—for additional market liberal-ization by foreign countries in tandem with an ever more intransigent protectionist stance at home.[26] The justification the United States puts for-ward for its multi-level approach to the attempt to maintain a free trade régime through GATT, a western hemisphere free trading area, and bi-lateral market liberalization negotiations is that without this all-out effort on all fronts, Congress and public opinion could not be persuaded and the United States government might be forced to move towards outright pro-tectionism. The United States argues that the consequences of such a step would be much more severe for the rest of the world than for the United States.

Those critical of the American government's trade policy argue that the United States should devote more energy to nurturing and enhancing the strong economic and technological foundations of United States power by intervening more directly to revitalize its own economy.[27] The resort of the United States government to negotiations with foreign governments on the premise that the deepening of economic interdependence through liberal-ization would ensure the maintenance of United States hegemony because the United States could continue to make the best use of institutionalized and non-institutionalized patterns of influence is criticized by its domestic opponents as disregarding the economic and technological basis of power underlying global hegemony. Thus, they propose that the United States should deploy those industrial and technology policies that Europe and Japan have been allegedly using so effectively to develop a regionally self-sufficient economic and technological base like those Europe and Japan have been nurturing and expanding in Europe and Asia respectively.

Whether the United States government surrenders power and policy to these forces in the United States is one of the most critical factors in the framing of Japan's policy in this area. The United States House of Represent-atives has recently given surprisingly strong support to the administration for a continuation of the 'fast-track' approach on the GATT talks, the North American free trade bloc agreements, and other trade talks. Japanese fears may thus be somewhat allayed, especially when one finds the name of Richard Gephardt among those who voted for the continuation. Perhaps the members of that alleged bastion of protectionism, the United States Congress, may be only surface protectionists.[28] For the time being, therefore, Japan's policy is to support further liberalization of the market, whether in rice, construction, finance, or retailing, so that global economic interdepend-ence can be strenghened. The Japanese government recognizes very clearly that Japan would be the first to suffer from a protectionist and regionalized world market.

The latest conference of G–7 finance minsters and central bankers seems to show once again that policy co-operation is not easily achieved despite all the rhetoric of the participants. When the issue was whether it was necessary to raise interest rates in Germany and Japan so that the United States, entering a recession, could effectively sustain a lower interest rate, neither Germany nor Japan followed the preference of the United States but instead gave priority to management of their domestic economies. The Bank of Japan's decision to lower the interest rate in the late spring of 1991 may have seemed to be a response to United States wishes, but it was in fact based primarily on domestic priorities.[29] The euphoria about policy co-ordination which followed the Plaza agreement of 1985 may have dissipated by 1991.

Yet the contrast between the military triumph of the United States and the inability of the United States to secure compliance in economic monetary policy should not be exaggerated. One can argue, after all, that the G–7 meetings have been more of a ritual by which the United States government negotiates with other major governments over world economic management in order to induce them to assist the United States in the management of its domestic economy than the more pluralistic discussions that the image-makers have tended to suggest.[30] By 1991, however, such major actors as Germany and Japan have become less hesitant about giving the world the impression that they are not seeking to comply blindly with the wishes of the United States.

Europe 92, NAFTA, and the EAEG

If more regionalized economic centres acting more or less autonomously on the basis of domestic and regional priorities are indeed the wave of the future, then one must look at three current regional projects/proposals: Europe 1992, the North American Free Trade Area (NAFTA), and the East Asian Economic Grouping (EAEG). How does Japan assess these groups and how should it respond to them? Needless to say, Japan does not welcome the growth of regionalism in world economic affairs for the obvious reason that its own prosperity rests on broad and stable access to the world market.[31] Yet for as long as regionalism seems to flourish, Japan must adapt to it.

The Europe 1992 project initially provoked a fear that Japan would be excluded from the European Community much more completely than is now thought likely.[32] As progress towards economic union has proven more difficult than initially expected, however, Japan's misgivings (perhaps originally exaggerated) have receded somewhat, and there is no more talk of Fortress Europe. For most Japanese the upheavals in Eastern Europe and the Soviet Union, including German reunification, have overshadowed the

Europe 1992 project. The apparent stalemate in negotiations over two core ideas of the enhanced European community—an economic and monetary union and a standing army—seems to suggest the road to its achievement is not going to be smooth. All the diplomatic furore surrounding the implementation of monetary union—starting with the Delors plan, then the German objection to its emphasis on the economic maturity argument, and finally the British proposal delaying the timetable and thus watering it down considerably—has convinced many Japanese that the path to monetary union is fraught with difficulties. The likelihood of a European standing army growing out of the Western European Union seems even more remote. The Europeans are not ready to replace the North Atlantic Treaty Organization (NATO) with their own alliance in the immediate future, nor do they wish to suggest that a United States presence in Europe is no longer necessary. The American approval of the plan to establish a European rapid deployment force for out-of-area-operations (for example, in Yugoslavia) is a compromise which will not weaken the primary importance of NATO to European defence.[33] And, of course, the member-countries of the new Europe are also at odds over many other issues: the Soviet Union, a united Germany, the instability of eastern Europe, the emigrant-exporting Islamic world in North Africa, and the Middle East. Indeed, to some, they seem to lack any common vision of the future Europe. Despite all these difficulties, most Japanese believe that the Europe 1992 project will come to fruition in the long run, if perhaps more slowly than was thought likely in 1985 or 1989. It will thus continue to present challenges to Japan which will have to respond to the actual impact of this regionalist thrust, be it over issues of money, defence, energy, or agriculture.

The North American Free Trade Area arises out of the free trade agreements the United States has been arranging with its neighbours to the north and south, Canada and Mexico. If one also takes into consideration the traditional links between the United States and its southern neighbours, these economic connections might well lead in time to the emergence of an economic region encompassing the whole of the western hemisphere. The major Japanese reaction to this development has been the attempt to establish themselves in Canada and Mexico before the consolidation of any potentially discriminatory barrier against outsiders.[34] Given the importance to Japan of North America in terms of the supply of primary commodities to Japan and the provision of a market for Japanese products, the stakes are high. This move into Canada and Mexico has been accelerated by some protectionist policies in the United States against Japanese direct investment in the United States. Moreover, in the context of the accumulated debts of Latin American countries, Japan has been steadily drawn into that region by the United States to fill the gap occasioned by the retreat of American financial interests.[35] The North American free trade agreements have not elicited as many apprehensive reactions from Japan as the Europe 1992 proposal, because they are perceived to be largely confined to trade and manufacturing whereas the latter scheme is all-encompassing. The United States government has insisted that the thrust of its agreements with Canada and Mexico is not protectionist but a move in the direction of free trade and thus compatible with the GATT. Nevertheless the regionalist thrust of the agreements does give a clear message to many Japanese. Thus when the United States government expressed its displeasure over the EAEG proposal and Prime Minister Kaifu's 'understanding' of that proposal during his visit to the countries of the Association of South-East Asian Nations (ASEAN) in the spring of 1991, some Japanese were somewhat perplexed by the American response but did not make a fuss about it.[36]

The East Asian Economic Grouping proposal of Prime Minister Mahatir Mohamad of Malaysia is a bold yet ingenuous one. In light of the trend to regionalism in other parts of the world and the increasing pressure of the United States government on most Pacific Asian countries for market liberalization, Malaysia wants to establish a regional grouping that includes Japan but excludes the United States and all other non-Asian countries. Malaysia argues that such a grouping is a way to cope more effectively with both these problems. The major difficulty with the proposal lies in the exclusion of the United States. If American unhappiness extends to censuring Japan for its participation in the scheme, the proposal is not very likely to win support in Japan. If the purpose is largely to enhance the bargaining position of Malaysia and some other Pacific Asian countries with respect to the United States, an assessment of its prospects is more difficult to make. Pacific Asia cannot hope to continue to thrive without embedding itself ever more firmly into markets everywhere, but especially in North America and western Europe. Thus, estranging the United States and regionalizing Pacific Asia, however unwittingly, is not in the interests of most Pacific Asian countries. Looked at from a different angle, the proposal which was originally focused on trade and manufacturing might take on a more lasting life if it were applied to a regionalist restructuring of the international financial system. The major difference between the global systems of trade and finance is that while the former is a network in which every component is directly connected to every other component, the latter works most efficiently with a hub-and-spoke system whereby regional centres absorb most of the uncertainty in financial transactions and link sub-centres to the global financial system. If this notion were to be pursued, then the Malaysian proposal might be implemented—though in somewhat different form from the one its creator imagined.[37]

Steering a course through domestic cleavages and conflicts

In steering the nation in a world in which uncertainties abound and in which both expectations about and apprehensions over a greater role for Japan intersect in a very complex manner, the Japanese government must also manoeuvre among the cleavages and conflicts within the domestic political system. There are four major ones which should be noted, however briefly: left versus right, private sector versus public sector, politicians versus bureaucrats, and bureaucratic politics.

Left versus right

The traditional left versus right ideological cleavages die hard. The leftist influence on public policy in Japan is much smaller now than it once was. The lower growth in the economy after 1974 forced the left to make greater compromises over social policy than would have been necessary if the previous higher growth rates had continued. The decline of the public sector, including the privatization or disappearance of quasi-governmental agencies and companies such as the Japan National Railway and Nippon Telegraph and Telephone in the 1980s, has reduced the left's organizational base. The end of the Cold War has reduced the cleavage over defence issues. Nevertheless, a few issues remain that could revive this division, depending on circumstances; the most likely are defence, education, and taxes.[38]

Defence continues to arouse controversy as we have seen during the Gulf crisis of 1990–1.[39] The government introduced the United Nations Peace Co-operation bill in order to enable the Self-Defence Forces to participate in military and non-military operations in the war against Iraq. But the outcry among the public was so strong—more than two-thirds were opposed to it—that the government abandoned the bill during the National Diet session of 1990. Not only the opposition parties but also a sizeable portion of the governing party opposed sending the SDF overseas, citing the constitution and public opinion. The defeat of the government in this particular legislative game is not solely attributable to the strength of the leftists. Rather, the rightist position on defence was not as strongly supported as some in the governing circle hoped. Neither Prime Minister Kaifu nor the Ministry of Foreign Affairs seemed particularly willing to push the bill through against such obstacles. Yet after the war ended in March 1991 and the government and the public reassessed the impact of its actions during the war, a shift in the government's policy and public opinion became visible. In March 1991, immediately after the German government decided to send minesweepers to the Gulf, the Japanese government decided to send SDF ships.

Two-thirds of the public now support the government's decision, and the prospects for passage of a slightly revised bill have become brighter. The key to the change in the government and among the public seems to lie in the seriousness with which they have taken the negative impact that the original decision has had on American attitudes towards Japan and on American-Japanese relations. The two smaller opposition parties, the Democratic Socialist party and the Clean Government party, have shifted their positions and are ready to approve overseas operations for the SDF with some provisos with respect to non-combat activities and the need for a United Nations umbrella. Factions within the Socialist party have also modified their positions steadily in the same direction. The core of the leftist opposition will remain, however, opposing what it regards as a militarist revival in Japan.

Private sector versus public sector

A reversal in the balance of financial power between the private sector and the public sector took place during the 1980s in Japan, as the former accumulated unmistakable financial clout while the latter suffered deficits and a chronic shortage of funds. Accordingly, the private sector has become much more assertive. Given the ways of Japanese politics, namely, that they are very responsive to changes in demographic, technological, economic, social, and international forces, the private sector's voice has come to have more influence on public policy.[40] A good example of this influence is the market liberalization of the 1980s, which occurred largely in the context of bilateral negotiations between the United States and Japan. The Structural Impediments Initiative talks between the two governments, especially those in the spring of 1990, provided evidence of this change in a very twisted manner.[41] Each government put forward its requests, with the general aim of further market liberalization and trade deficit (or surplus) reduction. What is interesting is that the list of requests from the United States government to the Japanese government makes use of all kinds of proposals and opinions which have been raised and articulated within Japanese society. In essence the United States government has become the articulator of the demands of the Japanese private sector.

The Japanese government has two weaknesses in the execution of policy including any further market liberalization. One is the peculiar nature of the Japanese prime ministership in the eighteen years since Kakuei Tanaka lost power in 1974.[42] After the merger of the two conservative parties in 1955, all the prime ministers except one (Tanzan Ishibashi) had come from the largest faction of the governing party, whereas since 1974 only one prime minister has come from the largest faction (Noboru Takeshita). In consequence, most prime ministers for the last eighteen years have not enjoyed a strong power base within the governing party (with the notable exception of Yasuhiro Nakasone, 1982–7), which has been more or less continuously controlled by the largest faction, namely, the Takeshita (or former Tanaka) group. This faction, which is also in charge of collecting money for the party, has tended to be somewhat more vulnerable to corruption and was involved in the Lockheed and the Recruit scandals. The other weakness of the government grows out of the position of the prime minister; it is much more difficult for a weak prime minister to achieve a compromise among the competing interests in the party. Especially when bureaucratic rivalries are involved, achieving a consensus at the highest level is often difficult—at the very least it is time-consuming. Hence the value in the market liberalization talks of foreign pressures which reflect the interests of the Japanese private sector. Hence Kenichi Ohmae's remark that in the Structural Impediments Initiative talks, the United States government has taken on the role of a Japanese opposition party, pressing the Japanese government to undertake further market liberalization especially for urban consumers.[43]

Politicians versus bureaucrats

One consequence of the increasing strength of the private sector and especially of the power of corporations is the steady ascendance of politicians vis-à-vis bureaucrats. This shift in influence is manifested in various forms, of which one is the rivalry between parliamentarians and diplomats over the conduct of foreign policy.[44]

Japan's relations with the Soviet Union have been improving slowly since the Japanese ruling party issued its 1990 election pledge to make 'genuine efforts towards rapprochement with the Soviet Union'. Yet the Ministry of Foreign Affairs has been reluctant to move in this direction. It has maintained the long-time position that a resolution of the territorial dispute should come first, to be followed by efforts at genuine rapprochement. The disparity between the views of politicians and bureaucrats on how to seek Soviet-Japanese rapprochement was laid bare in the spring of 1991. When the secretary general of the LDP visited Moscow to prepare for Gorbachev's visit to Tokyo, he brought with him a package of economic aid, amounting to US$26 billion, which had apparently been hastily drawn up by some MITI officials in their 'private capacity'. Ozawa probably wanted to make a deal, offering economic aid in exchange for the Northern Territories, but Gorbachev's advisers seem to have told him that the package did not appear to have the full support of the Japanese bureaucracy because some projects under way with major trading corporations were not included in the package.[45] In fact, projects negotiated by the Japanese-Soviet Economic Committee were not supposed to be included because this package was an initiative of the Ministry of International Trade and Industry involving private-sector money.[46]

When Gorbachev came to Tokyo, no compromise was made by either side. Gorbachev was in no position to give concessions to Japan when his domestic power base was eroding. Kaifu did not find it prudent to relax the hard line on the territories and on the collective security issue in general. The prime minister and the Ministry of Foreign Affairs were content with the fifteen accords that were concluded. They did not want any major policy shift to emerge from the meeting for by then it was clear that the United States government was somewhat apprehensive about the possibility of a sudden improvement in Soviet-Japanese relations at a time when American-Japanese relations were in severe trouble. While the discussions were going on, the governing party did make some representations to the Ministry of Foreign Affairs that without Soviet concessions on the territories, no joint communiqué should be issued, but to no avail. These differences between politicians and diplomats seem to stem largely from politicians' impatience and unhappiness about the policy direction of the Ministry of Foreign Affairs which they allege is too rigid, too tactless, and too pro-American. The increased assertiveness of politicians vis-à-vis bureaucrats has led to a number of similar contretemps. For example, when Shin Kanemaru, a former vice president of the LDP, met Kim Il Sung, secretary general of the Korean Workers' party, he pledged 'compensation' for Japan's neglect of North Korea during the post-colonial period, namely, after 1945. The Ministry of Foreign Affairs did start negotiations towards a rapprochement with North Korea, but its approach and its agenda are totally different.[47]

Bureaucratic politics

The Japanese political system is noted for its perennial ministerial in-fighting, with the highest political leader tending to adopt a consensual mode of decision-making rather than overcoming bureaucratic rivalries through decisive leadership. When the prime minister comes from a weak faction in the party, bureaucratic rivalries are especially evident. At the present time, with Japan's position in the international system clearly in a transitional stage, the consequent uncertainty has tended to spur bureaucratic conflict. The EAEG proposal, for example, seemed to trigger a good deal of bureaucratic shadow boxing. Because this issue is an extremely sensitive one, not much is known about the differences of view. But scattered evidence would appear to indicate that the Ministries of Finance, Foreign Affairs, and International Trade and Industry found something attractive in the idea.[48] They are apparently interested in establishing a Japanese yen economic area. The increasingly strong position of the yen in the region and the demand for a hub-and-spoke regime in international finance make the proposal both appealing and feasible. Furthermore, setting up a yen zone would mean that the strains on the current account surplus and its steady decrease (from a 1986 peak to one-fifth of that amount in 1990) might be somewhat eased if a large chunk of official development assistance went to countries in a potential yen zone such as China, Indonesia, and Vietnam. However it would be difficult to set up such a yen bloc at the present time for three reasons. First of all, Pacific Asia (and particularly the members of ASEAN) do not lack financial resources and hence there is no strong demand for yen-denominated short-term bonds (samurai bonds). Second, the structure of trade of most countries of Pacific Asia forces them to deal in dollars not yen because both their massive imports of energy and their massive exports of manufactured goods to the United States market are denominated in dollars. Finally, the economic structure of most Pacific Asian countries leads most rich investors from those countries to invest in countries other than their own because of the potential for political instability. Although the yen dominates the financial loans market in Pacific Asia, a yen bloc lies well in the future.[49] Once Prime Minister Kaifu's expression of 'understanding' for the EAEG when he met with Prime Minister Mahatir triggered a suspicion in the United States government, however, the Japanese government has backed away from this position. As soon as the United States government expressed its displeasure, it seems that the argument that a pro-United States line is primary has come to the fore again in the Ministries of Foreign Affairs, Finance, and International Trade and Industry.

Conclusion

The iridescent character of Japan can be condensed into two major streams. First, Japan adapts to changing circumstances remarkably steadily at home and abroad. Although Japan occasionally seems to behave in a slow and timid manner, it is able to move quickly and flexibly when its vital interests are thought to be in jeopardy. The speed and steadiness of the changes in Japan should not be underestimated. Second, Japan is stubborn at home and abroad. Although Japan often appears to be reasonable and understanding, it tends to stick to its own beliefs and mode of conduct when operating in an environment of uncertainty. Stubbornness and steadfastness in Japanese thinking should not be underestimated either. Given the dynamic quality of economic change in Japan, these seemingly contradictory character-istics manifest themselves much more dramatically in Japanese policy-making than in the decision-making of some other actors in the international system. At a time when the world is undergoing structural changes that many Japanese believe may jeopardize their nation's interests and when there is much uncertainty about the future throughout the world, both these characteristics are much in evidence when Japanese policy is examined. This article has sought to provide a glimpse at the multifaceted nature of Japanese foreign policy as it unfolds in the 1990s.

Acknowledgement

I gratefully acknowledge the helpful comments of Courtney Purrington on an earlier draft of this article.

Notes

1. Karel van Wolferen, *The Enigma of Japanese Power* (New York: Knopf 1989).
2. Robert A. Scalapino and Junnosuke Masumi, *Party Politics in Contemporary Japan* (Berkeley: University of California Press 1962).
3. Ronald Dore, *Flexible Rigidities* (London: Athlone 1989).
4. Inoguchi Takashi, *Gendai Nihon seiji keizai no kozu* [Contemporary Japanese Political Economy] (Tokyo: Toyo keizai shimposha 1983); Takashi Inoguchi, 'The nature and functioning of Japanese politics', *Government and Opposition* 26 (spring 1991), 185–98.
5. Robert M. Orr Jr., *The Emergence of Japan's Foreign Aid Power* (New York: Columbia University Press 1990); Shafiqul Islam, ed., *Yen for Development: Japanese Foreign Aid and the Politics of Burden-Sharing* (New York: Council on Foreign Relations Press 1991).
6. Takashi Inoguchi, 'Japan's politics of interdependence', *Government and Opposition* 25 (autumn 1990), 419–37.
7. *Yomiuri shimbun*, 22 May 1991, and Susumu Awanohara, ed., *Japan's Growing External Assets: A Medium for Regional Growth?* (Hong Kong: Centre for Asian Pacific Studies, Linnan College, 1989).
8. *Nihon o chushin to shita kokusai tokei* [Comparative Economic and Financial Statistics, Japan and Other Major Countries] (Tokyo: Bank of Japan 1990).
9. *Ibid*.
10. This point was brought up during the discussion after a speech I gave at the Maritime SDF Officers' College, 14 May 1991.
11. Inoguchi Takashi, 'The legacy of a weathercock prime minister', *Japan Quarterly* 34 (October–December 1987), 363–70.

12. *Asahi shimbun*, 25 April 1991.
13. Takashi Inoguchi, 'Japan's response to the Gulf crisis: an analytic overview', *Journal of Japanese Studies* 17 (winter 1991), 257–73.
14. Takashi Inoguchi, 'Japan's images and options: not a challenger, but a supporter', *Journal of Japanese Studies* 12 (winter 1986), 95–119; 'Four Japanese scenarios for the future', *International Affairs* 65 (winter 1988–9), 15–28; Takashi Inoguchi and Daniel Okimoto, eds., *The Political Economy of Japan*. 11: *The Changing International Context* (Stanford CA: Stanford University Press 1988).
15. Inoguchi, 'Japan's response to the Gulf crisis'.
16. *Yomiuri shimbun*, 21 May 1991.
17. *Mainichi shimbun*, 25 March 1991 (evening edition).
18. Peter Tarnov, as cited by Saeki Kiichi, vice-president of the Institute of Global Peace, Tokyo, in his 'Gorubachofu rainichi o sokatsu suru' [Summing up Gorbachev's visit to Japan], *Ajia jiho* (June 1991), 28–60.
19. Robert Delfs and Anthony Rowley, 'No deal, no money', *Far Eastern Economic Review*, 2 May 1991, 11–13. Courtney Purrington kindly shared with me some findings on the subject based on his interviews with bureaucrats and business leaders.
20. Takashi Inoguchi, 'Change and response in Japan's international politics and strategy', in Stuart Harris and James Cotton, eds., *The End of the Cold War in Northeast Asia* (South Melbourne: Longman Cheshire/Boulder Co: Lynne Rienner 1991).
21. Takashi Inoguchi,'The politics of decrementalism: the case of Soviet-Japanese salmon catch negotiations, 1957–1977', *Behavioral Science* 23 (November 1978), 457–69; Robert A. Scalapino, ed., *The Foreign Policy of Modern Japan* (Berkeley: University of California Press 1978).
22. Murray Sayle, 'The powers that might be: Japan is no sure bet as the next global top dog', *Far Eastern Economic Review*, 4 August 1988, 38–43.
23. Japan, Economic Planning Agency, *Keizai hakusho* [White Paper on the Economy] (Tokyo: Government Printing Office 1990).
24. Takashi Inoguchi, 'The ideas and structures of Japan-US relations', in his *Japan's International Relations* (London: Pinter/Boulder Co: Westview 1991); Takashi Inoguchi, 'Zen chikyu ampo kyoryoku kaigi o teishosuru' [A proposal for a Conference on Security and Cooperation on the Earth], *Chuo koron* (March 1991), 124–37.
25. Yujiro Hayami, *Japanese Agriculture under Siege: The Political Economy of Agricultural Policies* (London: Macmillan 1988); Homma Masayoshi, 'Kinkyu nogyo hojosakugen' [Reduction of agricultural subsidies urgently needed], *Nihon keizai shimbun*, 20 May 1991; 'Here comes farmer Giles-san', *The Economist*, 8–14 June 1991, 24.
26. I. M. Destler, *American Trade Politics* (Washington: Brookings Institution 1986); I. M. Destler and John S. Odell, *Anti-Protection* (Washington: Institute for International Economics 1987); Jagdish Bhagwati, *Protectionism* (Cambridge MA: MIT Press 1988); Helen V. Milner, *Resisting Protectionism* (Princeton NJ: Princeton University Press 1988); Robert Pastor, *Congress*

and the Politics of US Foreign Economic Policy (Berkeley: University of California Press 1980).

27. Stephen Cohen and John Zysman, *Manufacturing Matters* (New York: Basic Books 1987); Wayne Sandholtz et al., *The Highest Stakes: Technology, Economy and Security Policy* (New York: Oxford University Press, forthcoming); Robert Reich, *The Work of Nations* (New York: Knopf 1991).

28. *The Economist*, 18-24 May 1991, 42.

29. *Nihon o chushin to shita kokusai tokei.*

30. William A. Niskanen, 'G7 wa makuro keizai kyocho ni mueki' [G-7 is not useful for macro-economic co-operation], *Nihon keizai shimbun*, 27 May 1991.

31. *Keizai hakusho*; Ministry of International Trade and Industry, *Tsusho hakusho* [White paper on international trade] (Tokyo: Government Printing Office 1991).

32. Takashi Inoguchi, 'Japanese response to Europe 92', in this volume, pp. 71-90.

33. *Asahi shimbun*, 13 April 1991.

34. Two bilateral committees called wise men's committees, one with Canada, the other with Mexico, were recently formed.

35. Yanagihara Toru, ed., *Keizai kaihatsu shien to shiteno shikin kanryu* [Financial mediation as a support for economic development] (Tokyo: Institute of Developing Economies 1989); Islam, ed., *Yen for Development*.

36. *Nihon keizai shimbun*, 8 and 27 May 1991.

37. Takuma Takahashi, 'Alternative futures of the global financial market', paper prepared for presentation at the XVth World Congress of the International Political Science Association, 21-25 July 1991, Buenos Aires; 'Higashi Ajia keizai ken ni kyusekkin suru Okurasho-Nichigin rengo' [A coalition of the Ministry of Finance and the Bank of Japan move toward the formation of an East Asian economic region], *Infordia* (June 1991), 16-18.

38. Takashi Inoguchi, *Public Politics and Elections: An Empirical Analysis of Voters-Parties Relationship under One Party Dominance*, Papers in Japanese Studies 2 (Singapore: Department of Japanese Studies, National University of Singapore, February 1989).

39. Inoguchi, 'Japan's response to the Gulf crisis'.

40. Inoguchi, *Gendai Nihon seiji keizai no kozu* and 'The political economy of conservative resurgence under recession: public policies and political support in Japan, 1977-1983', in T. J. Pempel, ed., *Uncommon Democracies: The One-Party Dominant Regimes* (Ithaca NY: Cornell University Press 1990), 189-225.

41. Ohmae Kenichi, *Sekai no mikata, kangaekata* [How one should look at and think about the world] (Tokyo: Kodansha 1991).

42. Takashi Inoguchi, 'The emergence of a predominant faction in the Liberal Democratic party', paper prepared for presentation at the conference on 'Beyond the Cold War in the Pacific', Institute of Global Conflict and Cooperation, University of California, San Diego, 7-9 June 1990.

43. Ohmae, *Sekai no mikata, kangaekata*.
44. Donald Hellmann, *Japanese Foreign Policy and Domestic Politics: The Peace Agreement with the Soviet Union* (Berkeley: University of California Press 1969).
45. *Mainichi shimbun*, 25 March 1991.
46. My findings are based on Courtney Purrington's interviews with officials.
47. Okonogi Masao, *Nihon to Kitachosen* [Japan and North Korea] (Tokyo: PHP Institute 1991).
48. Compare the positions of the three ministries on the meanings of Pacific Asia to Japan: *Look Japan* (May 1991), 4–7.
49. Takahashi, 'Alternative futures of the global financial market'.

7

Japan's role in international affairs

A debate is under way—both in Japan and in capitals around the world—about the role Japan should play in international affairs. Some maintain that Japan should do more, given its position as one of the world's leading economic powers. Others worry that the emergence of an active, assertive Japan would alarm its neighbours and disrupt existing patterns of relations among the great powers. The worst-case scenario, according to some, is that an energetic Japan might become aggressive and militaristic.

In this article, the international and domestic factors that will shape the course of Japan's foreign and security policy in the near future are analysed. The article begins by examining the international and domestic pressures that are pushing Japan in the direction of a more activist role in international affairs. Next, the international and domestic impediments to a more active Japanese role are assessed. Finally, Japan's role in two issue areas of particular importance, international economic affairs and international security institutions, are examined.

The pressures on Japan to play a greater role in world affairs are beginning to overwhelm the countervailing obstacles. Japan, in short, will probably play a more active role internationally in the future than it has in the past. Moreover, this development should be encouraged, provided two conditions are met. First, Japan's policies must be in harmony with those of the international community as a whole. In practice, this means that Japan's actions should be linked to multilateral undertakings wherever possible. Second, Tokyo's initiatives need to be grounded by a solid domestic consensus about the broad course and content of Japan's foreign policy.

International pressures for a more active role in world affairs

A number of developments in the 1980s began to push Japan in the direction of a more active international role. In security affairs, the United States embarked on a systematic campaign to strengthen its military forces, both conventional and nuclear. The belief in Washington, at least during the first term of the Reagan administration, was that the Soviet Union had to be countered militarily if it was to be contained politically. With that in mind, the United States encouraged its allies, including Japan, to strengthen their own forces. Japanese Prime Minister Yasuhiro Nakasone supported this policy by increasing defence spending, increasing the amount of support provided to US troops stationed in Japan and entering into a number of joint technological ventures and wide-ranging joint military exercises with the United States. These exercises essentially overturned Japan's long-standing policy of restricting the activities of its Self-Defense Forces (SDF) to local venues.

At the same time, the economic fortunes of the United States and Japan began to go in opposite directions. By the mid-1980s, the United States was immersed in record budget deficits as a result of a severe recession, deep tax cuts and high levels of military spending. Its fiscal resources were limited, and its long-term economic competitiveness began to suffer. Japan's economy, on the other hand, was robust. Japan's industrial competitiveness, bolstered by favourable exchange rates, generated ever-higher levels of exports. This, in turn, embedded Japan even more deeply in the international economic system, giving it a wide range of international economic interests and making it highly interdependent with other countries.

By the time Yasuhiro Nakasone and Ronald Reagan left office in 1987 and 1988, respectively, the Cold War order was beginning to crumble. The US military build-up, combined with Soviet economic weaknesses and a commitment in Moscow to improve relations with the West, led to the signing of the Intermediate-range Nuclear Forces (INF) Treaty in December 1987. This treaty, the first to eliminate entire classes of nuclear weapons from the arsenals of the superpowers, marked an end to the most intense phase of the US-Soviet military competition and led many to conclude that further improvements in East-West relations were likely to be forthcoming. And, indeed, they were. The collapse of Soviet power in Eastern Europe in 1989, the Soviet decision to accept the reunification of Germany and the signing of the Conventional Armed Forces in Europe (CFE) Treaty in 1990 clearly indicated that the Cold War was over. The final chapter in the Cold War unfolded in December 1991, when the Soviet Union itself disintegrated.

These developments have had a tremendous impact on international relations as a whole and on Japan in particular. The old bipolar international order has collapsed, but a new order has not yet emerged in its place. What is clear, however, is that this new order will be multipolar in character and that all of the world's leading powers, including Japan, will have an important role in shaping it. Many world leaders would like to see Japan play a more active role in these deliberations.

Second, with the demise of the Soviet military threat, military power is not as important in international affairs as it once was. This is not to say that it has become unimportant, only that economic power has become increasingly significant. Many people around the world feel that Japan, with its immense financial, industrial and technological resources, should be more active in addressing international problem areas. The most pressing issues in the world today, many would argue, are not deterrence and defence, but economic reconstruction (in Eastern Europe and the former Soviet Union) and economic development (in the Third World). Few states are in a better position to deal with these economic problems than Japan. Policy-makers and analysts around the world are putting pressure on Japan to do more. Clearly, one of the driving forces behind Japan's growing role in world affairs has been the demand by the United States and others for Japan to assume more global responsibilities.

Other economic and political developments have also propelled Japan into a leading role in world affairs. Under President George Bush, the United States has maintained rigid tax and energy policies, and US industry, on the whole, has failed to become significantly more competitive internationally. As a result, the United States lacks significant financial or economic leverage in its international dealings. Second, a cascade of events in Europe—the liberation of Eastern Europe and the dissolution of the Warsaw Pact, German unification, the disintegration of Yugoslavia and the Soviet Union and the signing of the Maastricht Treaty on European economic and political union—has kept Europe preoccupied. Most of Europe's intellectual energy and economic resources are being devoted to local problems. Finally, other countries with large trade surpluses, such as Taiwan and some oil-exporting countries, are unwilling or unable to play a leading role in international affairs.

Thus, Japan with its high savings rates and large trade surplus has emerged as virtually the only country that can afford to underwrite large-scale international public policy actions.

Domestic pressures for a more active role in world affairs

'Occupying an honourable place in the international community' was an aspiration of Japanese people even before this phrase was written into the 1952 Constitution. Since 1952, Japan's desire to be accepted as a full-fledged member of the international community has been reflected in its membership in international institutions such as the United Nations Educational, Scientific and Cultural Organization (UNESCO), the General Agreement on Tariffs and Trade (GATT), the United Nations (UN), the Organization for Economic Co-operation and Development (OECD) and the Western Economic Summit.

More recently, Japan has begun to play a more influential role in institutions such as the International Monetary Fund (IMF) and the World Bank. This is not at all surprising, given Japan's position in the international economic hierarchy and the Japanese people's long-standing interest in multilateral organizations. In the World Bank, for example, Japan's capital share was 2.77 per cent in 1952 when it obtained membership and 6.69 per cent in 1987, second only to the United States. In the International Development Association, an arm of the World Bank, Japan's replenishment share was 4.44 per cent in 1961 and 20.98 per cent in 1990, again second only to the United States.[1]

Japan is also interested in attaining a prominent position on the UN Security Council and would like to establish closer ties to the North Atlantic Treaty Organization (NATO), the European Community (EC) and the Conference on Security and Co-operation in Europe (CSCE). If the international community encouraged and endorsed developments along these lines, Japan would not hesitate to pursue them. Japan's self-confidence in this regard is clearly growing.[2]

It is important to keep in mind, however, that there are internal debates in Japan on the international stance that country should take. For example, an inconclusive debate about the perennial US-Japan trade imbalance has been conducted between Japan's Economic Planning Agency and the Ministry of Finance. The US government has argued that Japan must eliminate structural barriers against imports to reduce Japan's trade surplus. In response, the Economic Planning Agency has argued that the root cause of the trade imbalance is macroeconomic: US savings rates must be raised, and the US fiscal deficit must be reduced. The Ministry of Finance, on the other hand, has argued that Japan needs to run a large trade surplus, given existing international demands for economic assistance and foreign direct investment. In addition, the Ministry worries that savings rates in Japan will decline as the population ages, and the country's capital resources will dwindle as a result. In short, the former is aggressive in calling for changes in an ally's savings and spending behaviour, while the latter is self-serving in its justification of the *status quo*.

Policy disputes also emerged in the internal deliberations leading up to the agreement reached between Japan and the EC in July 1991. According to the terms of this agreement, Japan and the EC are to hold regular consultative meetings on a wide range of issues, including security. The EC was reluctant to enter into discussions with Japan on security issues, especially European security issues; France, in particular, was adamantly opposed to this. Japan's Ministry of Foreign Affairs was anxious to move in this direction, but the Ministry of International Trade and Industry was apprehensive: it feared that pushing ahead in the security arena would create a backlash on trade issues, given that Japan had perennial trade surpluses *vis-à-vis* most EC members. In the end, Japan and the EC agreed that they would attempt to provide 'equitable access' to each other's market. The Ministry of International Trade and Industry is not unaware of the need to liberalize the Japanese economy in light of the fact that Japan is virtually the only country with a large trade surplus; criticism from abroad is likely to mount unless such efforts are vigorously undertaken by Japan.[3]

International impediments to a more active role in world affairs

Japanese misconduct in the 1930s and 1940s casts a long shadow over Japan's international activities even today.[4] It is important to recognize that Japan's actions in the 1930s and 1940s were indeed very cruel. Although most Japanese acknowledge this, many feel that Japan behaved no more brutally than other powers. In addition, abetted by the version of history propounded by the Allied occupation powers, most Japanese regard themselves as victims of a past engineered by the militarist cliques. As a resut, Japan has not always done enough to atone for past misconduct.

Not surprisingly, many of Japan's neighbours—the two Koreas, China, the Philippines, Singapore, Malaysia and Hong Kong—are apprehensive about Japan's growing economic influence. The concern is that economic preponderance could transform at some point into military dominance. Although official protests to the Japanese government have been rare, unofficial murmurings are not uncommon. Various newspapers in the region expressed concern, for example, about Prime Minister Nakasone's visit in 1985 to the Yasukuni shrine for the war dead, including war criminals; about Japan's decision in 1986 to build an advanced jet fighter (the FSX) on a largely indigenous basis; about Japan's growing levels of defence spending (which surpassed 1 per cent of gross national product in 1987); about Japan's decision to send mine-sweepers to the Persian Gulf in 1991; and about Japan's recent moves to pass legislation that would allow the SDF to be sent abroad.

Powers outside the region also have reservations about Japan's growing role in international affairs. The five victorious allies in World War II whose pre-eminent positions were institutionalized in the United Nations—the United States, Britain, France, China and (now) Russia—naturally do not want to give up their places of prominence. However, UN financial contributions of the vanquished powers of World War II—Germany and Japan, in particular—have been increasing at a faster rate than those of the victorious powers.[5] As a result, German and Japanese influence in UN debates has been growing. The funding issue is delicate, however, because although the victorious powers do not want to see the UN fall apart or their institutional positions deteriorate, they are not, by and large, able to increase their own contributions; the US Congress, for example, is adamant about any increase in US support for the United Nations. In addition, the five permanent members of the Security Council are reluctant to introduce the question of permanent membership for Germany and Japan.

Ironically, one of the main countries presenting a covert barrier to Japan's assumption of a greater role in world affairs is the United States, which has for many years publicly argued that Japan should assume more of the collective defence burden. As a recent US Defense Department memorandum indicates, there is a great deal of interest in some segments of the US policy establishment in maintaining a pre-eminent global military position. According to this memorandum, the United States should seek to maintain a military position that would enable it to dominate a unified Europe, a restructured Commonwealth of Independent States (CIS) or a more assertive Japan.[6] Thus, some in the United States would like to share the defence burden without relinquishing the pre-eminent military position the country now enjoys.

Two things work to moderate these impediments, however. First, those Pacific Asian countries with close economic ties to Japan—trade, investment, manufacturing and training—tend to have higher economic growth rates than countries that do not. Recognizing the increasing dependence on Japanese capital and technology for their own economic development, they have tended to moderate the otherwise harsh criticism of Japan. Japan's application of economic sanctions following the Tiananmen Square massacre in June 1989 is a good example of this.

Second, Japan's economic success has encouraged others to emulate the Japanese model—that is, the Japanese system of financing, manufacturing, distribution, education, health care and pollution control. Some South-east Asian countries have even adopted Japanese-style police and military institutions; others have attempted to hire Japanese forces to provide internal security at a time of rapid socioeconomic change.[7] This suggests that views in Asia are changing from what they were 30 or 40 years ago.

Domestic impediments to a more active role in world affairs

The increasing demands for Japan to assume more global responsibilities, in conjunction with the international and domestic opposition to such steps, has led Japanese policy to zigzag in a manner frequently characterized as 'two steps forward and one step backward'. In the words of Ichiro Ozawa, the former secretary-general of the ruling Liberal Democratic Party, it is 'the Japanese way of leaving everything in an ambiguous state and accumulating established facts through makeshift circumstantial judgments',[8]

For example, Prime Minister Zenko Suzuki visited the United States in May 1982 to meet President Ronald Reagan; they subsequently issued a communiqué in which the word 'alliance' was used. In terms of shouldering more responsibilities, confirmation of an alliance relationship by a Japanese prime minister was 'two steps forward'. However, Suzuki reinterpreted the word 'alliance' and insisted that this did not refer to a military alliance—thus, 'one step backward'. This was later followed by Suzuki's abrupt resignation, Yasuhiro Nakasone's assumption of power and Nakasone's subsequent championing of legislation that paved the way for military co-operation with the United States. This move represented another 'two steps forward'.

Similarly, the Japanese government's response to the Gulf crisis in 1990–91 was also characterized by zigzagging.[9] The Japanese government introduced a bill in the Diet that would have allowed Japan to send Self-Defense Forces abroad for peace-keeping operations, but the bill was killed in late 1990 because of pacifist sentiments at home. Following the Gulf War's end in March 1991, the Japanese government, emboldened by apparent public support for the SDF's mine-sweeping operation in the Gulf, tabled a revised bill, potentially opening the way for the SDF to be sent abroad. However, by failing to accommodate the Democratic Socialist Party demand for revision of the bill—which insisted that the Diet had to give prior approval before the SDF could be sent abroad—the bill was killed. In the spring 1992 session of the Diet, the government tried to advance its position by confining SDF missions to UN peace-keeping operations.

The reasons for such fluctuation in Japanese foreign policy lie in the domestic impediments to an activist policy. First, the pacifist tendencies that grew out of Japan's experiences in World War II are still strong. A particularly powerful domestic approach is 'pacifism in one country', which reasons that even if other states are aggressive, Japan should restrain itself from using force or participating in violent international conflicts.

Second, domestic vested interests oppose taking any steps that might undermine economic prosperity at home. Many believe that the preservation of Japan's economic dynamism is the key to overcoming global economic difficulties.

Third, decision-making in Japan is consensual, and it is undermined by a lack of strong political leadership. Consequently, it is difficult for the Japanese government to move quickly to shoulder new international responsibilities. Instead, the government tends to move incrementally. For example, it might attempt to develop a broader or more flexible interpretation of the Constitution. Thus, a consensus would be sought, which would seek to incorporate as many divergent positions as possible.

Net assessment

The pressures on Japan to assume a more active role in world affairs appear to outweigh the countervailing forces. Japan has the will, the need and the capacity to assume more global responsibilities. It is driven by a tenaciously held aspiration to occupy an honourable place in the world, increasingly dictated by the self-interested need to sustain international stability and economic prosperity. It is also likely to enjoy high savings rates and increasing technological accomplishment for some time. Thus, as long as Japan does not deviate substantially in its positions from the international community as a whole, the United States and other leading powers will, with but limited reservations, continue to prod Japan to do more. If the world economy avoids the beggar-thy-neighbour policies of the 1930s, economic interdependence will deepen. This, in turn, will strengthen Japan's overall international position.

Naturally, Japan's historical legacy, its weakly articulated vision of its international role and its feeble political leadership will prevent it from taking up some responsibilities with vigour. These, however, are constraints that Japan will have to live with for the foreseeable future.

Japan's role in international economic affairs

In examining Japan's role in international economic affairs, one has to consider both unilateral actions, such as economic aid, and multilateral activities in institutions such as the Group of Seven (G–7) and the World Bank.

The argument of 'yen for development' has been made by many and is fairly well accepted by Japan.[10] Acting within the financial constraints imposed by savings rates, energy and food needs, demographic structure and other factors, Japan's role in aiding development is bound to constitute a major pillar in its approach to shouldering global responsibilities.

Japan's financial contributions to Third World economic development, human and social needs and environmental protection are expected to be increasingly aimed towards Africa, South Asia and the Middle East, compared with previous support, which was largely concentrated on East and Southeast Asia. Staggering amounts of debt accumulated by countries such as Brazil and Mexico have also drawn Japanese banking interests to Latin America. In the 1980s, Japanese banks increasingly helped compensate for the difficulties associated with bad debts. In the Pacific, Japan has been encouraging both recipient and donor countries alike to consider not only what is essential for manufacturing and infrastructure development, but also the needs associated with environmental protection and social and political stability. Thus, Japan's role has become much more complex and wide-ranging in the Asian Pacific.

The sudden disappearance of command economies in many Eurasian countries has also expanded Japan's role. Prime Minister Toshiki Kaifu's pledge to aid East European countries in January 1990 was the first of its kind. The Japanese government's recent emergency aid to Mongolia to facilitate the transition to a market economy is another. Most recently, emergency aid was given to the Commonwealth of Independent States. In addition, a number of plans are being drawn up in Japan to help the CIS— especially the Russian Republic—move away from its tightly regulated economy. In light of the growing mood of reconciliation between the Russian Republic and Japan after the August 1991 abortive *coup d'état* in Moscow, these plans could become quite extensive, at least in the long term. Aiding the CIS has been made particularly attractive because of increasing needs by Japan for energy and other resources still to be exploited in Siberia, the Far East and Central Asia. In addition, there has been a steadily growing geographical division of labour among the European Community (Moscow and St Petersburg), the United States (the vast industrial area surrounding the Urals) and Japan (the vast Siberia, the Far East and Central Asia).[11]

The eagerness of North Korea to bring in Japanese capital and technology to make itself more competitive *vis-à-vis* South Korea has reinforced the expectation that Japan would help North Korea so that, should there be a sudden reunification of the two Koreas, South Korea would not be bankrupted by the heavy burden of absorbing North Korea.

Of course, Japan's contributions to the execution of the Gulf War included a large transfer of funds to the United States. Due in part to Japan's Gulf War contributions, the US current account deficit decreased from $92.1 billion in 1990 to $8.6 billion in 1991.[12]

Japan's unilateral actions increasingly include the dissemination of the 'Japanese development model'. Many would like to draw on this model and the Japanese development experience. The latest to import the Japanese model is Peru, under President Alberto Fujimori. Some of Japan's East and South-east Asian neighbours (for example, China and Malaysia) and former socialist countries (such as Hungary) find it relevant to their own development.

Japan's role in multilateral economic activities is no less important. Japan's multilateral activities take place in such international institutions as the IMF, the World Bank, the Inter-American Development Bank, the Asian Development Bank, the OECD, the Bank for International Settlement (BIS), the G–7, the European Bank for Reconstruction and Development and the Post-Ministers' Conference of the Association of South-east

Asian Nations (ASEAN). Japan makes a significant contribution in two areas of multilateral activities: surveillance and systems design.

In this context, surveillance is the monitoring of data pertaining to global management and to the improvement of indicators and measurement for such monitoring. Japan's surveillance activities involve wide-ranging policy areas, detailing economic, technological and social activities.[13] These contributions have been quite robust, and Japanese technical expertise has had considerable impact on organizations such as the OECD and Asian-Pacific Economic Co-operation (APEC). Befitting its status as an economic superpower, Japan has moved ahead steadily in consolidating economic surveillance, in part because organizations such as the IMF and World Bank have become less vigorous in this task.

Systems design includes envisioning, conceptualizing and institutionalizing devices and mechanisms for global management. Requests for such a role have been increasingly heard from within and outside Japan. The need for systems design covers virtually all major fields, including manufacturing (for example, the Intelligent Manufacturing System, a system of jointly constructing and utilizing manufacturing technologies), environmental protection (for example, a system of controlling carbon dioxide emissions around the globe), administrative institutions (for example, a system of recruiting and training bureaucrats) and economic development (for example, a system of state-led, yet market-based, economies, much like Japan's in the 1950s and 1960s).[14]

The latest Japanese development in systems design can be found in the way in which US-led World Bank lending strategies were called into question by World Bank Executive Director Masaki Shiratori, who pushed successfully for the publication of a controversial study on the industrial strategies of South Korea, Indonesia and India. The study argued that select government intervention can complement market mechanisms and thus promote economic development.[15] If World Bank lending policies change in the direction envisioned by Shiratori, then economic development policy of recipient countries will also change to an enormous extent.

Growing interdependence of finite financial resources force donors like Japan to weigh many different options before arriving at the best portfolio of contributions. This process requires donors to have a much more global outlook and a clearer sense of global citizenship. In other words, the Japanese need to depart from the all-too-often narrowly conceived calculations of national interest. Domestically, the Japanese must rectify and restructure their often opaque system to ensure that the Japanese entry into global systems design is more apparent and acceptable to the rest of the global community. Japan's role in envisioning, conceptualizing and designing global systems in the future is bound to grow when the Japanese are convinced of such needs.

Japan's role in international security institutions

Japan's role in international security is an area that creates controversy, as the attendant phrases 'cheque-book diplomacy' and 'revival of militarism' imply. However, Japan's role in international security has begun to take shape steadily, albeit slowly. Aside from bilateral regimes and devices such as the Japan-US Security Treaty and the Japan-Republic of Korea Basic Treaty, which are not covered here, the five most important institutions for Japanese security are the UN, NATO, CSCE, the G–7 and the Post-Ministers' Conference of ASEAN. As long as Japan's role is to consolidate global peace and development, its role in relation to these five institutions must be discussed, even if one has difficulties envisioning how this might unfold. The Japanese government has several concerns regarding the United Nations: deletion of the 'enemies' clause in the UN Charter, accession to permanent membership on the Security Council, participation of Japan's SDF in the UN peace-keeping forces and monitoring of arms transfers. The Japanese government also wants to enhance its current 'observership' status in the CSCE and in NATO. The Japanese government wants to see the G–7 raise several global issues, including security, as part of their agenda for discussion and co-operation. Finally, the Japanese government would like to see the Post-Ministers' Conference of ASEAN take up regional security issues.

Japanese participation in the UN

The United Nations, an organization established by the major victors of World War II, originally excluded Japan as a defeated country. It was not until 1956 that Japan was able to become a member, and today Japan still lives with the 'enemies' article (Article 107) of the UN Charter. Although the three original 'enemies' of the UN—Japan, Germany and Italy—make financial contributions that together match that of the United States—some 25 per cent—none of these countries is represented on a permanent basis on the Security Council. Italy has recently proposed that the 'enemies' clause be deleted from the UN Charter. Japanese Prime Minister Kiichi Miyazawa, too, has expressed Japan's long-term desire to enhance its representation, albeit in a characteristically vague expression in a speech at a UN Security Council meeting engineered by British Prime Minister John Major.

Because of the torrent of resistance likely to face Japan when it moves onto the world stage, especially in the political and military arenas, the Japanese government prefers to move slowly. Even though permanent membership on the Security Council is one of the Japanese government's goals, the time is not yet perceived to be ripe for both the current permanent members and non-members, particularly for Japan itself, to move boldly in this direction. Japan would have difficulties fully abiding by a number of key clauses of the UN Charter that pertain to political and military roles, particularly those that apply to permanent members. A still-influential interpretation of Japan's Constitution forbids Japan from using military force for the resolution of international disputes. However, the special deliberative council of the ruling party has recently put forward a document asserting that the SDF's participation in the UN forces (as distinguished from UN peace-keeping operations) is fully constitutional.

Two bills, which were not addressed in the autumn session of 1991, have much to do with this point. If the interpretation of the Cabinet Legislative Bureau is accepted, these bills would allow Japan's SDF to participate as part of UN peace-keeping forces and would allow Japanese emergency relief forces to work on world disasters. These would clearly be two steps forward.

In autumn 1991, the two bills met with fierce opposition by some in the ruling party (which opposed the SDF's participation in the UN peace-keeping forces, if not the UN peace-keeping operations) and by the small opposition party, the Democratic Socialist Party, which demanded the Diet's prior approval before sending the SDF to those missions. Perhaps recognizing the lack of wisdom in skirting the well-established practice of consensus formation, Foreign Minister Michio Watanabe has been hinting of late about a 'moderated' version of the two bills, clearly eyeing the spring 1992 Diet session.

Aside from the zigzagging domestic legislative process, reinforced by the scandals of the ruling Liberal Democratic Party (LDP), international policies have been steadily shaped in favour of greater Japanese contributions. Cambodia is one example. Yasushi Akashi has been made head of the UN Transitional Authority in Cambodia (UNTAC), and the UN High Commissioner for Refugees is Sadako Ogata; both appointments are widely regarded as conducive to greater Japanese financial (and other) contributions to the United Nations. Domestically, the latest changes in the SDF's officers' assignments suggest the SDF's preparedness to meet the likely contingency of being sent to join peace-keeping and other types of operations in Cambodia, and possibly elsewhere.[16]

Permanent membership on the Security Council will be no less difficult. Japan was not able to be elected as a non-permanent member in 1978, was barely able to get elected in 1986 and got elected with a handsome vote only in 1991. The permanent membership issue was raised in 1990 at a meeting between Mikhail Gorbachev and Helmut Kohl when the Treaty on German Reunification was concluded. At that meeting, Gorbachev suggested that

Germany become a permanent member of the Security Council. Reacting to this conversation, Italian Foreign Minister Gianni de Michelis suggested that the two West European members—Britain and France—be replaced by the EC and Japan, with the EC participant rotating among the four major EC members: Germany, Britain, France and Italy. Although the Japanese government has not made any comment on these events, its position is in stark contrast to Germany's. Germany has repeatedly expressed a lack of interest in seeking permanent membership on the Security Council, if only for tactical reasons.

One positive step the Japanese government has taken in relation to UN participation is to propose that the UN pass a resolution whereby all member countries register all arms transfers with the United Nations. Although the proposal does not go very far, it reflects Japan's concern about arms proliferation and takes a positive step towards conflict management. Although arms control expertise in Japan needs further development, Japanese technical expertise in monitoring and surveillance urges favourably for such a role for Japan.[17]

Japan's relations with NATO

Japan's interest in improving its observership status in NATO is somewhat different from its interest in the UN. The steady development of the notion of international security or co-operative security, which has developed extensively in the context of US-Soviet disarmament negotiations, has been a major factor driving Japanese interests. This has two related components. One is that the United States and the former Soviet Union, the two major nuclear superpowers, have had a strong interest in promoting steady and stable arms reductions, along with joint research and development, manufacturing and monitoring of military weapons. Japan, a US ally, feels that it should be kept informed of developments in this area to a greater extent than has been the case in the past. Indeed, Japan feels that it should be kept abreast of developments to the extent to which NATO members are informed. The second component is that, as an ally of the United States, Japan feels that it cannot help but be part of the broader US-led international security coalition, which includes NATO and the Republic of Korea (ROK). Bilateral arrangements function well with respect to US-Japan and Japan-ROK security consultations. Regarding NATO, however, no such forum existed until 1991, when Japan's observership in NATO began. Today, Japan's participation is still nominal, and much remains to be done if Japan is to take up global security responsibilities in the future. Exposure to regular meetings of NATO and to NATO-sponsored seminars and conferences would provide an impetus for Japan to provide training for more personnel in the realm of international security—one precondition for Japan's ability to monitor arms transfers and arms control actions.

Japan's interest in CSCE

Japan's interest in the CSCE, although overlapping its interest in NATO, does have somewhat different origins. In Japan, there is apprehension that Europe may evolve independently, possibly leaving Japan outside its consideration. With the end of the Cold War, the notion of Europe has clearly changed. According to US Secretary of State James Baker, Europe now extends 'from Vancouver to Vladivostok'. This suggests that emphasis is being given to a 'greater Europe', particularly in regard to the CSCE, perhaps because of the tendency on the European continent to think more narrowly. Although Baker's statement did not arouse a strong negative reaction in Japan, the fact that Japan is the only major developed country excluded from the CSCE or from Baker's notion of a greater Europe is disturbing to some Japanese.

The recently concluded agreement between Japan and the European Community on establishing regular consultative mechanisms underlines the same sort of apprehension. In addition, the CSCE has introduced new criteria for judging societal behaviour. Human rights and arms control are two international relations criteria that have not been particularly familiar to the Japanese government; until recently, the government had favoured more traditional concepts of relations between sovereign states.

Japan and the G-7

Although having started as a loose organization through which advanced countries could consult and co-ordinate their policies on global, regional and national economic issues, by 1991, the G-7 had become a global custodian for many international security issues. Its 1991 declaration on arms control with respect to nuclear weapons, proliferation, arms production and trade is a major step forward, particularly for Japan, because the G-7 represents an international institution in which Japan has been anchored for some time. The Japanese government would like to see the G-7 continue its work in the security area.

Japan and ASEAN

Although ASEAN functions largely as a regional organization, the Post-Ministers' Conference of ASEAN includes non-members such as the United States, Japan, South Korea and Australia. Although started as an anti-communist alignment of Asian nations, since the demise of the Cold War, ASEAN has developed into a more all-encompassing institution, with emphasis given to free trade and regional security.

The East Asian Economic Grouping proposal by Prime Minister Mahathir Mohamad of Malaysia has sought to develop an East Asian Free Trade Area. This then resulted in a pronouncement by the Post-Ministers' Conference about regional security. ASEAN has long been regarded largely as a mouthpiece, taking little significant action, and, since that pronouncement, ASEAN has manifested its fissiparity in developing jointly executable ideas on regional security. Yet, to Japan, which has long been concerned about regional security, as the United States steadily reduces its military presence in the region, ASEAN's initiatives present significant value as a local initiative. Japan cannot envisage regional security arrangements that are not driven by regional powers. Because of Japan's historical debts, its economic preponderance and the potential rivalry with the United States, it feels it must be deferential to regional preferences and pursue joint activities wherever possible.

Conclusion

In sum, as far as international security policy is concerned, more time is needed for the Japanese to articulate their thoughts, given the large-scale structural transition taking place around the globe and Japan's traditional piecemeal adaptation to change. At present, Japan's interests derive largely from its 'search for an honourable place in the world community', from its apprehension of being isolated and from its genuine desire to make positive contributions to international security.

Those who complain that Japan's international efforts have been half-hearted should keep in mind that Japan has been a global power for only two decades. Another constraint has been that many in Japan worry about the future: an aging population and declining savings rates could lead to a deterioration in Japan's international position some time after the turn of this century. It is not surprising, therefore, that Japanese policy has been tentative in the past. In some respects, this might well continue into the future.

Overall, though, Japan's readiness to play a more active role in international affairs is growing. This should be encouraged as long as Japan's policies are compatible with those of the international community and Japan's initiatives are, by and large, undertaken in conjunction with multilateral ventures. Japan appears to be ready, willing and quite able to shoulder more global responsibilities. In all probability, therefore, Japan's contributions will steadily rise in tandem with the increase in the global demand for them and the rise in Japan's own capacity to supply them. As time goes by, Japan's international role is certain to broaden and deepen.

Acknowledgement

The author is grateful to Koreshige Anami, Takoshi Isayama, Kohel, Yo Takeuchi and Kyoji Janagisawa for taking the time to answer his questions. Naturally, they bear no responsibility for the arguments expressed.

Notes

1. Sadako Ogata, 'Shifting power relations in the multilateral development banks', *Journal of International Studies*, no. 22, January 1989, pp. 1–25.
2. Kuriyama Takakazu, 'New directions for Japanese foreign policy in the changing world of the 1990s', *Gaiko Forum*, no. 20, May 1990, pp. 12–22.
3. See Ministry of Industrial Trade and Industry, *White Paper* (Tokyo: Government Printing Office, 1991).
4. See Barry Buzan,'Japan's future: old history versus new roles', *International Affairs*, vol. 64, no. 4, Autumn 1988, pp. 557–73.
5. In 1946, 33.9 per cent of the UN's budget came from the United States, 0 per cent from Japan, 6.6 per cent from France, 12 per cent from Britain and 6.3 per cent from China. In 1968, 31.6 per cent came from the United States, 3.8 per cent from Japan, 14.6 per cent from the Soviet Union, 0 per cent from West Germany, 6 per cent from France, 6.6 per cent from Britain and 4 per cent from China. In 1989–90, 25 per cent came from the United States, 11.4 per cent from Japan, 10 per cent from the Soviet Union, 8.1 per cent from West Germany, 6.3 per cent from France, 4.9 per cent from Britain and 0.8 per cent from China. See Ministry of Foreign Affairs, *The UN and Japan* (Tokyo: Government Printing Office, May 1990), p. 11.
6. Patrick E. Tyler, 'Pentagon's new world order: US to reign supreme', *International Herald Tribune*, 9 March 1992, pp. 1–2.

7. Personal communication with Atsushi Shimokobe, president of the National Institute for Research Advancement, 24 September 1991.

8. Quoted in 'Ozawa heads new committee', *Liberal Star*, 15 June 1991, p. 2.

9. Takashi Inoguchi, 'Japan's response to the Gulf War: an analytic overview', *Journal of Japanese Studies*, vol. 17, no. 2, Summer 1991, pp. 257–73.

10. Shafiqul Islam, ed., *Yen for Development* (New York: Council on Foreign Relations, 1990).

11. The Japanese government is now thinking of providing official development assistance to the Central Asian republics.

12. 'US current account deficit greatly improved to 8.6 billion dollars for 1991', *Mainichi shimbun* (evening edition), 18 March 1992, p. 1.

13. Included in Japan's surveillance are monetary policies, commodity prices, exchange rates, economic growth rates, unemployment figures, energy demand and supply rates, climatic changes, environmental deterioration, population and migration statistics, details on criminals and terrorists, literacy rates, arms production and trade, telecommunications and airline networks, transportation data, depletable resources, health and hygiene, scientific and technological developments and income distribution. Thus far, Japan has not done much monitoring of civil liberties, political freedom or human rights.

14. See 'Training customs officials from Asian countries', *Nihon keizai shimbun*, 25 August 1991, p. 3; 'Japan extends co-operation in environmental protection', *Nihon keizai shimbun*, 23 September 1991, p. 9; Okita Saburo, 'Contributions should be based on Japanese experiences', *Asahi shimbun* (evening edition), 19 August 1991, p. 3.

15. Steven Brull, 'Japan wants strings on aid', *International Herald Tribune*, 9 March 1992, pp. 9, 11; Susumu Awanohara, 'Question of faith', *Far Eastern Economic Review*, 12 March 1992, p. 49.

16. 'SDF personnel changes', *Asahi shimbun* (evening edition), 10 March 1992, p. 2.

17. 'Consolidating the pool of arms control experts', *Nihon keizai shimbun*, 1 October 1991, p. 31.

Part IV:
Two historical appreciations

8

Asia and the Pacific since 1945: a Japanese perspective

Looked at from the vantage point of the late 1980s, the history of the countries of the Asia-Pacific region evokes two major images: One is that of war devastation and struggles for national development; the other is that of decolonization overshadowed by the cold war and the emergence of the region during a slow decline of what may be called 'Pax Americana'. The Asia-Pacific region has experienced polar extremes—from devastation to development, from humiliation to self-confidence—in a period of little more than 40 years since World War II. What is most striking about this region is the tenacity and vigor with which its peoples rebound from adversity.

War and devastation

War has been a recurrent theme in the history of the Asia-Pacific region.[1] In China alone more than 10 million people were killed during the war with the Japanese in the years 1937–45, and about 20 million were killed during the political turmoil of the Chinese Cultural Revolution of 1966–76.[2] One can give no less awesome figures for the Korean War and the Vietnam War, as well as for the suppression of Communists in Indonesia after 1965 and the massacre in Cambodia between 1975 and 1979. It is not an exaggeration to say that the Asia-Pacific region has been one of the most conflict ridden during the 20th century.

The colonization drives of the Western powers, and later of Japan, swept across the region in the 19th and 20th centuries. Colonization left few countries unscathed.[3] China was half colonized, with Hong Kong and Macao, Taiwan, Manchuria and Mongolia, Tibet and Sinkiang coming under the direct control or 'spheres of influence' of the colonial powers. Korea was colonized by Japan; Vietnam, Laos and Cambodia by France; and Burma (now Myanmar) and Malaya by Great Britain. Indonesia was colonized by the Netherlands; the Philippines first by Spain and later by the

United States; and various islands in the Pacific by France, Britain, Germany, Japan, and the United States.

Colonization had three major consequences. First, it robbed people of self-confidence. At the same time, it planted the seeds of a deep sense of national pride, which was to manifest itself dramatically in the movement for independence. Second, it integrated the economy with that of the colonial powers. The incorporation of colonial economies with the world economy dramatically increased production and population. This effect is sometimes called the 'modernizing' influence. At the same time, it skewed and distorted the local economy in many ways, subsequently slowing down self-sustained economic development. Third, it bred war among the colonial powers themselves. The consequences were devastating. So humiliated were those elites who sided with the colonial powers that their political foundation became tenuous and their subsequent political development was detoured. Most directly, war made it plain that the destinies of the colonized were at the mercy of the colonial powers and that the only alternative was national independence. With the region a battlefield for colonial powers and economic mobilization for war making life more miserable, it appeared foolhardy for local elites to cooperate with these powers. Thus, in many ways, World War II prepared the ground for most of the countries of Asia and the Pacific to start anew in its aftermath.

There was virtually no place that was unaffected by war. Throughout China, war permeated the lives of ordinary people for more than eight years. Korea and Manchuria were transformed into a base of military production for the Japanese war machine. Taiwan became the supply base of food for the Japanese.[4] The Philippines was a battlefield between the Japanese and the Americans. So, too, were many Pacific islands. The forced export of food from Vietnam brought about acute food shortages, which gave momentum to the Communists to assume the leadership in peasant-led uprisings. Burma was a battlefield between the Japanese and the British, as were Malaya and Singapore, and Indonesia was a battlefield between the Japanese and the Dutch.

When the war was finally over, virtually no one could predict what would happen. For instance, as late as the mid-1950s an American mission made a recommendation that the scheme for bullet trains between Tokyo and Osaka was unrealistic. It was only about a dozen years later that this 'unrealistic' plan was realized. This presaged the rapid recovery and steady development of Japan, and later the region as a whole. Also, in 1945 it was unthinkable that Communist countries would go to war with each other.[5] As late as the early 1960s, when the Sino-Soviet ideological conflict came to the surface, many people refused to admit that the two countries were really at odds with each other. Yet war was waged in 1969 between China and the

Soviet Union, and in 1979 between Cambodia and Vietman and between China and Vietnam. These wars underlined the fluidity of power realignments in the region. Furthermore, it was inconceivable that South Korea would propose to the United States that it should have independent military command, which was precisely the case in 1987 during the talks between the then ruling party chairman Roh Tae Woo and US President Ronald Reagan. This seems to signify the growing self-confidence of South Korea and perhaps the region as a whole in the late 1980s. Thus, the rapidity and steadiness of economic recovery and development, the fluidity and uncertainty of power configuration, and the growing self-confidence seem to capture the basic tone of the history of the Asia-Pacific region since 1945.

The Asia-Pacific region has achieved a great deal since 1945. However, it was accomplished despite almost insurmountable adversities and achieved at incalculable cost.

Decolonization and the cold war

The impact of World War II on the peoples of the Asia-Pacific region was twofold. First, it set them free from colonial powers to chart their own course—but at their own risk. Second, it introduced a new dimension of international politics to the newly emerging countries of the region. Decolonization in the aftermath of war forced people to organize themselves and to manage their own politics and economics. Prior to independence, the influence of world economic and political forces was through the filter of the colonial powers. After independence, the newly independent countries had to cope with these forces directly. One of the most important new forces was that of the cold war between the United States and the Soviet Union, the two major victors of World War II.[6]

The process of decolonization took a number of years. Roughly by the end of the 1950s most countries had achieved independence, with some exceptions such as Singapore, Brunei, Hong Kong, Papua New Guinea and many in the Pacific. The Asia-Pacific countries were able to accelerate their independence due to war. Especially important in this respect were the humiliation of colonial powers at the hands of the Japanese and the dominance of the US liberating spirit after World War II. There are important exceptions, however. Formerly British Brunei became independent only in 1985, while British Hong Kong is destined to return to Chinese sovereignty in 1997. French New Caledonia, among others in the Pacific, has been refused independence. From north to south in this region, the situation is as follows.

First, China was independent but full sovereignty was restored to a number of former colonies including Manchuria and Taiwan.[7] Civil war between the Communists and the Nationalists erupted soon after World War II. The victory of the Communists was followed half a year later by the outbreak of the Korean War, which was to bring China into the conflict. Thus China was engaged in a succession of wars before and after its revolution—1937-45, 1946-49 and 1950-53. The adversities that confronted the Chinese Communists during these years, especially in 1949-50, made it natural for them to 'lean to one side', that of the Soviet Union. The Sino-Soviet alliance of 1950 had enormous consequences for the Chinese Communists, affecting the way they have run their government and economy ever since. It also contributed to the polarization of international politics in the region. Although the alliance lasted 30 years, at least in form, its spirit virtually evaporated 10 years after the conclusion of the treaty. One of the Chinese complaints was the manner in which the Soviet Union, reminiscent of colonial powers, dealt with China on such matters as the utilization of manufacturing and mining facilities, ports and railways in China's northeastern region, which had been a Japanese colony. Taiwan had been controlled by the Nationalists since 1945, but its fate changed by their defeat on the mainland in 1949. From then on Taiwan became overwhelmingly dependent on the protection offered by the United States. It is ironic that the Nationalists, whose cause célèbre was the redemption of sovereignty and national pride lost since the late 19th century, became so tightly subordinated to the will and whim of the United States. It must be noted, however, that Mao Zedong appreciated Chiang Kai-shek's refusal to allow foreign armies on the soil of Taiwan. China, while waiting for the return of Hong Kong, along with Macao has been trying to 'unite' with Taiwan under the 'one country—two systems' idea.

Second, Korea was divided in 1945 by the United States and the Soviet Union in terms of their respective spheres of influence.[8] The division was further given institutional basis in 1948 when the Republic of Korea in the south and the Democratic People's Republic of Korea in the north were established under the aegis of their patrons. Like China and Taiwan, South and North Korea were placed in an ironic situation, in which vehemently nationalistic regimes were subordinated largely to the logic of the two major powers. Even before the advent of the Japanese defeat, Korean nationalists and Communists alike had been fighting to achieve independence and power. Their efforts continued after 1945. The Communists were especially active in South Korea, as the postwar economic, social and political conditions there were conducive to rebellion and revolution. Local rebellions erupted intermittently, and the Communists in the north and the south saw them as a golden opportunity, especially when the United States hinted that it would not defend South Korea against the Communists' onslaught—which in fact took place later that year. The Korean War that ensued reinforced the cold war structure in the region as China stood on the side of the North Koreans in opposition to the American-led forces allied with the South Koreans.

The consequence of the Korean war on both Koreas was immense. After decolonization the fate of both Koreas was tightly linked to their neighboring powers, the United States, the Soviet Union and China. Because of the cold war, the course of Korea's development since then has been constrained. Even after these neighboring powers reached accord and accommodation with each other, both Koreas continued to find it difficult to do what both Germanys did after the 1961 construction of the Berlin Wall.

Third, Japan was incorporated into the cold war structure, relinquishing the status of a vanquished and occupied power.[9] The outbreak of the Korean War precipitated the conclusion of the peace treaty between Japan and the Allied powers (except the Soviet Union) and the US-Japanese security treaty. The United States reversed its policy of punishing Japan to one of creating a strong Japan—sans military power—in order to cope with Communist threats in the Asia-Pacific region. An exception to Japan's independence was Okinawa. The Ryukyu Islands, which accommodate large US military bases, were kept outside the control of Japan, an arrangement that lasted until 1972. Since then the US bases in Japan, including those in Okinawa, have been indispensable to the United States. The US forces in Japan since the end of the Vietnam War have been the largest in the entire region.

In the late 1940s and early 1950s the United States concluded security treaties whereby the US unilateral security umbrella was accorded to such countries as the Philippines, South Korea, Taiwan, South Vietnam and Thailand, thus forming the US-led cold war blockade against communism in the Asia-Pacific region.[10] Taiwan, however, did not allow US forces to be stationed there. Furthermore, in the wake of the rapprochement between the United States and China, in 1971, relations with the United States underwent a qualitative change. Yet the US commitment to deter China from 'repatriating' Taiwan militarily has kept Taiwan where it is. With the United States having downgraded its China connection in its dealings with the Soviet Union around 1981–82, Taiwan has considerably revived its US ties. South Vietnam was liberated by North Vietnam in 1975; subsequently, Vietnam has allowed the Soviet Union to make use of air bases and naval facilities. In part to counter these moves, the United States has been strengthening its maritime strategy in the Asia-Pacific region. Thailand relinquished the US bases in 1975 in response to widespread demands. An antimilitary protest and democratization movement in that year proclaimed itself vehemently against the stationing of the US bases there. In the 1980s,

however, Thai-US military cooperation was greatly enhanced as the United
States saw the need to strengthen Thai defense capability against Soviet-
aided Vietnam. For years the Philippines has been negotiating the terms of
retaining US bases. But the intensified activities of the New People's Army,
the Philippine Communist party's military wing, apparently prompted the
United States to encourage the anti-Marcos forces to take power in February
1986. The Aquino government is no less insistent on getting better terms
vis-à-vis the US bases. Irrespective of the bargains between the Philippines
and the United States on the US bases, the New People's Army has been
increasing its strength steadily, with the future of the Subic Bay and Clark
air bases somewhat uncertain. In South Korea the demand for an independent
military command reflects the growing nationalism and self-confidence of
the South Koreans.

All this does not mean that Japan alone lacks groups opposed to the
stationing of the US forces on domestic soil. There have been, and are, such
forces in Japan. But it is clear that Japan has been the consistent and reliable
core of the US-led cold war alignment in the Asia-Pacific region. It should
be mentioned, however, that other allies have been more directly involved
in cold war-related conflicts, and have thus shouldered more burdens and
made greater sacrifices than Japan. South Korea fought one of the largest-
scale conventional wars since 1945; even now its vigilance has not been lost
concerning North Korea. Taiwan has retained until recently a watchful posture
toward China, spending enormous sums for military preparedness. South
Vietnam collapsed after having fought a war of attrition for so many years.
Thailand has long been a frontline state while Vietnam, Cambodia and
Laos were engaged in a war against communism, and since 1975 it has been
a neighboring state to Communist Cambodia under the Khmer Rouge and
later the pro-Vietnamese Heng Samrin government. The Philippines has
been in intermittent confrontation with communist forces for years.

The crux of the problem is that the process of decolonization and the
incorporation into the cold war structure of these newly independent
countries coincided, and thus the task of nation building and development
was made more complex. This combination had both positive and negative
effects from the viewpoint of the newly independent countries. Positively,
they could obtain economic assistance in large amounts at a time when
resource scarcity posed a serious constraint on their nation-building task. In
a similar vein, they could rely on the generosity and largesse of the United
States in terms of their access to the US market, while maintaining their own
protectionism. Also, they could arm themselves against external Communist
foes and domestic antagonists, Communist or otherwise. Without foreign
backing many of them, unable to cope with vast demands from the masses
below, could not have consolidated their political-economic-military foun-

dations in the relatively short span of time after independence.[11] Negatively, the fact that these newly independent nations were allied with foreign powers made them appear as pawns in many ways, thus sometimes undermining the very basis of their legitimacy. That was exactly the fate the government of South Vietnam faced. Also, the facile dependence on foreign aid tended to weaken self-reliant efforts at widening and consolidating their power bases. That has been the tendency of the government of the Philippines for years, from the time of Roxas and Magsaysay through Marcos and Aquino. In other words, all the counties in the Asia-Pacific region had to cope with the long and difficult transition from colonialism and occupation to independence and national development in the shadow of the cold war structure, which sometimes took on the character of neocolonialism, in both its capitalist and communist variants.[12]

It has already been mentioned that China felt it was unjustifiably subjected to the demands and pressures of the Soviet Union during the decade of their alliance. North Korea perhaps felt that these two Communist brothers were not sufficiently supportive of North Korea at the critical time of the fledgling revolutionary state in 1950-53. Similarly, it felt that they were not generous enough thereafter in the difficult process of socialist construction on the ruins of devastation, which was to lead North Korea to develop its overtly nationalistic autarkic strategy of *juche*. North Vietnam apparently felt that the two big brothers did not appreciate the commitment and sacrifice of a fledgling revolutionary movement-cum-front-line state in the world Communist movement. The feeling of resentment was intense, especially when North Vietnam was forced by them to come to terms with South Vietnam, France and the United States in the form of imposed geographical division in 1954, and when it was not fully supported by them in its execution of the war of liberation in 1965-75.[13] Like the newly independent countries of the non-Communist world, the Communist counterparts experienced the very difficult process of revolutionary struggle and socialist construction at almost the same time. The cold war environment worked both positively and negatively for them. Positively, they could justify their revolutionary struggle and socialist construction in terms of the expansion and consolidation of national liberation and world socialism, thus obtaining support from the Soviet Union and China. Negatively, the alignment with the Communist bloc has tended to invite intervention from the big brothers, which is deemed unjustifiable in light of the spirit of world socialism.

In other countries that are more remote from the cold war frontiers— countries such as Indonesia, Malaysia, Singapore and Papua New Guinea— the road to independence took somewhat different paths. Indonesia had to fight an independence war against the Dutch, becoming independent in 1949, but its drive was further directed at Portuguese Timor (now Indonesian

Timor), Western Borneo (now eastern Malaysia) and western New Guinea
(now Indonesian Irian Jaya). Indonesia's incorporation of Timor and western
New Guinea is sometimes viewed as a new colonialism. Malaya was plagued
by the Communist insurrection led largely by ethnic Chinese Communists,
and had to wait until the threat subsided in the late 1950s. Papua New
Guinea won independence from Australia in 1975, while western New
Guinea was incorporated into Indonesia by plebiscite in 1969.

Despite the difficulties of decolonization and the constraints posed by
cold war developments, the Asia-Pacific countries have in fact grown much
more steadily than many expected. They have shown remarkable tenacity
and vigor in pursuing their goals of power and plenty. Even though feeble
and desolate in the aftermath of war and independence, they pursued their
struggle for national development.

Struggles for national development

It has been seen thus far that, placed in the broader context of
decolonization and the cold war, the newly independent countries in the
Asia-Pacific region had to cope with many complex problems in the international arena. Vulnerable to the penetration of international forces, they
were exceedingly fragile in terms of their domestic foundation. These
countries were not sufficiently able to monopolize allegiance from the populace, since they were still competing with many social forces that remained
resistant to centralized control. National identity was not strong enough to
cement the societies as nations. Thus, these countries were too often unable
to create sufficiently robust infrastructures for taxation and administration
of popular public policies. The ability of these countries to penetrate society
was shallow at best, and too often was dependent on the protection and
largesse of the major powers.

First, the problem of national identity was difficult to resolve in many
newly emerging countries, largely because, under colonialism, a sense of
being a part of a distinctive and proud nation was curtailed and budding
nationalism was repressed. In many islands in Indonesia it was difficult,
first, to conceive that one was an Indonesian when one did not understand
the national language and when state officials were not normally present. It
was ironic that the war of independence against the Dutch, as well as the
confrontation with major and neighboring powers, and territorial expansion
into Timor and western New Guinea, was one of the most instrumental
forces to enhance national identity, along with the diffusion of the national
standard language. External confrontation and expansion were the primary
forces fostering nationalism.

The colonial legacy of arbitrary political division and a deliberate policy of playing one ethnic group against another made this problem all the more difficult for the newly emerging countries to resolve. In Malaya, the Malays, Chinese and Indians were the three largest ethnic groups, with a fairly clear division of labor maintained by the British colonialists. The Malays worked in the countryside, the Chinese in commerce, and the Indians in mining and on plantations. The Malay predominance in politics after independence further forced the other ethnic groups to work in commercial activities. National identity was slow to develop among them when the preferential policy was adopted by the Malay-dominated government. Ethnic antagonism was difficult to hide and sometimes manifested itself in violent forms.[14]

Even where national identity did not pose a grave problem, the government was not able to enjoy wide acceptance of its legitimacy. Similarly, the rule of the government was not perceived as working for public purposes. South Vietnam was a good example. In Vietnam independence was not realized in the 1945 settlement. France came back shortly after the end of World War II, and war ensued between the Communists and the anti-Communists. The latter were backed by France and subsequently by the United States. The Geneva agreement of 1954 temporarily stopped the colonial-civil war, but the step-up of civil war in 1960 led to large-scale US intervention by 1964. The 1973 armistice agreement was followed by the 1975 liberation of South Vietnam. During the period 1945–75 the government was unable to enjoy strong support from the populace. The Communist challenge reinforced the persistence of personalistic authoritarianism and overdependence on foreign powers. Political participation was severely circumscribed by governmental authoritarianism, which in turn fundamentally limited government penetration into society. Shallow rule gave rise to difficulties of taxation, poverty of public policy and dependence on external forces.

South Korea has shown another contrasting example. National liberation came in 1945, but the ensuing occupation by Soviet and American forces in the north and south, respectively, led to the formation of two republics with different ideological foundations. The sporadic civil war between Communists and anti-Communists became an international war between the countries, backed by foreign powers in 1950 under the shadow of the cold war. After the armistice agreement of 1953 South Korea was plagued by the problem of legitimacy. Its authoritarian government was not so different from that in South Vietnam. But the democratic overthrow of the government in 1960 and the military coup of 1961 significantly changed its orientation.

By the mid-1960s South Korea had embarked on the ambitious task of economic development with the help of four factors. One was the government's orientation, often called 'developmental authoritarianism', whereby freedom and democracy are kept at a minimum for the sake of economic development.[15] In other words, wealth must be accumulated before people are permitted more freedom. The engine of economic development was the presumably enlightened and powerful government showing the 'correct' developmental path for the country. The second factor was the security guarantee by the United States. The third was access to the US and Japanese markets. These markets, having been opened up by the diplomatic normalization with Japan in 1965, were also important in enabling South Korea to import a large bulk of capital goods from Japan and to export its products to the United States. Fourth, although less visible, was the Japanese colonial legacy that had integrated Korea with Japan during the wartime period of the 1930s and 1940s. As the economic performance of South Korea improved, the government was able to steadily consolidate its hold over society. Although its legitimacy had always been questioned to a certain degree because of its military origin, the government's penetration into society was considerable. The record of years of high economic performance and a goal-oriented government seem to be major reasons for the considerable success in this regard.

Legitimacy was not a major problem for the government of Japan.[16] Vanquished in 1945, the country was occupied by foreign powers, the government changed and the emperor was deprived of power. Under the Allied occupation the core of the state bureaucracy retained its prewar power and worked more effectively than before under the new constitution. Despite the temporary prominence of the left in the late 1940s, the occupation reforms led many potentially antigovernment social groups, such as workers and farmers, to support the government in the 1950s and thereafter. The rise of Japan from the ranks of the vanquished to become Asia's first newly industrialized country and finally an economic giant is explained primarily by economic factors. But no less important were favorably international factors, such as the US guarantee of security that led Japan to devote its energy and attention almost exclusively to economic development. The continuously impressive economic performance helped the government to enjoy relatively strong public support over the years.

China was thrown back into a civil war between Communists and anti-Communists shortly after 1945. The Communists had already expanded their influence among Japanese-occupied areas before 1945.[17] The civil war was strongly overshadowed by the cold war. Thereafter China was confronted by the anti-Communist regime on Taiwan with its claim of sovereignty over the mainland. Shortly after the Communist victory in 1949 the Korean War erupted, and late in 1950 China entered the war supporting North Korea. Thus, the Chinese government experienced almost continuous war in the early years of its foundation. This affected Chinese national development significantly. The revolutionary restructuring of the society like the liberation of tenant farmers and the collective ownership of factories, was facilitated by the warlike emergency, as was the monopoly of power by the Communists. In the period 1949–50 legitimacy was basically strong because millions of people were liberated and the Chinese state was able to cope with external threats. However, the revolutionary fervor evaporated and politics of intrigue in Beijing and in the provinces became increasingly evident. Political participation took on the character of political mobilization from above, and the government tended to lose touch with the masses. Cruelty at its most extreme was manifested during the years 1966–76 in the course of the Cultural Revolution. The trials and errors of economic management over the 30 years following liberation, especially during the period 1958–78, turned out to be an immense failure. With the advent of economic reform in 1978, pent-up energy was unleashed in many ways. The basic cynicism of the masses, however, has been and will be difficult to eradicate unless reforms bring tangible results, both economic and political, especially since China's immediate neighbors, including Taiwan, have shown such astonishing achievement for the last 40 years, beginning from a similarly low income level.

The emergence of the Asia-Pacific region

In the midst of the Vietnam War, the Asia-Pacific region did not really exist as an entity. As an extension of the United States it reflected the sphere of influence it achieved during World War II. America's leading position was backed by the preponderant role it played in running the world economy. Despite the 'miracle of Japan' (so dubbed by the *Economist* magazine as early as 1960), the prevalent perception was that Japan was an exception in the region. No one anticipated that The Association of Southeast Asian Nations (ASEAN) and what were later to be called Asia's Newly Industrialized Countries (NICs) would subsequently follow no less remarkable economic development patterns. When the double dust of the Vietnam War and the first oil crisis settled in the mid-1970s, it was clear that the picture had changed drastically.

First, while the United States was exhausted by the Vietnam War, the Watergate scandal, the dollar crisis and the oil crisis, both in terms of political will and economic health if not military might, the Asia-Pacific region prospered in the aftermath of war.[18] The upward turn of the world economy coincided in the 1960s with the emergence of the NICs. It was during this period that they were able to switch from import substitution to export-led industrialization, with open access to the US export market and Japanese capital goods for import. In that direction, Taiwan started off early in the

1960s and South Korea in the mid-1960s. Second, as the first oil crisis hit every country hard, the Asia-Pacific region was particularly affected since most of those countries were not rich in energy resources. But contrary to the expectation of some pessimists, the NICs began to flourish in the post-oil crisis period. They were able to make full use of their comparative advantage as latecomers with low wages, long working hours, fast technological catch-up, intensive capital utilization and good developmental planning. Thus, by the late 1970s, when the NICs joined the redoubtable Japan, which among the industrialized countries was least harmed by the oil crises, the emergence of the Asia-Pacific region was visible and tangible.[19] Third, the international alignment pattern was steadily changing the way in which many political leaders looked at the region. The cold war division began to erode. In 1969 China and the Soviet Union clashed on their common borders. In 1971 the United States and China normalized diplomatic relations. In 1973 the United States and North Vietnam negotiated an armistice agreement. In 1975 Vietnam was unified. In 1978 Japan and China concluded a treaty of peace and friendship. In 1979 the Sino-Soviet treaty of peace and mutual assistance was automatically terminated. Also in 1979 Vietnam occupied Cambodia and China invaded Vietnam, two incidents involving Communist neighbors. These developments complicated, or at least blurred, the image of the traditional cold war antagonism between the Communist and the anti-Communist blocs in the Asia-Pacific region. The picture of Pacific dynamism has become more salient. Though political uncertainties continue, economic vigor has become the foremost feature of the region.[20]

The emergence of the Asia-Pacific region was further consolidated by two movements in the 1980s: One was the increasing integration of the regional economy with the US economy; the other was the tighter strategic integration with the United States of Japan, South Korea and the Philippines, and to a lesser extent Thailand, Taiwan, China and Australia. Economic integration between the US economy and the Asia-Pacific economies has kept a steady pace, with the US trade pattern shifting from the Atlantic to the Pacific in the late 1970s. But the trend broadened in the 1980s. Manufacturing patterns have become truly cross-Pacific, with capital, technology, resources and labor factors all flowing freely across national borders. Trade has thrived, with Japan-United States activity annually registering the largest transoceanic volume and the NICs-United States commerce steadily catching up. International monetary interdependence became extraordinary in the 1980s. The acceleration of capital movements between the United States and Japan in particular was enormous. The economic management of both countries would have been difficult to conceive without fuller coordination between them. Despite often insurmountable problems, the reality of inexorable economic interdependence and penetration resides there. All in all, the phrase 'the Pacific economy' has come to take on an authentic character. Not only Japan and the United States but also the NICs and the ASEAN countries have begun to do more business with each other. Pacific dynamism has also attracted the attention of Communist neighbors, including China, the Soviet Union, Vietnam and North Korea, encouraging economic reforms and the opening to the West.

Strategic integration among the Asia-Pacific countries and the United States has gone forward significantly. The vigorous military buildup of the United States, unprecedented in peacetime, has permeated the northwestern Pacific region. The US maritime strategy, with forward defense and horizontal escalation concepts, has been applied to the region to a considerable degree. Enhanced deterrence efforts along the Asia-Pacific corridor have solidified with an increase in the number of submarine-launched ballistic and cruise missiles. Especially important is US-Japanese defense cooperation, which has deepened with the latter's participation in the US Strategic Defense Initiative program. The US defence umbrella has been very tight vis-à-vis South Korea, Japan and the Philippines; defense cooperation with Thailand and Taiwan has also been strong, although there are no security treaties with the United States. The US defense arrangements with China and Australia, especially the one allowing installation of high-technology equipment for intelligence in the midst of desert areas, are indispensable to the US international security network, given their geographical location. Despite the steps toward complete abolition of land-based intermediate-range nuclear missiles, agreed on in 1987 between the United States and the Soviet Union, competition between the two countries in the northwestern Pacific has intensified.[21]

The emergence and achievement of the Asia-Pacific region merit special attention. In addition to having suffered from colonialism, imperial rivalries and the cold war, many of the region's countries, especially those regarded as dynamic cores, do not enjoy bounteous natural resources. However, as Eric Jones argues in his book *The European Miracle*, this smaller endowment of resources, along with the hardships of disease, hunger and war, may exert a strong drive for power and plenty.[22]

Alternative future scenarios

The history of Asia and the Pacific in the minds of most Japanese has until recently been confined to East and Southeast Asia. South Asia was regarded as relatively unimportant for a number of reasons, including the different trajectories of its history; the absence of international, extraregional war in this area; and its lower rates of growth and lower degree of involvement in world trade. South Asia had attracted Japanese attention mainly for the following reasons: (1) the Japanese role of encouraging nationalists in Burma and India toward independence during World War II; (2) Judge Pal's position in the Far Eastern Tribunal of World War II; (3) Jawaharlal Nehru's role in the nonalignment movement; (4) regional wars among India, Pakistan, China, Sri Lanka and Bangladesh; and (5) Soviet intervention in Afghanistan. It was only in the 1980s that South Asia came to occupy a more than negligible place in the minds of many Japanese. First, the Soviet intervention in Afghanistan brought a sense of strategic need to help the region cope with its difficulties. Second, economic development was expanded noticeably in the region. The fact that many countries neighboring Japan—most notably South Korea, Taiwan, Singapore, Thailand and Malaysia—can no longer supply low-wage manufacturing bases has been pushing Japan to farther peripheral areas, such as the Philippines, China and South Asia. Japan is now the number-one donor of official development assistance to most South Asian countries, including India, Pakistan and Bangladesh. The significance of South Asia has become apparent. In less than a decade it will be covered in any Japanese-written history of the Asia-Pacific region in full depth.

How has the Japanese elite perceived the place of Japan in Asia and the Pacific in the decades since 1945? In that year Japanese self-confidence was completely lost. Japan was discredited in Asia and the Pacific and had no role whatsoever in the region. All efforts were directed at recovery and reconstruction under the benevolent umbrella of the United States. In 1955 the accelerating recovery of their country encouraged the Japanese to announce the end of the postwar era in a white paper of the Economic Planning Agency. Also, Japanese war reparations were under way to a number of East and Southeast Asian countries. With the departure of the occupation forces, the armistice agreement in the Korean peninsula and the inauguration of rapid economic development, Japan's role in Asia and the Pacific was motivated by the combination of the debt of history and economic opportunities in such forms as reparations, foreign aid and export markets.

By 1965 the Japanese elite recovered its self-confidence significantly as Japan's profile expanded in the region. Most noteworthy were increased economic transactions with South Korea and Taiwan. These two former colonies revived their close economic ties with Japan. Also important was Japan's role in the implementation of the US war in Vietnam, a role that was primarily economic, however, as it was during the Korean War. In 1975 Japan and other countries in the region were coping with the oil crisis and the collapse of South Vietnam. Determined to achieve what they called economic security, including assured energy supply when the United States no longer seemed to provide as solid a security umbrella, the Japanese elite started to talk about the Asia-Pacific region in a determined manner. In 1985 Japan's role was redefined as that of a good member of the Western alliance when President Reagan and Prime Minister Nakasone coordinated their policies against the Soviet threat. Japan's role was a supporting one, making up for the reduced role played by the United States in the region— hence the enhanced official development assistance and the enlarged defense perimeter of the Japanese Self-Defense Forces in the western Pacific. Yet the debt of history was felt by the Japanese elite, as the history-textbook controversies and others with South Korea and China demonstrated in the 1980s. At the same time their improved profile in the world has given most Japanese self-confidence and a sense of national pride.

Japan's role in the region is primarily conceived as economic but with increasing security components as well. The Japanese elite have come to acquire a sense of mission through representing the interests and concerns of the regional countries in international forums such as the Organization for Economic Cooperation and Development (OECD) and the Western summits. They have also moved to forge and/or promote regional institutions such as the Pacific Economic Cooperation Council and the Asian Development Bank. This is indicative of their concern for shaping and sharing the benefits of the Pacific dynamism encompassing northern Mexico, the Pacific areas of the United States and Canada, East and South Asia and the South Pacific, as North America and Western Europe appear to be moving toward the formation of regional protectionist blocs. The Japanese defined their role in this respect as shaping a Pacific economic community in an open multilateral form, which would create a zone of prosperity with free trade, and rolling back the protectionist and regionalist trends that might accelerate in other parts of the world.

As to the alternative futures now being articulated by the Japanese elite, the question is: In which direction will the Asia-Pacific region go? Considering the differing way in which the world—and this region—will be organized, there seem to be four major possibilities at the beginning of the 21st century.[23] They are what have been called: (1) Pax Americana Phase II; (2) Pax Ameripponica; (3) Pax Consortis; and (4) Pax Nipponica. Although the focus in this article is on the two leading protagonists in the region, the United States and Japan, the following images should convey the alternatives for the Asia-Pacific region.

Pax Americana Phase II: This image of the future is that of the United States retaining its leading position, making full use of the advantage of being the creator of institutions of post-World War II order and security, after somehow riding out the current difficulties into the 1990s. It is an America experienced in forging the 'balanced', or globalist, view of the Western alliance, and deftly prodding and cajoling allies into an enlightened joint action. Japan's roles in Pax Americana Phase II would not be significantly different from those it now plays.[24] Essentially, they would be economic in nature, the bulk of global security roles being shouldered by the United States. Even if Japan-United States security cooperation is accelerated, this basic division is unlikely to change. Similarly, if Japan increases its security-related assistance to some Third World countries such as Pakistan, Turkey, Papua New Guinea and Honduras, the security leadership of the United States will remain strong. Needless to say, there are those who argue that Japan will in due course start to exert influence by accumulating credit to the United States and recipient countries. Japan's regional roles will be heavily economic. More concretely, Japan will become the vital core of the Pacific growth crescent encompassing three areas: (1) northern Mexico and the Pacific areas of the United States and Canada; (2) Japan; and (3) the NICs, coastal China, the ASEAN countries, and Australia and New Zealand. The incorporation of the second and third economic groups into the extended US economic role would link the United States with the Asia-Pacific economies in a more balanced manner.

Pax Ameripponica: This image of the future focuses on the increasingly steady development and integration of what Robert Gilpin calls the '*nichibei* [Japanese-US] economy'.[25] That is to say, the economies of Japan and the United States will have become one integrated economy of a sort. Since the major external activities of Japan and the United States are found in the Asia-Pacific region, this image is sometimes called the Pax Pacifica.

Japan's roles in this Pax Ameripponica, primarily economic, are not fundamentally different from those envisaged in Pax Americana Phase II. However, as economic power almost inevitably becomes military power Japan would not likely constitute the historic exception of this rule. But the form in which Japan's economic power would translate into military power needs close attention. The techno-economic-strategic cooperation and integration between the United States and Japan could become formidable and of the largest scale in history. The strategic integration of many countries in the region may make it hard to accommodate the Soviet Union within an invigorated structure of US-Japanese dominance, thus consigning it to a far less important status than it has now.

Pax Consortis: The third image portrays a future world of many consortia in which the major protagonists are busily forging coalitions to effectuate policy adjustments and agreements among themselves and no single actor is allowed to dominate the rest.[26] The thrust of this image rests on the pluralistic nature of policy adjustments among interested parties. This is a good contrast to the first image of Pax Americana Phase II, which subtly conveys the desirability or necessity—or even hoped for inevitability—of the 'administrative guidance' by, or 'moral leadership' of, the primus inter pares—that is, the United States. This third image will be favored by many actors in the Asia-Pacific region because of their resentment of America's arrogant behavior, especially when it only grudgingly admits its relative decline.

Japan's roles in the Pax Consortis are essentially two. With the strategic nuclear arsenals increasingly nullified either by the de facto US-Soviet détente process or by a technological breakthrough, Japan's role would be primarily one of quiet economic diplomacy through forging coalitions and shaping policy adjustments among peers. Its secondary role would be to help create a world spared of the need for military solutions. That would include, if possible, the diffusion of an antinuclear defensive system to all the countries, and the extension of massive economic aid tied to cease-fires or peace agreements between belligerents. Japan's primary regional role therein would be that of coordinator-promoter of interests of the Asia-Pacific countries, which have not been fully represented either in the US system or in economic institutions of industrialized countries such as the OECD. It is remarkable that despite the fact that Japan, Taiwan and South Korea have accumulated most of the world's trade surpluses, not one has been adequately represented in world economic institutions. Japan's secondary regional role would be that of moderator, especially in security areas, and might involve relations between South Korea and China or neutral peacekeeping forces in Cambodia and Afghanistan.

Pax Nipponica: This is the world in which Japanese economic power reigns supreme. This image has been most vigorously propagated by those Americans who are concerned about the visible contrast between the relative loss of technological and manufacturing competitiveness of the United States and the concomitant gain of Japan in those terms.[27] As in Pax Consortis at its most effective, strategic nuclear arsenals must be eliminated or the antinuclear defense system perfected before the advent of Pax Nipponica. Without the nullification of nuclear weapons, Japan's leading role in security areas would be minimized, hence the difficulty of a true Pax Nipponica being realized. In this image, Japan's regional roles would coincide with its global roles, as its pre-eminent position would enable it to assume paramount importance in the Asia-Pacific region as well.

The above scenarios do not exhaust all possible alternatives. However, one common theme can be discerned: the increasing centrality of the region in world economic-political development—a view strongly shared by the Japanese elite. In their view, the future of the Asia-Pacific region—

and indeed the rest of the world as well—seems to rest to a considerable extent on how the peoples of the area manage this centrality. The challenge is immense, both exciting and risky. But the balance and moderation that will be acquired gradually as economic maturity advances and permeates the region will make the transition to a new future smoother and more manageable.

Notes

1. For useful overviews of the history of Asia and the Pacific, see, inter alia, John K. Fairbank et al., *East Asia: The Modern Transformation* (Boston: Houghton Mifflin, 1965); David Joel Steinberg et al., *In Search of Southeast Asia* (Honolulu: University of Hawaii Press, 1987).
2. These figures are cited as the Chinese official view in *Yomiuri Shimbun*, 16 October 1981.
3. See, inter alia, Fairbank et al., *East Asia*; Steinberg et al., *Southeast Asia*; Lloyd G. Reynolds, *Economic Development in the Third World, 1850–1980* (New Haven; Yale University Press, 1985); W. H. Morris-Jones and Georges Fisher, eds., *Decolonization and After: The British and French Experience* (London: Frank Cass, 1980).
4. Ramon H. Myers and Mark P. Peattie, eds., *The Japanese Colonial Empire, 1895–1945* (Princeton, New Jersey: Princeton University Press, 1984).
5. Benedict O. Anderson, *Imagined Communities: Reflections on the Origin and Spread of Nationalism* (London: Verso, 1983).
6. John Lewis Gaddis, *Strategies of Containment: A Critical Appraisal of Postwar American National Security Policy* (New York: Oxford University Press, 1982).
7. See, inter alia, Jonathan Spence, *The Gate of Heavenly Peace: The Chinese and Their Revolution, 1895–1980* (New York: Viking Press, 1981).
8. Bruce Cumings, *The Origins of the Korean War* (Princeton, New Jersey: Princeton University Press, 1981); Peter Lowe, *The Origins of the Korean War* (London: Longman, 1986).
9. Robert Ward and Yoshikazu Sakamoto, eds., *The Democratization of Japan* (Honolulu: University of Hawaii Press, 1986).
10. See Gaddis, *Strategies of Containment;* Bruce Cumings, ed., *Child of Conflict: The Korean-American Relationship, 1943–1953* (Berkeley: University of California Press, 1988).
11. See Frederic Deyo, ed., *The Political Economy of the New Asian Industrialism* (Ithaca, New York: Cornell University Press, 1986).
12. On the Philippine political economy, see Gary Hawes, *The Philippine State and the Marcos Regime: The Politics of Export* (Ithaca, New York: Cornell University Press, 1986.
13. William J. Duiker, *The Communist Road to Power in Vietnam* (Boulder, Colorado: Westview Press, 1981).

14. For Malaysian politics, see Karl von Vorys, *Democracy Without Consensus: Communalism and Political Stability in Malaysia* (London: Oxford University Press, 1976).
15. For the economic development of South Korea, see Kwang Suk Kim and Michael Roemer, *Growth and Structural Transformation (Korea)* (Cambridge, Massachusetts: Harvard University Press, 1979); Deyo, *Political Economy of the New Asian Industrialism*.
16. Takashi Inoguchi, *Gendai Nihon seijikeizai no kozu* (Contemporary Japanese Political Economy) (Tokyo: Toyo keizai shimposha, 1983).
17. Chalmers Johnson, *Peasant Nationalism and Communist Power: The Emergence of Revolutionary China, 1937–1945* (Stanford, California: Stanford University Press, 1962); Lowell Dittmer, *China's Continuous Revolution* (Berkeley: University of California Press, 1987).
18. Robert Gilpin, *War and Change in World Politics* (New York: Cambridge University Press, 1981); Robert Gilpin, *The Political Economy of International Relations* (Princeton, New Jersey: Princeton University Press, 1987).
19. Deyo, *Political Economy of the New Asian Industrialism*.
20. Takishi Inoguchi, *Tadanori to ikkoku hanei shugi o koete* (Beyond Free Ride and One-Country-Prosperity) (Tokyo: Toyo keizai shimposha, 1987); Takashi Inoguchi and Daniel I. Okimoto, eds., *The Political Economy of Japan*, Vol. II: *The Changing International Context* (Stanford, California: Stanford University Press, 1988).
21. Takashi Inoguchi, 'Trade, Technology and Security: Implications for East Asia and the West', *Adelphi Papers*, no. 218 (Spring 1987): 39–55.
22. E. L. Jones, *The European Miracle: Environment, Economies and Geopolitics in the History of Europe and Asia* (Cambridge: Cambridge University Press, 1981).
23. The following is adapted from Takashi Inoguchi, 'Japan's Gobal Roles in a Multipolar World', paper prepared for presentation at the Council on Foreign Relations, New York, May 18, 1988.
24. Takashi Inoguchi, 'Japan's Images and Options: Not a Challenger, But a Supporter', *Journal of Japanese Studies* 12, no. 1 (Winter 1986): 95–119.
25. Gilpin, *Political Economy of International Relations*.
26. Kuniko Inoguchi, *Posuto-haken Sisutemu to Nihon no sentaku* (The Emerging Posthegemonic System: Choices for Japan) (Tokyo: Chikuma shobo, 1987).
27. Ronald Morse, 'Japan's Drive to Pre-eminence', *Foreign Policy*, no. 69 (Winter 1987–88): 3–21.

Further reading

Cady, John F. *The History of Post-war Southeast Asia*. Athens: Ohio University Press, 1974.
Cumings, Bruce. *The Origins of the Korean War*. Princeton, New Jersey: Princeton University Press, 1981.

Fairbank, John King. *The Great Chinese Revolution, 1800–1985*. New York: Harper & Row, 1986.

Frost, Ellen L. *For Richer, For Poorer: The New US-Japan Relationship*. New York: Council on Foreign Relations, 1987.

Gaddis, John Lewis. *The Long Peace: Inquiries into the History of the Cold War*. New York: Oxford University Press, 1987.

Hofheinz, Roy, and Calder, Kent E. *The East Asia Edge*. New York: Basic Books, 1982.

Inoguchi,Takashi, and Okimoto, Daniel I., eds. *The Political Economy of Japan*. Vol. 2: *The Changing International Context*. Stanford, California: Stanford University Press, 1988.

Iriye, Akira. *The Cold War in Asia*. Englewood Cliffs, New Jersey: Prentice-Hall, 1974.

Steinberg, David Joel, ed. *In Search of Southeast Asia: A Modern History*. 2nd ed. Sydney: Allen & Unwin, 1987.

Thorne, Christopher. *The Issue of War: States, Societies, and the Far Eastern Conflict of 1941–1945*. London: Hamish Hamilton, 1985.

9

Awed, inspired, and disillusioned: Japanese scholarship on American politics[1]

It may not be a surprise to many to learn that Japanese interest in American politics first sprang from the fact that Americans repulsed English tyranny in the colonies and achieved independence without killing kings or subsequently exercising repressive politics.[2] This interest was kindled during the mid-nineteenth century, when the Japanese were confronted by successive attempts by Westerners to open up the country. The Japanese were keen to know which countries were successful in averting colonization by, or gaining independence from, Western countries. India or Vietnam were not encouraging examples. Siam, which kept its independence throughout the nineteenth and twentieth centuries, did not inspire them very much either. The only one remaining, even though it was a western country, was the United States. It is remarkable that the Japanese, busy with handling Westerners, were already anticipating the need to establish a new political system different from the existing one. The point here, however, is that this Japanese interest in American politics is indicative of, and presaging, the recurrent pattern in Japanese research in foreign areas. Japan is, above all, driven by the need to learn from foreign countries in order to survive and make itself a better place in which to live. This means studying foreign countries, selectively adopting essential foreign elements and weaving them into Japanese life. In other words, Japan is driven by the pragmatic need for learning with discriminating eyes. Japan was very fortunate in not having been colonized throughout its modernization drive of the nineteenth and twentieth centuries or even during the sixteenth and seventeenth centuries, when Westerners began arriving in Pacific Asia. While colonization invariably forces those colonized to borrow in toto both ideas and institutions from foreign countries, independence allows those noncolonized to borrow very selectively—that is, to borrow only to the extent to which they find it necessary. Selective borrowing and absorption to meet the domestic market demands of the day seem to have enabled the noncolonized to add strength to their indigenous modernization efforts.

Another useful example is the strong penchant in Japan for learning. In 1534, a Chinese ship drifted onto one of the southernmost islands of Tanegashima.[3] The ship carried approximately one hundred Chinese and eight Portuguese. The Lord of Tanegashima, Tokitaka, met the leaders of the ship in person three days after the ship landed. He showed intense interest in their guns and, within a dozen days of the ship's arrival, learned how to shoot. He then ordered local smiths to manufacture guns. Within five months, the smiths had produced more than six hundred guns, which Tokitaka used to conquer the adjacent island of Yakushima. It is worth noting that these guns were imperfect, with some parts not well finished by the inexperienced gunsmiths. Thus, when the next Chinese ship arrived at Tanegashima, it brought a Portuguese smith to produce perfect guns. Mendes Pinto, one of those Portuguese who first introduced guns to the Japanese in 1534, was told by a reliable merchant in 1556, when he returned to Japan, that there were more than 300,000 in the country, of which 25,000 were exported to the Ryukyu Islands. Thus, it took only 13 years for the Japanese to start exporting guns that they had neither heard nor seen nor produced before. Furthermore, two decades later, Oda Nobunaga, the first unifier of the country after ten decades of the Warring Period, amassed new homemade guns and conducted his campaigns with a brand new military strategy called musketry volleys. This strategy led to Nobunaga's overwhelming success at the Battle of Narashino in 1575. Yet it was only in 1594 that William Louis of Nassau first suggested using musketry volleys to his cousin Maurice. William Louis's idea was tested on a large scale in Europe only when Gustavus Adolphus of Sweden used the strategy at the Battle of Breitenfeld, near Leipzig, in September 1631.[4] This is a dramatic example of how the Japanese focused their attention on learning from foreign countries and mastered a new idea with extraordinary speed and effectiveness while tailoring it to local conditions.

Thus, it should not be too difficult to see how Japanese research of foreign areas is significantly affected by Japan's domestic demands. In the mid-sixteenth century, Japanese warlords needed weapons to enlarge their territories and unite the country militarily. In the mid-nineteenth century, Japan needed to repulse foreigners and establish a political system that could make the country strong and wealthy. The needs of the day forced the Japanese to learn from foreigners. Thus, in order to see the 'political culture' of American political studies in Japan, it is useful first to examine the general features of the relationship between the two countries.

Awed, inspired, and disillusioned

It seems safe to say with some oversimplification that during the process of learning, the Japanese have repeated the cycle of being awed, inspired, and disillusioned in their historical relationship with the United States for the last 150 years. Schematically, the first cycle started with Commodore Matthew C. Perry's gunboat diplomacy. Then, American examples, along with other Western models, provided intellectual and practical inspiration for Japanese reformers during the formation of the early state in the late nineteenth century. Finally, the immigration issue and economic rivalry aggravated their bilateral relations, leading the two countries eventually to clash militarily in 1941. The second cycle, which the author hopes will not evolve as the first one, started with the convincing defeat of Japan by the United States in 1945. Then, the Occupation reforms were, on the whole, supported by the Japanese, who were convinced of the good reformist intentions of the Americans. But gradually, the increasingly visible tensions and tangible strains between the two countries—the Japan-US Security Crisis, the Vietnam War, the trade and economic disputes of the late 1960s, a spate of burden-sharing contentions in the 1980s, and the Gulf War in the 1990s—have disillusioned many Japanese about Americans and the American system. It seems that because the Japanese were first awed and then inspired by Americans, they tend to borrow from them, while entertaining somewhat idealized images of Americans. However, because they tend to idealize Americans, the Japanese become disillusioned more quickly than they would have had they not been inclined to borrow from the Americans.[5]

Clearly, this is an oversimplification. But the change in topics and tone of Japanese scholarship on American politics closely paralleled those of the vicissitudes of the bilateral relationship.[6] According to Kamei Shunsuke, a Japanese Americanist, two key phrases most often used to characterize the Japanese reaction to Americans are *sasuga Amerika* (i.e., 'Great! Only in America are such things possible') and *koredemo Amerika* (i.e., 'Terrible! Such things should not take place in America').[7] Both phrases capture the dominant Japanese reactions to the United States; the Japanese have both a strong core of admiration and appreciation, yet when their somewhat idealized image is destroyed in reality, they are more easily disillusioned. This is not to deny the obvious fact that a large majority of academic research on US politics does not necessarily follow the trend of the day and has only a remote connection with the secular demands of the day. At any rate, such an oversimplified characterization obviously needs more elaboration and refinement.

Following the opening of its ports by the Treaty of 1853 with the United States, the Japanese drive to modernize the country—a rich country, a

strong army—was accelerated. The Meiji Restoration of 1868 accelerated
the modernization drive even further. A number of government-sponsored
missions were sent abroad to learn from advanced countries. However, the
three earliest Japanese Americanists who went abroad alone were not spon-
sored by the government. Niijima Jo left Japan illegally in 1864 and studied
at Amherst College. Upon his return, he founded Doshisha University in
Kyoto, one of the bastions of American studies in Japan thereafter.
Uchimura Kanzo, a Christian, also studied at Amherst in 1885. Nitobe
Inazo, another Christian, studied at Johns Hopkins from 1889 to 1891.
Nitobe was later to play a large role in consolidating Japan-US relations and
establishing American studies courses in Japan.[8] In regard to political ideas
and institutions, the American model competed with the English, Prussian,
and French models. Because it preached liberal republican ideas, the
American model enjoyed considerable influence. It attracted many poor
students who believed that the United States was a country of great
opportunities.[9] And, of course, Americans entertained, as is often the case,
a missionary zeal vis-à-vis the Japanese. Commodore Perry, for instance,
wrote in his diary: 'It seems not altogether inappropriate that the United
States should be the instrument of breaking down these barriers and of
opening Japan to the rest of the world.'[10] One can immediately see that this
sentence could stand very well in 1990 as the statement of the US government when it attempted to liberalize the Japanese market further in the
Structural Impediments Initiative talks. Fukuzawa Yukichi, a well-known
writer, preached many ideas essentially derived from the political writings
of Thomas Paine and Thomas Jefferson. The United States was portrayed as
'the sacred land of liberty'.[11] To quote Fukuzawa:

The United States of America is republican in the best sense of the word.
This is the country in which real representatives of the people meet and discuss
national politics without any private interests. Although nearly a century
has passed since it was established, the laws of the country have never been
thrown into confusion.[12]

The American model appealed very much to those freedom fighters working
toward 'freedom and people's rights' in the 1870s and 1880s. These were
the people left behind by the political upheavals of the Meiji Restoration—
most notably former warriors, who were not able to join the ruling establishment, and local landlords, who were easy targets for heavy taxes. (The
new government lacked a large tax-collecting apparatus and had no major
industry to tax; the result, therefore, was a small revenue base.[13]) Those two
decades represented the formative period of political ideas and institutions,
more or less, with each sector of Japanese society adopting its own model

without much coordination at the top. Thus, for instance, the navy adopted the English model, the army adopted the Prussian model, and the metropolitan police adopted the French model. But with the petering out of the 'freedom and people's rights' movement by the late 1880s, the British and the Prussian models of constitutional monarchy and bureaucratic authoritarianism, rather than the American model of republicanism and representative democracy, held sway in the 1890s and 1900s.[14] Already in the 1870s and 1880s, many leaders took note of the basic inapplicability of the American model. In the democratic society of America, it was observed that 'people persist in their private rights, bribery is practiced among officials, and political parties collide with each other'.[15]

Two major factors changed the relative weight of Japanese interest in foreign areas from models of Western countries to the concerns of their Asian neighbors. First, the Japanese political system was consolidated by the turn of the century,[16] hence their reduced interest in Western countries as models from which to learn. Second, Japanese imperial expansion required more knowledge of neighboring countries; colonial governments need knowledge of colonies[17] In 1895, Japan came to possess Taiwan; in 1905, Manchuria, Sakhalin, and the Kuriles; and in 1911, Korea. Japan regarded these colonies as suppliers of primary products and as military bastions for Japanese defense. Yet much had to be developed in order to achieve these two objectives. Hence, the second strand of foreign areas studies, colonial studies, was developed. This strand metamorphosed and flourished when Japanese economic expansion brought firms and government officials to Third World countries. However, since this strand of foreign area research is not of principal concern here, the author will not elaborate further on this subject.[18]

Despite the shift of focus, Japan remained interested in Western countries for two major reasons. One was, of course, its need to cope with international power politics in the first half of the century when the world order was crumbling, and a new order to replace it had not yet emerged.[19] The other was its continuous interest in Western models and inspirations. Taisho Democracy in the 1910s and 1920s was responsible for this interest. During this time, political participation was enlarged, and two alternating parties on the center-right political continuum emerged to contest each other.[20] The latter events were influenced by American democratic ideals, as propounded by Woodrow Wilson and others. A number of major Japanese Americanists, such as Takagi Yasaka, the first holder of the chair in American politics at the University of Tokyo, and Matsumoto Shigeharu, the founder of the International House of Japan, were essentially the product of American democracy in the 1910s, 1920s, and 1930s. Takagi Yasaka, whose two books depicted two major organizing factors of American politics, the frontier and

Puritanism, was widely regarded as one of the few founders of academic American studies in Japan.[21] Yet the period of renewed interest in the United States coincided with one countertrend in the bilateral relationship, the increasing barriers to Chinese and Japanese immigration to the United States since the dawn of the century. This injured the pride of many Japanese who were hurt by the restrictions and rejections. Having psychologically already departed from Asia, as Fukuzawa Yukichi did in the 1890s in his famous essay calling for Japan's departure from inferior Asia and its joining the West, the Japanese were distressed to find that, in the 1900s, 1910s, and 1920s, Americans continued to treat them as they treated other Asians. The increasingly sour relations between Japan and the United States reflected the changed power balance in the Pacific. Russia was badly beaten by Japan in 1905, and the United States found it to be in its best interest to side with Russia and favor China to curb the steadily emerging Japan. Uchimura Kanzo, a Christian missionary, could not help expressing his disappointment in the United States when an anti-Japanese land law was passed in California in 1913. Said Uchimura,

The United States does and does not exist. In the sense that the Mississippi River leisurely flows into the ocean and the Rocky Mountains stand gently in the sky, the United States exists. But in the sense that the voice of Lowell, Bryan, and Whittier is heard no more in the land, and the spirit of Lincoln, Sumner, and Garrison rules it no more; in that sense, America is no more.[22]

In addition to the immigration issue of the 1910s and 1920s, the China issue became a major point of contention between Japan and the United States in the 1930s. As the two countries competed with each other in a naval arms race, and as each tried to lure China into a friendship of its own making, Japanese writings on the United States increasingly came to discuss the latter's might and menace.[23]

When war came, mutual images of Japan and the United States reached their nadir. Each side mobilized conceivable racist prejudices and slurs about each other, as John Dower has so vividly and richly documented.[24] Yet ironically, war mobilization efforts created some grounds for the blossoming of studies about each other after the war. This is more evident in the case of America's Japanese studies than in the case of Japan's American studies. The former was fully encouraged for war mobilization.[25] But the latter was discouraged to the extent that teaching English was temporarily suspended in schools during the war. Yet underneath the government's oppression, a small core of intellectuals like Takagi and Matsumoto survived the war and came to bridge the prewar and postwar appreciation of American studies in Japan.

In Japan, the preparation for the blossoming of American studies started during the Occupation. The Japanese accepted Americans who naturally had reformist-cum-missionary zeal, not only in politics but also in intellectual research agenda-setting in American studies in Japan. Awed and inspired by Americans, the Japanese wanted to start afresh with new ideas and institutions, many of which naturally came with the Americans. Moreover, various institutional devices were utilized in order to encourage and enhance Japan's American studies, including the American Center, the Fulbright Program, and the Japan Association of American Studies, as well as a host of funding organizations.[26] All of these were necessary to fill the great demand in Japan for knowledge of, and friendship with, the United States. Much of the 1940s and 1950s was dominated by the absorption of Americans' research on US politics by adherents of what is called *sengo minshushugi* (postwar democracy)—that is, believers in freedom, democracy, and peace—as enunciated in the 1952 constitution. For instance, Hidaka Meizo portrayed Andrew Jackson as a hero of independent farmers, à la Frederick Turner's thesis.[27] It is, according to Yasutake Hidetake, a Japanese Americanist, an essential self-contradiction. The Japanese cry against American imperialism (in daily life), yet they overlook the racist prejudice against American Indians, as shown in the famous film by John Ford, and applaud the populism expounded in the film.[28]

But the seeds of departure from a tutelage-type scholarship were already sown in the late 1940s. Communists and some socialists felt betrayed by Americans when the cold war intensified and the reverse course was enacted, countering New Deal reformist policies.[29] They were the first to write critically on American politics. For instance, Kikuchi Kenichi, a Marxist, wrote an article in 1950 on Jacksonian democracy, concluding: 'The frontier communities in the Southwest which constituted the most vigorous movement toward democracy during the period were under the control of the cotton kingdom. Jacksonian democracy was the outcome of the hegemony of southern plantation owners without farmers being represented in the end'.[30] Kikuchi's conclusion preceded R. E. Brown's article 'The Missouri Crisis, Slavery, and the Politics of Jacksonianism',[31] which was published at the beginning of the Vietnam War era.

The Security Treaty Crisis of 1960 involved a far larger number of intellectuals.[32] Yet its impact on Japan's American studies was overwhelmed by the Vietnam War, which brought about a spate of work on the imperial nature of American political development and external expansion, such as those by Shimizu Tomohisa and Kugai Saburo. They were ironically influenced by Americans' works on US politics, such as William Williams, Gabriel Kolko, and Robert Wiebe.[33]

Perhaps most importantly, as Japan-US economic competition intensified, the basic tone of Japanese scholarship changed. Instead of following the American lead in conceiving and conducting research on American politics, an increasing number of Americanists have focused on their own domestic academic demands. First, the fairly large number of Japanese Americanists has enabled them to live in their own, more or less, parochial academic community. Although there has been a constant influx of American works, the relative influence of American Americanists on Japanese Americanists seems to have shrunk significantly, if one looks at the fact that Japanese Americanists cite each other more frequently than they do American Americanists.

Second, practical demands for knowledge of the United States in Japan have been growing so fast that many Americanists tend to confine themselves to more academic research, which separates them from secular trends. But the large trend of disillusionment and detachment has become more visible in opinion polls and more tangible in nonacademic writings and in works done by non-Americanist social scientists, perhaps because the latter are more in tune with the secular trends of Japanese market demands for these kinds of works on the United States.

Overwhelmed by Americans and pulled by domestic market demands

If Japanese Americanists have been overwhelmed by American Americanists such as Merrill Jensen, Charles Beard, and C. Vann Woodward for a long time, they have been increasingly pulled by domestic market demands, popular, business, and bureaucratic. When the Japanese were content, as they were in the 1940s and 1950s, with introducing American works, they were not necessarily worried about their own original contributions very much. But once they recognized the need to do their own work, they felt simply overwhelmed by American Americanists. Keeping abreast of American Americanists required hard work, which Japanese Americanists had been assiduously doing for a long time. More depressing from their point of view, the fact that massive primary documents were mostly available in the United States often discouraged them from continuously conducting original research for as long as they based their professional life in Japan. So Japanese Americanists started to write what is called *keimosho* (books for enlightenment), a genre consciously tailored to those popular demands for basic knowledge of subjects with social significance. Homma Nagayo, an Americanist and former vice president of the University of Tokyo, laments as follows: 'American studies specialists in Japan are caught in a dilemma: they are faced with a hard choice of either pursuing a specialization at the expense of meaningful generalization, or trying desperately to influence both policymakers and general public by the force of their expertise'.[34]

Domestic market demands have grown very steadily as the scope and depth of Japan-US relations grew so as to make the relationship what former US Ambassador to Tokyo Mike Mansfield aptly called 'the most important bilateral relationship—bar none'.[35] Both the immense importance of the bilateral relations and the relative ease of using English for educated elites place Japanese Americanists in a difficult position; namely, non-Americanists, be they social scientists, businessmen, or bureaucrats, enter the field of American studies without feeling the need to 'pay any dues'. In other words, non-Americanists flourish in publication, as domestic market demands go up, and they do not bother to obtain membership in the Japanese Americanists' academic community. Furthermore, their academic training and interests, which are tailored to the needs of the day, tend to prevent Americanists from meeting those domestic demands. Hence, the oft-heard criticism of businessmen and bureaucrats that Japanese Americanists have not shouldered their responsibilities very much.[36] Yet they cannot compete well with American Americanists on their home ground because of the differences in language, style, and the number of readers of publications. Moreover, the strong pull of domestic market demands means that they publish overwhelmingly in Japanese instead of English. If they publish in English, it is often in Japanese journals specializing in American politics, such as the *Japanese Journal of American Studies* or university bulletins, the circulation of which tend to be pitifully small and normally restricted to members only.

By emphasizing the overwhelming effect of American Americanists for Japanese Americanists, I should not give a false impression that the latter have been feeble and meager in producing research. The number of works, books, and articles alone does not necessarily indicate the vigor of academic production, but it can be used as a crude indicator of such vigor. For instance, we can look at the *Annual* of the Center for American Studies, University of Tokyo. Published since 1977, the *Annual* lists a series of excellent critical bibliographical works on major topics in American studies that have been published recently. The time span of the works ranges from 'since 1954' to 'for the last five years', and those works annotated or cited herein do not seem to be exhaustive of all such bibliographical works. Thus, the utmost caution is necessary in drawing any conclusions from the following figures in Table 9.1.

Table 9.1   *Bibliographical essays consulted*

Subject (Author)	Publication Year	Number of Japanese Works Cited
Contemporary politics (Abe Hitoshi)	1979	130
Social history (Aruga Natsuki)	1979	123
Reformist era (Takahasi Akira)	1982	124
Diplomacy at the turn of the century (Matsuda Takeshi)	1982	145
Politics since 1945 (Yui Daizaburo)	1982	138
Independence (Tomita Torao)	1983	147
Politics/diplomacy around American independence (Aruga Tadashi)	1983	57
American contemporary politics (Sunada Ichiro)	1985	97
History of American women (Aruga Natsuki)	1985	94
Japan-US relations (Hayashi Yoshikatsu)	1986	758
Jacksonian era (Yasutake Hidekatsu)	1987	159
The economy in the latter half of the nineteenth century (Muroya Takeshi)	1987	319
Japan-US relations since 1945 (Iokibe Makoto et al.)	1988	201
American south (Taninaka Toshiko et al.)	1989	245

The overwhelming predominance of the topic of bilateral relations is easy to notice. Yet even without them, the number of academic publications on American politics is impressive indeed. David Chalmers, an American Americanist, wrote, 'despite the barriers in language and basic materials, I can say that, besides the United Kingdom, Canada and the United States, Japan has produced most excellent, serious works on the United States in the world'.[37]

Favorite topics include American independence, slavery, overseas expansion, progressivism, and the New Deal. One can only guess why these topics are favored by Japanese Americanists. First, the topic of independence supposedly informs one of the spirit and nature of the American political system. Given the very brief history of the United States, two hundred years compared to Japan's two thousand, the argument is that Japanese Americanists must start from the year 1776 at least. Second, a sizable number of Marxian economic historians in American studies tend to focus on slavery, overseas expansion, and the New Deal. They discuss how the American ruling establishment handled inner social and economic contradictions. Third, many Japanese Americanists are struck by the self-restructuring capacity of the American political system at times of great upheavals, as expressed by Samuel Huntington, hence, such topics as slavery, progressivism, and the New Deal. Moreover, the fact that works by such authors as C. Vann Woodward, Richard Hofstadter, Charles Beard, Frederick Turner, Henry Commager, Merrill Jensen, Robert Fogel and Stanley Engerman, Walter LaFeber, Elmer Schattschneider, and Valadimir Key are studied, discussed, and often challenged in Japanese journals and books suggests the serious nature of American studies in Japan. It is a bit like the situation in which a disciple keeps reading and discussing and sometimes goes beyond his teacher, challenging his teacher's work without the latter's being informed because of the language difference.

Yet the dilemma of Japanese Americanists' wandering between meeting domestic market demands and aspiring to make academic inroads into America's American studies on their home ground remains. What are the ways out of this dilemma for Japanese Americanists? Where can they hope to make more original contributions most successfully and efficiently?[38] They normally find opportunities in two fields of study: bilateral relations and Japan-US comparisons. The former has been explored and developed very heavily by Japanese Americanists.[39] Looking back, one can readily find major works by Japanese Americanists on Japan-US relations, often in cooperation with American Americanists. Normally, their American counterparts do not use Japanese materials. Moreover, American Japanologists have not done very much in the area of Japanese foreign relations, including Japan-US relations. They tend to devote themselves more to Japan's domestic history and politics. Although it is not quite clear why this is so, it seems to me that it occurs, in part, because American Japanologists were born and bred as informants to the government during the wartime mobilization and the Occupation, even though they have written works that have been humanistic and historical.[40] In other words, topics of Japan's international relations have tended to be left until recently to American academic and government specialists in international relations, to whom Japanologists are expected to give some background knowledge and a modicum of historical insight. Thus, bilateral relations are a good target. It is no wonder that there are more topics regarding Japan-US relations than others.[41] If one looks at an English-language journal published by the Japanese Association of American Studies, a journal published once every four years since 1981, each as a special issue, one is struck by how much Japanese Americanists favor bilateral subjects. The 1981 issue deals with US policy toward East

Asia 1945–50, the 1985 issue with the American Revolution, and the 1989 issue with Japanese immigrants and Japanese-Americans.

Another path is one suggested and practiced, for instance, by Aruga Natsuki. She argues that in order to make original contributions, Japanese Americanists can make the best use of Japanese materials and Japanese perspectives when they compare Japanese cases with American ones.[42] Her choice is the social history of women in Japan and in the United States, specifically female and child labor mobilization during World War II in the United States and in Japan and their social significance in terms of job and family compatibility. Another example is Fujimoto Kazumi's study of Jacksonian politics: How were American political parties born out of faction-ridden politics? What he has in mind is clearly the Japanese ruling party's factional dynamics in the latter half of this century.[43] This is also evident in Fujimoto's study of American political reform and the salience of ethical codes of Congress. In this study, he asks the question: Why are Japanese political reform attempts basically devoid of the ethical considerations of politics?[44] Somewhat similarly, Japanese Americanists can focus more on conceptual frameworks developed from a comparative reading of American and Japanese political science studies in order to come up with an original analysis of American politics. This seems to be represented, for instance, by Kubo Fumiaki. He has studied Warren Wallace's agricultural policy formation during the New Deal, discussing pluralist, statist, and corporatist frameworks.[45] Although he does not venture to make any explicit, or even implicit, comparisons with Japanese social and agricultural policies, Fumiaki's conclusion that direct bureaucratic policy initiative was crucial to the agricultural policy of the New Deal rather than interest group pressure and bargaining reminds one of the bureaucratically initiated Japanese social policy during the interwar period.[46]

Yet another path is increasingly represented by non-Americanist social scientists' or policy analysts' works on American politics. The starting point of their research is, first, the subject that attracts their curiosity, whether it is a local content bill or foreign policy attitudes and, second, their methodology, whether it is through interviews or through quantitative methods. This is represented by several people. Yamamoto Yoshinobu has conducted extensive interviews in the US Congress to examine US energy policy; Nobayashi Takeshi has painstakingly studied US steel protectionism; Kabashima Ikuo and Hideo Sato have analyzed US congressional behavior; Kawato Sadafumi has done a statistical analysis of US electoral outcomes; and Yui Daizaburo, an Americanist, has analyzed US foreign policy toward the Eastern Mediterranean in the 1940s within a Wallersteinian framework in the historical system tradition.[47] To this camp are added a vast number of policy analysts and writers in business, bureaucracy, and journalism who produce massive reports with increasingly greater research funding. They include Sakamoto Masahiro's analytic study of Pax Americana, Funabashi Yoichi's economic study of international monetary diplomacy,and Tomita Toshiki's economic analysis of the US-led international system.[48]

Whether these new approaches, distinct from the predominantly humanistic American studies in Japan, turn out to be a shining path or not is yet to be seen. Still, there are a number of encouraging factors. First, business, bureaucratic, and popular market demand is rapidly increasing. Where demand exists, supply will emerge in the long term. Second, penetration of the market by non-Americanists has been vigorous only if the subjects attracted them. Third, nonacademic sectors—whether they are in business, bureaucracy, or journalism—challenge the academic sector with vast funding, rich experience, and fast, accurate intelligence and data. It is this sector that the academic sector will perforce come to meet head-on sooner or later.[49]

This point can be seen when one compares two larger series in Japan-US relations published in the early 1970s and early 1990s, respectively. One is *Nichi-Bei Kankeishi* (History of Japan-US relations), four volumes, 1971–72, while the other is *Shirizu Nichi-Bei Kankei* (Series on Japan-US relations), 1988–.[50] The former is the product of a binational project focusing on the bilateral diplomatic and political history leading to Pearl Harbor. All the chapters are basically historical descriptions and analysis and are indicative of the predominant mood in Japan, which is to look at Japan-US relations in light of those events that led to, and were significantly shaped by, Pearl Harbor. The latter includes such titles as: *The Changing Japanese Industrial Structure and Its Impact on Japan-US Economic Disputes, The Cold War and Japan-US Relations: The Formation of Partnership, Lobbying US Congress: Japan-US Relations in Washington, DC, USTR: US Commercial Policy Making and USTR's Roles, US Logic and Japan's Response: US-Canada Free Trade Agreement and Japan*, and *America's Jewish Community*.[51] The dominant approach in the series is a political science one, bordering on policy analysis, and is indicative of the mood in Japan regarding Japan–US relations in the early 1990s. Its primary focus is the evolving estrangement amid the ever-deepening interdependence between the two countries, its causes, its dynamics, and its prospects.

More broadly, the list of the latest books on American studies in the newsletter of the Japanese Association of American Studies can give one a sense of the scope of Japan's American studies as of 1990–91. They were all published in Japan circa 1990–91.

Asaba Yoshimasa, *A Historical Study of Land Banks in American Colonies*
Ochi Michio, *Gold in California*
Maruyama Naoki, *American Jewish Community*

Kugai Saburo, *Hollywood and McCarthyism*
Fujiwara Shinya, *America*
Nose Masako, *The Sacred Land Called Disneyland*
Okajima Shigeyuki, *Environment Movements in the US*
Fujimoto Kazumi, ed., *American Politics—Reaganite Era*
Miyasato Seigen, *USTR*
Akiyama Kenji, *American Commercial Policy and Trade Disputes*
Tanimitsu Taro, *Alfred Mahan*
Oba Minako, *Tsuda Umeko*
Oda Motoi, *A Story of Liberty Goddess*
Sengoku Kideyo, *Amidst White Whales*
Hiwatari Yumi, *Postwar Politics and Japan-US Relations*
Kitamura Takao, *America*
Furukawa Hiromi, *A Study of Afro-American Literature*
Homma Nagayo et al., eds., *Reconstructing the Views of Contemporary America*
Ozawa Kenji, *The Formation of American Agriculture and Peasant Movements*
Kaji Motoo, *International Economic Relations*
Ishizaki Akihiko, *The Reversal of Japanese and US Economies*
Fukuda Shigeo et al., *The United States of America*
Yamazaki Tadashi, *Finance of State Governments in the US*

The major features of American studies in Japan can be discerned here also. They are the predominance of humanistic studies, a significant portion of books for enlightenment, and the increasing attention to domestic demands for knowledge that relates to American economics, politics, and Japan-US relations. The humanistic dominance in the academic community does not seem to be abating in the near future, given the position of Japanese Americanists in academia. Pitifully fewer courses are offered on American politics and economics than on American literature and history. The number of books for enlightenment also does not seem to be decreasing, given the sure prospect for the ever-widening and deepening interdependence-cum-friction between Japan and the United States. Yet compared to the 1940s through the 1960s, the last two decades have seen a reversal of fortune for authors of books on enlightenment. During the former period, Americanists tended to monopolize the market, while during the latter period, non-Americanists have been much more vigorous and have started to flourish. For the same reason, the third feature seems to grow in importance.

Conclusion: admiration, appreciation, and ambivalence

Foreign area research is often characterized by ambivalence, a love/hate relationship toward the area under study. Japanese American political studies seem to show such ambivalence, as shown by the phrases *sasuga Amerika* and *koredemo Amerika*. A sense of admiration and appreciation remains hard when sometimes difficult times lead Japanese Americanists to distance themselves from the United States. Japanese Americanists seem to experience this kind of ambivalence all the more because Japan has seen the United States in the past as a staunch enemy, militarily threatening to destroy Japan, and as a reliable ally, steadfastly helping Japan to recover. This ambivalence is further reinforced by the concurrent, irreversible movement of the continuous Americanization of Japanese daily life[52] and the increasingly strident criticisms of Japan coming from the United States.[53] Yet one cannot exaggerate the tendency of academics to change the subject with newspaper headlines. As far as Japanese American studies are concerned, a good majority of Japanese Americanists live a proper academic life even when their writings are not likely to be read by American Americanists very much. A small but growing number of them are increasingly confident about the standard and quality of some of their work. Whether their fledgling self-confidence will be borne out or not is what the rest of the world may be interested in knowing at a time when Japanese affluence and influence are slowly changing the map of the world.

Notes

1. I am grateful to Igarashi Takeshi and Yui Daizaburo for taking the time to enlighten me on American political studies in Japan, and to Sunada Ichiro, Peter Katzenstein, Tsunekawa Keiichi, and Courtney Purrington for making helpful comments on an earlier draft of this essay. Richard Samuels's editorial comments are also most appreciated. At a conference in Sydney, Australia, in late February 1991, Richard Holbrooke kindly enlightened me about Commodore Perry's diary and, furthermore, gave me, gratis, a copy of Michael Lewis's book in which Commodore Perry's words are cited. Japanese names in the text are spelled with a family name first and a given name last, as they are in Japanese.
2. Aruga Natsuki, *Amerika Feminizumu no shakaishi* (Social history of American feminism).
3. Kurosawa Yo, 'Nichi-O kankei' (Japanese-European relations), in *Joso o hajimeta 21 seiki* (The twenty-first century approaching), pp. 173-98.
4. Geoffrey Parker, *The Military Revolution: Military Innovation and the Rise of the West, 1500-1800*, pp. 18-24 and 140-42.
5. As for Japan-US relations, see Iriye Akira, *After Imperialism: The Search for a New Order in the Far East, 1921-1931; Pacific Estrangement: Japanese and American Expansion, 1879-1911;* and *Mutual Images: Essays in American-Japanese Relations*; Dorothy Borg and Okamoto Shumpei, eds., *Pearl Harbor as History: Japanese-American Relations, 1931-1941*; Hosoya

Chihro, ed., *Shirizu Nichi-Bei Kankei* (Library on Japan-US relations); Hosoya Chihiro et al., eds., *Nichi-Bei Kankeishi*, 4 vols. (A history of Japan-US relations); Masuda Hiroshi and Asada Sadao. 'Japanese-American Relations Since 1952', in Asada Sadao, ed., *Japan and the World, 1853–1952: A Bibliographic Guide to Japanese Scholarship in Foreign Relations* (New York: Columbia University Press). For the most recent occasion revealing the schism of both countries, see Inoguchi Takashi, 'Japan's Response to the Gulf Crisis: An Analytic Overview'.

6. Kamei Sunsuke, *Nihonjin no Amerika ron* (Japanese discuss the United States); Saito Makoto, 'Nihon niokeru Amerika zo to Amerika kenkyu: senzen Nihon' (Perceptions of and studies on the United States in prewar Japan) in Saito Makoto and Sigmund Skard, eds., *Sekai niokeru Amerika zo* (Perceptions of the United States in the World), pp. 11–35; Aruga, *Amerika Feminizumu;* Masuda and Asada, 'Japanese-American Relations Since 1952'; Homma Nagayo, 'America in the Mind of the Japanese', in Iriye Akira and Warren Cohen, eds., *The United States and Japan in the Postwar World*, pp. 209–22; Sunada Ichiro, *The Study of American Politics in Japan: Its State, Trends, and Problems*.

7. Kamei, *Nihonjin no Amerika ron.*

8. Saito, 'Nihon niokeru Amerika'.

9. Ibid.

10. Michael Lewis, *Pacific Rift: Adventures in the Fault Zone Between the US and Japan*, p. 9.

11. Kamei Shunsuke, 'The Sacred Land of Liberty: Images of America in Nineteenth-Century Japan', in Iriye, *Mutual Images*, pp. 55–72.

12. Kamei Shunsuke, *Jiyu no seichi—Nihonjin no Amerika* (The sacred land of liberty: America as perceived by the Japanese).

13. Masumi Junnosuke, *Nihon seitoshiron* (A treatise on Japanese political parties).

14. Saito, 'Nihon niokeru Amerika'.

15. Kamei, *Nihonjin no Amerika ron*, p. 62.

16. Masumi, *Nihon seitoshiron*; Banno Junji, *Meiji kempo taisei no kakuritsu* (The establishment of the Meiji constitutional system).

17. Ramon H. Myers and Mark R. Peattie, eds., *The Japanese Colonial Empire, 1895–1945.*

18. Inoguchi Takashi, 'Japan', in William G. Andrew, ed., *International Handbook of Political Science*, pp. 207–18; Inoguchi Takashi, 'The Study of International Relations in Japan', in Hugh C. Dyer and Leon Mangasarian, eds., *The Study of International Relations: The State of the Art*, pp. 25–264. As for the four distinct traditions of Japanese political science, the legalist-institutionalist, Marxist, historicist, and behavioral-empiricist, see Inoguchi Takashi, 'Democracy and Development of Political Science in Japan'. As to the place of social sciences and intellectuals in prewar Japan, see Ishida Takeshi, *Nihon no shakaikagaku* (Japanese social sciences), and Andrew Barshay, *Intellectuals and the State in Imperial Japan.*

19. Iriye, *After Imperialism;* Hosoya, *Shirizu Nichi-Bei Kankei.*
20. Mitani Taichiro, *Nihon seito seiji no keisei* (The formation of Japanese party politics); Peter Duus, *Party Rivalry and Political Change in Taisho Japan.*
21. Saito, 'Nihon niokeru Amerika'.
22. Kamei Shunsuke, 'Jiyu no seichi' (The sacred land of liberty) in Kato Hidetoshi and Kamei Shunsuke, eds., *Nihon to Amerika* (Japan and the United States), pp. 83–144; Kamei, 'Sacred Land of Liberty', pp. 55–72.
23. Borg and Okamoto, *Pearl Harbor as History.*
24. John Dower, *War Without Mercy.*
25. Richard J. Samuels, 'Japanese Political Studies and the Myth of the Independent Intellectual'.
26. Center for American Studies, *Amerika kenkyu shiryo senta nempo* (Annals of the Center for American Studies, University of Tokyo).
27. Hidaka Meizo, *Jackusonian Demokurashi* (Jacksonian democracy).
28. Yasutake Hidetake, 'Jackson jidai no seiji to shakai, 1815–1859' (The society and politics during the Jacksonian era, 1815–1850), pp. 12–23.
29. Yui Daizaburo, *Mikan no Senryo Kaikaku* (The unfinished Occupation reform); Igarashi Takeshi, *TaiNichi kowa to Reisen* (Peace with Japan and the cold war); Iokibe Makoto, *Beikoku no Nihon senryo* (US Occupation policy in Japan).
30. Yasutake, 'Jackson jidai no seiji'.
31. R.E. Brown, 'The Missouri Crisis, Slavery and the Politics of Jacksonianism'.
32. George B. Packard, *Protest in Tokyo.*
33. Shimizu Tomohisa, *Amerika teikoku* (The American empire).
34. Homma, 'America in the Mind'.
35. Mike Mansfield, 'Together Toward Peace and Prosperity'. Address delivered to the Japan Society, New York, March 19, 1985.
36. Kitamura Hiroshi, et al., *Nichi-Bei kankei o kangaeru* (Thinking about Japan-US relations); Inoguchi, 'Study of International Relations'; Kusano Atsushi, *Nichi-Bei Orenji kosho* (Japan-US negotiations over Orange).
37. David Chalmers, 'Amerikajin kara mite' (As seen by an American) in Saito and Skard, eds., *Sekai niokeru Amerika zo* (Perceptions of the United States in the world), pp. 80–98.
38. Igarashi Takeshi, conversation with author, April 25, 1991.
39. Iriye, *After Imperialism*; Masuda and Asada, 'Japanese-American Relations Since 1952'.
40. Samuels, 'Japanese Political Studies'.
41. Hayashi Yoshikatsu, 'Nihon ni okeru Nich-Bei kankeishi kenkyu no genjo' (The state of affairs in Japanese research on Japan-US relations).
42. Aruga, *Amerika Feminizumu.*
43. Fujimoto Kazumi, *Amerika kindai seito no keisei* (The formation of modern American political parties).
44. Fijimoto Kazumi, *Gendai Amerika no seijikaikaku* (Contemporary American political reform).

45. Kubo Fumiaki, *New Deal to Amerika minshusei* (The New Deal and American Democratic politics).
46. Sheldon Garon, *The State and Labor in Modern Japan*.
47. Yamamoto Yoshinobu, *Beikoku no seisaku kettei niokeru gikai staff no yakuwari: Enerugi seisaku o rei to shite* (The role of legislative staffs in US policymaking on energy); Nobayashi Takeshi, *Hogo boeki no seiji rikigaku* (Political dynamics of protectionist trade); Kabashima Ikuo and Sato Hideo, 'Local Content and Congressional Politics: Interest Group Theory and Foreign Policy Implications'; Yui Daizaburo, *Sengo sekai chitsujo no keisei: Amerika shihonshugi to higashi Chichukai chiiki 1944–1947* (The formation of the postwar world order: American capitalism and the east Mediterranean region, 1944–1947).
48. Sakamoto Masahiro, *Pakkusu Amerikana no kokusai shisutemu* (The international system of Pax Americana); Funabashi Yoichi, *Managing the Dollar: From the Plaza to the Louvre;* Tomita Toshiki, *Kokusai kokka no seiji keizaigaku* (The political economy of the international state).
49. Abe Hitoshi and Igarashi Takeshi, eds. *Gendai Amerika seiji no bunseki* (Analyses of contemporary American politics); Naganuma Hideyo and Shinkawa Kenzaburo, *Amerika gendaishi* (A contemporary history of the United States).
50. Hosoya et al., *Nichi-Bei Kankeishi;* Hosoya Chihiro, *Ryotaisenkan no Nihon gaiko* (Japanese diplomacy during the two world wars).
51. Marumo Akinori, *Kawariyuku Nihon no sangyo kozo* (The changing Japanese industrial structure and its impact on Japan-US economic disputes); Ishii Osamu, *Reisen to Nichi-Bei kankei* (The cold war and Japan-US relations: the formation of partnership); Nobuta Tomohito, *Amerika gikai o robi suru* (Lobbying US Congress: Japan-US relations in Washington, DC); Miyasato Seigen, *Beikoku tsusho daihyobu* (US trade representative); Okita Saburo, *Amerika no ronri, Nihon no taio* (US logic, Japan's response); Okuda Kazuhiko, *Bei-Ka jiyu boeki kyotei to Nihon* (US-Canada free trade agreement and Japan); Maruyama Naoki, *Amerika no Yudayajin shakai* (America's Jewish community).
52. Kamei Shunsuke, *Amerika no kokoro—Nihon no kokoro* (American heart, Japanese heart).
53. Samuels, 'Japanese Political Studies'.

References

Abe, H., and T. Igarashi, eds. 1991. *Gendai Amerika seiji no bunseki* (Analyses of contemporary American politics). Tokyo: University of Tokyo Press.

Aruga, N. 1988. *Amerika Feminizumu no shakaishi* (Social history of American feminism). Tokyo: Keiso shobo.

Aruga, T. 1987. *Amerika gaikan* (American history: a general outline). Tokyo: University of Tokyo Press.

Asada, Sadao. 1989. *Japan and the World, 1853-1952: A Bibliographic Guide to Japanese Scholarship in Foreign Relations*. New York: Columbia University Press.

Banno, J. 1971. *Meiji kimpo taisei no kakuritsu* (The establishment of the Meiji constitutional system). Tokyo: University of Tokyo Press.

Barshay, A. 1988. *Intellectuals and the State in Imperial Japan*. Berkeley: University of California Press.

Borg, D. and S. Okamoto, eds. 1973. *Pearl Harbor as History: Japanese-American Relations, 1931-1941*. New York: Columbia University Press.

Brown, R.E. 1966. 'The Missouri Crisis, Slavery and the Politics of Jacksonianism'. *South Atlantic Quarterly* 65 (Winter): 52-77.

Center for American Studies, University of Tokyo. 1978-. *Amerika kenkyu shiryo senta nempo* (Annals of the Center for American Studies, University of Tokyo). Tokyo: University of Tokyo Press.

Chalmers, D. 1972. 'Amerikajin kara mite' (As seen by an American). In *Sekai niokeru Amerika zo* (Perceptions of the United States in the world), ed. M. Saito and S. Skard, pp. 80-98. Tokyo: Nanundu.

Dower, J. 1986. *War Without Mercy*. New York: Pantheon.

Duus, P. 1968. *Party Rivalry and Political Change in Taisho Japan*. Cambridge: Harvard University Press.

Fujimoto, K. 1981. *Amerika kindai seito no keisei* (The formation of modern American political parties). Tokyo: Ochanomizu shobo.

——. 1991. *Gendai Amerika no seijikaikaku* (Contemporary American political reform). Tokyo: Sairyusha.

Funabashi, Y. 1988. *Managing the Dollar: From the Plaza to the Louvre*. Washington, D.C.: Institute for International Economics.

Garon, S. 1987. *The State and Labor in Modern Japan*. Berkeley: University of California Press.

Hayashi, Y. 1986. 'Nihon ni okeru Nich-Bei kankeishi kenkyu no genjo' (The state of affairs in Japanese research on Japan-US Relations). *Amerika kenkyu shiryo senta nempo* 9 (March): 44-88.

Hidaka, M. 1948. *Jackasonian Demokurashi* (Jacksonian Democracy). Tokyo: University of Tokyo Press.

Homma, N. 1990. 'America in the Mind of the Japanese'. In *The United States and Japan in the Postwar World*, ed. A. Irihe and W. Cohen, pp. 209-22. Lexington: University of Kentucky Press.

Hosoya, C. 1989. *Ryotaisenkan no Nihon gaiko* (Japanese diplomacy during the two world wars). Tokyo: Iwanami shoten.

——. ed. 1988-. Shirizu Nichi-Bei Kankei (Series on Japan-US relations). Tokyo: Japan Times.

Hosoya, C. et al., eds. 1971-72. *Nichi-Bei Kankeishi*. (A history of Japan-US Relations). 4 vols. Tokyo: University of Tokyo Press.

Igarashi, T. 1986. *TaiNichi kowa to Reisen* (Peace with Japan and the cold war). Tokyo: University of Tokyo Press.

Inoguchi, T. 1981. 'Japan'. In *International Handbook of Political Science*, ed. W. Andrew, Westport, Conn.: Greenwood Press.

——. 1989. 'The Study of International Relations in Japan'. In *The Study of International Relations: The State of the Art*, ed. H. Dyer and L. Mangasarian. London: Macmillan.

——. 1990. 'Democracy and the Development of Political Science in Japan', forthcoming in David Easton, John Gunnel and Michael Stein (eds), *Regime and Discipline: Democracy and Development of Political Science*, Ann Arbor, University of Michigan Press.

——. 1991. 'The Nature and Functioning of Japanese Politics'. *Government and Opposition* 26 (Spring): 185–98.

——. 1991. 'Japan's Response to the Gulf Crisis: An Analytic Overview'. *Journal of Japanese Studies* 17 (Summer): 257–73.

Iokibe, M. 1988. *Beikoko no Nihon senryo* (US Occupation policy in Japan). 2 vols. Tokyo: Chuo koronsha.

Iriye, A. 1965. *After Imperialism: The Search for a New Order in the Far East, 1921–1931*. Cambridge: Harvard University Press.

——. 1972. *Pacific Estrangement: Japanese and American Expansionism, 1879–1911*. Cambridge: Harvard University Press.

——. 1975. *Mutual Images: Essays in American-Japanese Relations*. Cambridge: Harvard University Press.

Ishida, T. 1984. *Nihon no shakaikagaku* (Japanese social sciences). Tokyo: University of Tokyo Press.

Ishii, O. 1989. *Reisen to Nichi-Bei kankei* (The cold war and Japan-US relations: the formation of partnership). Tokyo: Japan Times.

Kabashima, I. and H. Sato. 1986. 'Local Content and Congressional Politics: Interest Group Theory and Foreign Policy Implications'. *International Studies Quarterly* 30 (September): 295–314.

Kamei, S. 1975. 'The Sacred Land of Liberty: Images of America in Nineteenth-Century Japan'. In *Mutual Images: Essays in American-Japanese Relations*, ed. A. Iriye. Cambridge: Harvard University Press.

——. 1977. *Nihonjin no Amerika ron* (Japanese discuss the United States). Tokyo: Kenkyusha.

——. 1978. *Jiyu no siechi—Nihonjin no Amerika* (The sacred land of liberty: America as perceived by Japanese). Tokyo: Kenkyusha.

——. 1989. *Amerika no kokoro—Nihon no kokoro* (American heart, Japanese heart). Tokyo: Kodansha.

——. 1991. 'Jiyu no seichi' (The sacred land of liberty). In *Nihon to Amerika* (Japan and the United States), ed. H. Kato and S. Kamei. Tokyo: Japan Society for Promotion of Sciences.

Kawato, S. 1987. 'Nationalization and Partisan Realignment in Congressional Elections'. *American Political Science Review* 81 (December): 1235–50.

Kikuchi, K. 1950. 'Namboku senso no shisoteki haikei' (The ideological backgrounds of the American Civil War). Vol. 2: *Amerika shisoshi* (Intellectual history of America). Tokyo: Nihon Hyoronsha.

Kitamura, H., et al. 1983. *Nichi-Bei kankei o kangaeru* (Thinking about Japan-US Relations). Tokyo: Sekai no ugoki sha.

Kubo, F. 1988. *New Deal to Amerika minshusei* (The New Deal and American

Democratic politics). Tokyo: University of Tokyo Press.

Kurosawa, Y. 1991. 'Nichi-O kankei' (Japanese-European relations). In *Joso o hajimeta 21 seiki* (The twenty-first century approaching), ed. Seventeen Top Leaders, pp. 173–98. Tokyo: Yuhikaka.

Kusano, A. 1984. *Nichi-Bei Orenji kosho* (Japan-US negotiations over Orange). Tokyo: Nihon keizai shimbunsha.

———. 1988. 'Nihon niokeru Amerika kenkyu' (American studies in Japan). *Leviathan* (March): 190–201.

Lewis, M. 1991. *Pacific Rift: Adventures in the Fault Zone Between the US and Japan.* New York: Whittle Direct Books.

Marumo, A. 1989. *Kawariyuku Nihon no sangyo kozo* (The changing Japanese industrial structure and its impact on Japan-US economic disputes). Tokyo: Japan Times.

Maruyama, N. 1990. *Amerika no Yudayajin shakai* (America's Jewish community). Tokyo: Japan Times.

Masuda, H. and S. Asada. 1988. 'Japanese-American Relations Since 1952'. In *International Studies in Japan: Japan and the World*, ed. S. Asada, pp. 1–20. Tokyo: Japan Association of International Relations.

Masumi, J. 1968–80. *Nihon seitoshiron* (A treatise on Japanese political parties). 7 vols. Tokyo: University of Tokyo Press.

Mitani, T. 1967. *Nihon seito seiji no keisei* (The formation of Japanese party politics). Tokyo: University of Tokyo Press.

Miyasato, S. 1989. *Beikoku tsusho daihyobu* (US trade representative). Tokyo: Japan Times.

Myers, R. and M. Peattie, eds. 1984. *The Japanese Colonial Empire, 1895–1945.* Princeton, N.J.: Princeton University Press.

Naganuma, H. and K. Shinkawa. 1991. *Amerika gendaishi* (A contemporary history of the United States). Tokyo: Iwanami shoten.

Nobayashi, T. 1987. *Hogo boeki no seiji rikigaku* (Political dynamics of protectionist trade). Tokyo: Keiso shobo.

Nobuta, T. 1989. *Amerika gikai o robi suru* (Lobbying US Congress: Japan-US relations in Washington, DC). Tokyo: Japan Times.

Okita S. 1989. *Amerika no ronri, Nihon no taio* (US logic, Japan's response). Tokyo: Japan Times.

Okuda, K. 1990. *Bei-Ka jiyu boeki kyotei to Nihon* (US-Canada free trade agreement and Japan). Tokyo: Japan Times.

Packard, G. 1966. *Protest in Tokyo.* Princeton, N.J.: Princeton University Press.

Parker, G. 1988. *The Military Revolution: Military Innovation and the Rise of the West, 1500–1800.* Cambridge, Eng.: Cambridge University Press.

Saito, M. 1972. 'Nihon niokeru Amerika zo to Amerika kenkyu: senzen Nihon' (Perceptions of and studies on the United States in prewar Japan). In *Sekai niokeru Amerika zo* (Perceptions of the United States in the world), ed. M. Saito and S. Skjard. Tokyo: Nanundo.

Sakamoto, M. 1986. *Pakkusu Amerikana no kokusai shishutema* (The international system of Pax Americana). Tokyo: Yuhikaku.

Samuels, R. 1991. 'Japanese Political Studies and the Myth of the Independent Intellectual'. Paper presented at the Conference on the Political Culture of Foreign Area Studies, Dedham, Mass., May 28–30.

Shimizu, T. 1986. *Amerika teikoku* (The American empire). Tokyo: Aki shobo.

Sunada, I. 1991. *The Study of American Politics in Japan: Its State, Trends, and Problems*. University of California Institute of Governmental Studies, Working Papers 91–92. Berkeley: University of California Press.

Tomita, T. 1989. *Kokusai kokka no seiji keizaigaku* (The political economy of the international state). Tokyo: Toyo keizai shimposha.

Yamamoto, Y. 1984. *Beikoku no seisaku kettei niokeru gikai staff no yakuwari: Enerugi seisaku o rei to shite* (The role of legislative staffs in US policymaking on energy). Tokyo: National Institute for Research Advancement.

Yasutake, H. 1987. 'Jackson jidai no seiji to shakai, 1815–1850' (The society and politics during the Jacksonian era, 1815–1850). *Amerika kenkyu shiryo senta nempo* 10 (March): 12–23.

Yui, D. 1985. *Sengo sekai chitsujo no keisei: Amerika shihonshugi to higashi Chichukai chiiki 1944–1947* (The formation of the postwar world order: American capitalism and the east Mediterranean region, 1945–1947). Tokyo: University of Tokyo Press.

——. (1990) *Mikan no Senryo Kaikaku* (The unfinished Occupation reform). Tokyo: University of Tokyo Press.

Select bibliography

1. History matters in any serious attempt to understand foreign policy. This applies especially to Japan's foreign policy. Given the nature of this book, it would suffice to suggest the following general and comprehensive volumes which together cover the last four centuries of Japanese history.

The Cambridge History of Japan, Vols. 4, 5, and 6 (Cambridge: Cambridge University Press, 1991, 1989, and 1988, respectively).
Janet Hunter, *The Emergence of Modern Japan* (London: Longman, 1989).

2. The study of Japan's foreign policy requires good understanding of the Japanese economy. Again given the nature of this book, it would suffice to suggest the following general and comprehensive volumes.

Takatoshi Ito, *The Japanese Economy* (Cambridge, Mass: MIT Press, 1992).
Penelope Francks, *Japanese Economic Development: Theory and Practice* (London: Routledge, 1992).

3. Japan's foreign policy did not arouse intense curiosity outside Japan until recently, hence the relative shortage of books dealing with Japan's foreign policy in the English language. Given that knowledge of the domestic workings of the Japanese economy, society, and politics is indispensable in understanding Japan's foreign policy, I have included some important works on these as well.

Roger Buckley, *US-Japan Alliance Diplomacy 1945-1990* (Cambridge: Cambridge University Press, 1992).
Kent E. Calder, *Crisis and Compensation: Public Policy and Political Stability in Japan, 1949-1986* (Princeton: Princeton University Press, 1988).
Richard Doner, *Driving a Bargain: Automobile Industrialization and Japanese Firms in Southeast Asia* (Berkeley: University of California Press, 1990).
John W. Dower, *War without Mercy: Race and Power in the Pacific War* (New York: Pantheon, 1986).
Reinhard Drifte, *Japan's Foreign Policy* (London: Routledge, 1990).

Peter Drysdale, *International Economic Pluralism: Economic Policy in East Asia and the Pacific* (New York: Columbia University Press, 1988).

Richard Finn, *Winners in Peace: MacArthur, Yoshida, and Postwar Japan* (Berkeley: University of California Press, 1992).

William Miles Fletcher, III, *The Japanese Business Community and National Trade Policy, 1920-1942* (Chapel Hill: University of North Carolina Press, 1989).

Jeffrey A. Frankel and Miles Kahler (eds), *The US and Japan in Pacific Asia* (Chicago: University of Chicago Press, forthcoming).

H. Richard Friman, *Patchwork Protectionism: Textile Trade Policy in the United States, Japan, and West Germany* (Ithaca: Cornell University Press, 1990).

Jeffrey Hart, *Rival Capitalists: International Competitiveness in the United States, Japan and Western Europe* (Ithaca: Cornell University Press, 1993).

Yujiro Hayami, *Japanese Agriculture under Siege: The Political Economy of Agricultural Policies* (Basingstoke: Macmillan, 1988).

Laura E. Hein, *Fueling Growth: The Energy Revolution and Economic Policy in Postwar Japan* (Cambridge, Mass.: Council on East Asian Studies, Harvard University, 1990).

Takashi Inoguchi, *Japan's International Relations* (London: Pinter Publishers, 1991).

Takashi Inoguchi and Daniel I. Okimoto (eds), *The Political Economy of Japan, Vol. 2: The Changing International Context* (Stanford: Stanford University Press, 1988).

Kenji Ishikawa, *Japan and the Challenge of Europe 1992* (London: Routledge, 1990).

Shafiqul Islam, *Yen for Development* (New York: Council on Foreign Relations, 1991).

Chalmers Johnson, *MITI and the Japanese Miracle: The Growth of Industrial Policy, 1925-1975* (Stanford: Stanford University Press, 1982).

Sheila K. Johnson, *The Japanese through American Eyes* (Stanford: Stanford University Press, 1988).

Peter J. Katzenstein and Yutaka Tsujinaka, *Defending the Japanese State: Structures, Norms, and the Political Responses to Terrorism and Violent Social Protest in the 1970s and 1980s* (Ithaca: Cornell University East Asia Program, 1991).

Paul Krugman (ed.), *Trade with Japan: Has the Door Opened Wider?* (Chicago: University of Chicago Press, 1991).

Shumpei Kumon and Henry Rosovsky (eds), *The Political Economy of Japan, Vol. 3: Cultural and Social Dyanmics* (Stanford: Stanford University Press, 1992).

Edward Lincoln, *Japan's Unequal Trade* (Washington: Brookings Institution, 1990).

John Makin and Donald Hellmann (eds), *Sharing World Leadership? A New Era for America and Japan* (Washington: American Enterprise Institute for Public

Policy, 1989).

Masao Miyoshi, *Off Center: Power and Culture Relations between Japan and the US* (Cambridge, Mass.: Harvard University Press, 1991).

William R. Nester, *The Foundations of Japanese Power* (London: Macmillan, 1989).

William R. Nester, *Japan and the Third World* (London: Macmillan, 1992).

Kathleen Newland (ed.), *The International Relations of Japan* (London: Macmillan, 1990).

Daniel I. Okimoto, *Between MITI and the Market* (Stanford: Stanford University Press, 1988).

Robert M. Orr, Jr., *The Emergence of Japan's Foreign Aid Power* (New York: Columbia University Press, 1990).

Hugh Patrick (ed.), *Pacific Basin Industries in Distress: Structural Adjustment and Trade: Policy in the Nine Industrialized Economies* (New York: Columbia University Press, 1991).

T.J. Pempel (ed.), *Uncommon Democracies* (Ithaca: Cornell University Press, 1990).

Kenneth B. Pyle, *The Japanese Question: Power and Purpose in a New Era* (Washington: AEI Press, 1992).

Frances McCall Rosenbluth, *Financial Politics in Contemporary Japan* (New York: Columbia University Press, 1989).

Gilbert Rozman, *Japan's Response to the Gorbachev Era, 1985–1991* (Princeton: Princeton University Press, 1992).

Shiro Saito, *Japan and the Summit: Japan's Role in the Western Alliance and the Asia-Pacific Region* (London: Routledge, 1990).

Richard Samuels, *The Business of the Japanese State* (Ithaca: Cornell University Press, 1987).

Robert A. Scalapino, *The Politics of Development: Perspectives on Twentieth-Century Asia* (Cambridge, Mass.: Harvard University Press, 1989).

Michael Schaller, *The American Occupation of Japan: The Origins of the Cold War in Asia* (New York: Oxford University Press, 1985).

Howard B. Schonberger, *Aftermath of War: Americans and the Remaking of Japan, 1945–1952* (Kent, Ohio: Kent State University Press, 1989).

Michele Schmiegelow and Henrik Schmiegelow, *Strategic Pragmatism: Japanese Lessons in the Use of Economic Theory* (New York: Praeger, 1989).

Masahide Shibusawa, Zakaria Haji Ahmad, and Brian Bridges, *Pacific Asia in the 1990s* (London: Routledge, 1991).

Christopher Thorne, *Allies of a Kind: The United States, Britain, and the War with Japan, 1941–1945* (London: Hamish Hamilton, 1978).

Laura D'Andrea Tyson, *Who's Bashing Whom: Trade Conflict in High-Technology Industries* (Washington, DC: Institute for International Economics, 1992).

Robert Wade, *Governing the Market: Economic Theory and the Role of Government in East Asian Industrialization* (Princeton: Princeton University Press, 1990).

John Welfield, *Eclipse of an Empire: Japan in the Postwar American Alliance System* (London: Athlone Press, 1988).

Allen Whiting, *China Eyes Japan* (Berkeley: University of California Press, 1989).

Kozo Yamamura and Yasukichi Yasuba (eds), *The Political Economy of Japan, Vol. 1: The Domestic Transformation* (Stanford: Stanford University Press, 1987).

John Zysman *et al.*, *The Highest Stake* (New York: Oxford University Press, 1992).

4. A number of periodicals that often deal with Japan's foreign policy are worth mentioning.

Japan Forum
Journal of the Japanese and International Economies
Journal of Japanese Studies
Monumenta Nipponica

Asian Survey
Pacific Affairs
Pacific Review
Journal of Asian Studies
Journal of Northeast Asian Studies

Foreign Affairs
Foreign Policy
International Affairs
International Economic Insights
International Journal
International Organization
International Security
International Studies Quarterly
Review of International Studies
Survival
World Politics

Japan Echo
Look Japan
Economic Eye
Journal of Japanese Trade and Industry
Japan Review of International Affairs

Index

Note: Page numbers followed by 'n' refer to notes. Page numbers in **bold** refer to tables.

Abe, Fumio, 94
Action Program (1985), 37–8
administrative reform, 37
aerospace, 62
agriculture, 58, 125
aid
    foreign, 4, 6, 45n, 146–7, 148
    to Communist countries, 94
    to South Asian countries, 118
Akashi, Yasushi, 150
American studies, 185–6
Americanists, Japanese, 186–92, 192–3
anti-colonialism, 104–5
APEC (Asian Pacific Economic Ministers
    Conference), 84, 85
Armacost, Michael, 99, 105
arms, 41, 80, 87, 109, 151
Aruga, Natsuki, 190
ASEAN (Association of South-east Asian
    Nations), 83–4, 95, 129, 153, 169
Asia
    North-east, 40
    South 95, 171–2
    South-east, 144
    see also newly industrialized countries
        (NICs); Pacific Asia
Asian Development Bank, 6
assets, external, 6–7
automobile industry, 32, 78–9

Baker, James, 152
Bank of Japan, 79, 109, 127
Bank of Tokyo, 7
banks, Japanese, 7, 79, 146–7
bigemony, 75, 76
bilateralism, 85–6
Borneo, Western, 166
Brown, R.E., 185
burden sharing, 4, 21, 71–2, 74, 117, 144
bureaucrats, 132–3

Bush, George, 141
butter-first policy, 23, 27

Cambodia, 124, 150
Canada, 128–9
Casey, William J., 5
Chalmers, David, 188
Chiang Kai-shek, 162
China, 40–1, 43, 83–4, 124, 165
    deaths, 159
    growth rate, 95
    'issue', 184
    and legitimacy, 168–9
    wars, 161–2, 168–9
Cipolla, Carlo, 106
Clean Government Party, 100, 131
Cold War, 140, 161–6
colonial studies, 183
colonization, 159–60, 183
Comecon countries, 86–7
Commonwealth of Independent States
    (CIS), 147
Communists, 162
competitiveness, 72, 106
conservatives, 10–11
constitution, 107–8
Conventional Armed Forces in Europe
    (CFE) Treaty (1990), 140
credit expansion, 13
CSCE (Conference on Security and
    Cooperation in Europe), 149,
    152
current account surplus, 103

Daihatsu, 86
Daimler Benz, 62
de Michelis, Gianni, 151
debt-of-history factor, 64, 104
decision-making, 145
decolonization, 161–6

defense, 130
  budget, 4
  build-up, 74, 91
  expenditure, 23-6, **24-5**, **26**, 143
  national, 110
  and right-left cleavage, 107
  White Paper (1979), 20
  White Paper (1989), 82
  zoku (Diet), 109-10
  see also burden sharing; security
Defense Agency, 110
demand
  domestic, 95, 124
    scholarship, 186-92
  foreign, 32
Democratic Socialist Party, 121, 131, 145, 150
Deng Xiaoping, 93
détente, 18-19, 63, 71
  refusal to recognize, 81, 101
development
  model, 147
  official development assistance (ODA), 4, 172
diplomacy, 107, 108
  incrementalism, 122, 145
dollar, 66-7
  -gold convertability, 59
  world standard system, 12-13
Dore, Ronald, 117
Dower, John, 184

EAEG (East Asian Economic Grouping), 127, 129, 133-4, 153
Economic Research Centre, 95
economy
  expansion, 17
  growth, 9, 27-8, 118
  management, 27-8
  multilateral activities, 147-8
  performance, 28, **30-1**
  power, 141
  relations with Europe, 78-80
EFTA (European Free Trade Association), 86, 87
Environment Agency, 34-5
equilibrium, internal, 33-5
Europe, 1992, 77-85, 123-4, 127-8
Europe
  Eastern, 86-7, 94, 147
  Western, 39, 95
European Community (EC), 85-6
  -Japan agreement (1991), 142-3
  and EFTA integration talks, 87
  monetary union, 128
  see also trade

exchange-rate system, floating, 12-14, 16-17
exports, 58, 78

Fauroux, Roger, 79
finance, 15-16, 103
  international, 5-6
  private versus public sector, 131-2
  reform, 29, 37
fiscal policy, 28-9
food security, 86, 125
Fortress Europe, 79
France, 79
FSO, 86
FSX fighter plane, 61-2, 80, 143
Fujimori, Alberto, 147
Fujimoto, Kazumi, 190
Fukuzawa, Yukichi, 182, 184

G-7, 127, 152
GATT (General Agreement on Tariffs and Trade), 39, 58, 85-6, 125-6
Gaullist scenario, 76-7
Gephardt, Richard, 126
Germany, 150-1
  West, 79, 83
Gibbon, Edward, 42
Gilpin, Robert, 174
globalization, 65-6
'good corporate Europeans', 95
Gorbachev, Mikhail, 81, 83, 132-3
  and Gulf War, 119-25
  and Security Council membership, 150-1
  Tokyo visit (1991), 82, 83, 133
Gotoda, Masaharu, 118
government
  bonds, 16, 29
  expenditure, 29
  outlays, ratio to GNP, 28-32
Great Britain, 79
Group of, 5 (G5), 59-60
Gulf crisis, 118-19
  response, 98-114, 145
    factors shaping, 101-6
Gulf War (1991), 99-100, 147
  and Gorbachev, 119-25
guns, 180

Hashimoto, Ryutaro, 124
Hawke, Bob, 84
Hidaka, Meizo, 185
Homma, Nagayo, 186-7
Hu Yaobang, 64
Human Frontier Project, 80-1
Hungary, 86, 87

Ikals, 86
immigration issue, 184
imports, 58, 59
incrementalism, 122, 145
independence, Pacific-Asian region, 161-6
India, 95
Indonesia, 83, 84, 165, 166
industrial relations, 117
inflation, 28
insecurity, national, 9
interest rates, 127
Intermediate-range Nuclear Forces (INF)
    Treaty (1987), 140
International Development Association,
    142
international role, 58-65, 108-10, 120-1,
    139-55
  domestic issues, 141-3, 144-6
  economic, 146-8
  international issues, 139-41, 143-4
  typology (Lake), 57, 66
  see also responsibilities; Self-Defense
    Forces (SDF)
investment
  diversification, 124
  in Europe, 79, 86
  foreign, 7, 16, 17
    in United States, 102, 124
isolationism, 21, 103

Japan-bashing, 11-12, 92, 106, 107
Japanese Association of American Studies,
    189-90, 191-2
Johnson, Chalmers, 5
Jones, Eric, 171

Kabashima, Ikuo, and Sato, Hideo, 190
Kaifu, Toshiki (Prime Minister, 1989-92),
    95, 99, 120
  aid pledge, 147
  and EAEG proposal, 129, 134
  and Gorbachev visit, 133
Kamei, Shunsuke, 181
Kanemaru, Shin, 124, 133
Kawato, Sadafumi, 190
keimosho (books for enlightenment), 186
Keynesian management, 29
Kikuchi, Kenichi, 185
Kim Il Sung, 133
Kohl, Helmut, 150-1
Kondratieff criteria, 8-9
Korea, 162-3
  North (Democratic People's Republic),
    124, 133, 147, 162, 165
  South (Republic of Korea [ROK]), 84,
    151, 161-2, 164, 170

legitimacy problem, 167-8
Korean War (1950-3), 162-3
Kubo, Fumiaki, 190

Lake, David, 57, 66
Latin America, 146
learning, 180
  historical, 103-5
Liberal Democratic Party (LDP), 33-5, 58,
    94

Macao, 162
McKinnon, Ronald, 12-13
Maekawa Report (1985), 118
Major, John, 149
Malaysia, 84, 129, 166, 167
Mansfield, Mike, 187
manufacturing, 4-5
  hi-tech products, 87-8
Mao Zedong, 162
market
  Europe, 78
  forces, international, 17
  liberalization, 59, 72, 91
    Asian NICs, 86
    global trend, 72-3
    policy weaknesses, 131-2
    and private sector strength, 110-11
    and protectionism, 125-6
    under Nakasone, 74
  world, liberal access to, 10
markets, enlargement need, 95
Masumi, Junnosuke, and Scalapino, Robert,
    117
Matsumoto, Shigeharu, 183, 184
Meiji Restoration (1868), 182
memory, 64-5
Mexico, 128-9
Miki, Takeo (Prime Minister, 1974-6), 23
military
  bases, 163-4
  build-up, 6, 139-40, 171
  capability, 22
  expenditure, 10
  power, 140-1
  role, 22-3
  scepticism about, 103-4
  see also Self-Defense Forces (SDF)
minesweeping operations, 118, 120, 130-1,
    143, 145
Ministry of Foreign Affairs, 110
Ministry of International Trade and Industry
    (MITI), 123, 142-3
Mitsubishi Heavy Industries, 62
Miyazawa, Kiichi (Prime Minister, 1992-   ),
    149

Mohamad, Mahatir, 129, 134, 153
money, 59–61
    policy, 28
Mongolia, 147
Morita, Akio, and Shintaro, Ishihara, 80
musketry volleys, 180

NAFTA (North American Free Trade Area), 127, 128–9
Nakasone, Yasuhiro (Prime Minister, 1982–7), 20–1, 33, 107, 108, 173
    minesweeping support, 118
    policies, 73–5
        internationalisation, 91
        military, 140, 145
    power base, 132
    reforms, 37
    Yasukuni shrine visit, 83, 143
National Diet, 99, 100
national identity, 107, 110, 166–7
nationalism, 106
NATO (North Atlantic Treaty Organization), 128, 151–2
New Guinea, Western, 166
Newby, Laura, 93
newly industrialized countries (NICs), 14
    Asian, 83–4, 86, 95, 169
    Far Eastern, 15
    post-oil crisis emergence, 170
Nichi-bei Kankeishi (History of Japan-US relations), 191
NICs see newly industrialized countries
Nihon keizai shimbun, 3
Niijima, Jo, 182
Nissan, 86
Nitobe, Inazo, 182
Nobayashi, Takeshi, 190
Nomura Securities, 7
nontariff barriers, overt, 14–15
Northern Territories issue, 81, 83, 121–2, 132–3
nuclear armaments, 41, 140

Occupation, 10–11, 168
Oda, Nobunaga, 180
official development assistance (ODA), 4, 172
Ogata, Sadako, 150
Ohira, Masayoshi (Prime Minister, 1978–80), 20, 37
    policy study groups, 36–7
Ohmae, Kenichi, 132
oil crisis
    first (1973), 20, 27–8, 98, 105, 170
    second (1980), 28, 98
Okinawa, 163

Ozawa, Ichiro, 99, 109–10, 120–1, 124, 132–3, 144–5

Pacific Asia, 95, 109, 172–3
    Cold War impact, 161–6
    and EAEG, 129
    economy, 83–4, 85, 123–4
    emergence, 169–71
    and Japan criticism, 144
    national development, 166–9
    profile, 83–4
    war recurrence, 159–61
    World War II impact, 160, 161
    and yen zone, 134
Pacific Asian scenario, 77
Pacific region, 146–7, 170–1
    Western, 15, 40
pacificism, 20, 21–2, 103, 145
    and constitution, 107–8
Papua New Guinea, 166
party system, 117
Pax Americana Phase II, 75, 76, 77, 173–4
Pax Ameripponica, 174
Pax Consortis, 75–6, 174–5
Pax Nipponica, 76, 77, 175–6
Pax Pacifica, 174
Perry, Commodore Matthew C., 181, 182
Peru, 147
Philippines, 83, 84, 164, 165
Pinto, Mendes, 180
Poland, 86, 87
policy, 28
    during Nakasone period, 73–5, 91, 140, 145
    options, 39–41, 42–3
        long-term, 75–6
        short-term, 76–7
    pro-American, 73–4
    redirection, 92–3
    security, 19–20, 41, 63, 122–3
    Soviet and Northern Territories issue, 81
politicians, 132–3
politics
    American
        academic publications 188, 188
        Japanese scholarship on, 179–200
    bureaucratic, 133–4
    management, 33
    right-left cleavage, 107–8, 110–11, 130–1
    see also Clean Government Party;
        Democratic Socialist Party; Liberal
        Democratic Party (LDP)
private sector, 16, 110–11, 131–2
productivity, relative, 57–8
protectionism, 39
    Japan's image, 66

and market liberalization, 125-6
technological, 62
unilateral, 85-6
United States, 39-40
Western Europe, 39
Provisional Council on Administrative and
    Financial Reform (1981), 29
public sector, 16, 131-2

rapprochement
  Korean-Japanese, 124
  Soviet-Japanese, 121-2, 132-3
Reagan, Ronald, 71-3, 140, 145, 161, 173
recession, 28
regionalism, 39-40, 127
  networking, 74-5
  North-east Asia, 40
  and response to Europe, 1992, 83-5
regionalization, economic, 85
relations
  Japanese-US, 191
      works by Japanese Americanists,
          189-90, 191
  Sino-Japanese, 93
  Sino-Soviet, conflict, 160-1
  Soviet-Japanese, 121-2, 124, 132-3, 191
research, foreign area, 192-3
reserves, foreign, 60
responsibilities
  global, 102, 123
  international
      political, 103, 108-9, 117-18
      security, 120
  see also international role
rice market, 125
rivalry, bureaucratic, 133
robotics, 5
Roh Tae-Woo, 161
Russian Republic, 147
Ryukya Islands, 163

Sato, Hideo, and Kabashima, Ikuo, 33, 190
Scalapino, Robert, and Masumi, Junnosuke,
    117
security, 18-19
  comprehensive, 20, 36
  economic, 20, 36
  and Europe, 80-3
  increased burden sharing, 7
  international, 124
      role, 62-4, 120-1, 149-53
  Japan-US alliance, 20-2, 93-4
      in, 1990s, 82-3, 87, 122-3
      cost-benefit calculations, 41-2
      departure from, 41-2
      see also Security Treaty, Japan-US

military force strengthening, 139-40
  and Pacific Asia, 84, 163
  policy, 19-20, 41, 63
      international, 122-3
  regional, 153
  shyness, 108
  strategies re-evaluation, 80
  see also defense
Security Treaty
  Japan-US (1951), 23, 63, 101, 119-20
      Crisis (1960), 185
self-confidence, 105-6, 172
Self-Defense Forces (SDF)
  early years, 23
  FS-X fighter plane for, 61-2, 80, 143
  New Defense Capability Consolidation
      Plan (1986-90), 37-8
  purchase from British Aerospace, 80
  role, 62-3
      Gulf War, 100, 145
      overseas, 130, 131, 143
      in UN peacekeeping and relief
          forces, 150
  see also minesweeping operations
semiconductors, 78
sengo minshushugi (postwar democracy),
    185
Shintaro, Ishihara, and Morita, Akio, 80
Shiratori, Masaki, 148
Shirizu Nichi-Bei Kankei (Series on Japan-US
    relations), 191
Sino-Soviet alliance (1950), 162
social security, 32
social welfare, 34-5
socialist states, 83
socioeconomic infrastructure, 27, 42
Soviet Union, 10, 40, 87
  tension reduction, 82, 94, 124
Spain, 79
spending, 105
Strategic Defense Initiative (SDI), 61, 62,
    171
Structural Impediments Initiative (SII), 58-
    9, 66, 92, 131, 132
surveillance, 148, 155n
Suzuki Automobiles, 86
Suzuki, Zenko (Prime Minister, 1980-2), 20,
    29, 73, 145
  reforms, 37
  and US 'alliance', 73, 145

Taisho Democracy, 183
Taiwan, 84, 162, 163, 164, 169-70
Takagi, Yasaka, 183-4
Takeo, Nichioka, 99
Takeshita, Noboru, 108

Tanaka, Kakuei (Prime Minister, 1972–4),
    23, 33
Tanegashima, 180
tax increases, 37
technology, 61–2, 66, 80, 86, 124
Thailand, 83, 84, 163–4
Third World, 117–18
Timor, 165–6
Tokyo Round Free Trade Agreement
    (1979), 15
trade, 4–5, 123
    European Community, 78, 82, 123–4
    imbalances, 142
    international role, 58
    liberalization, and protectionism, 14–15
    regulations in Europe, 78
    surplus, 60
    unequal, 58
    US interdependence, 15
trilateralism, 41

Uchimura, Kanzo, 182, 184
unilateralism, 21
United Nations
    financial contributions, 143–4, 154n
    participation in, 149–51
    Peace Co-operation bill, 99, 119, 120,
        130, 145
    Security Council, 142, 144
United States (US), 92–3
    and Europe, 1992, 85–8
    fiscal policy, 101–2

hegemonic umbrella, 10, 12, 19, 42, 43–
    4, 171
Japanese security policy, 23
    military bases, 163–4
    military build-up, 6, 139–40, 171
    overdependence reduction, 82, 123–4
    protectionism, 39–40, 102
    trade policy, 15, 125–6, 142
    see also security, Japan–US alliance; Secu-
        rity Treaty, Japan–US (1951)
USSR see Soviet Union

Vietnam, 163
    North, 165
    South, 164, 165, 167
Vietnam War (1965–75), 11, 165, 185

war recurrence, 159–61, 168–9
Watanabe, Michio, 150
weapons, 41, 80, 87, 109, 151
West Germany see Germany
World Bank, 142, 148
world economy, 11
World War II, 160, 161, 184

Yakovlev, Aleksandr, 82, 94
Yamamoto, Yoshinobu, 190
Yasutake, Hidetake, 185
yen, 59–60
    for development, 146
    economic area, 134
Yui, Daizaburo, 190